HAWTHORNE

HAWTHORNE·

A Critical Study
By Hyatt H. Waggoner

THE BELKNAP PRESS
of HARVARD UNIVERSITY PRESS

CAMBRIDGE · MASSACHUSETTS · 1955

ACKNOWLEDGMENTS

I am indebted to many people for help in the writing of this book. The students in English 511 at the University of Kansas City have contributed a great deal that can no longer be specifically identified and so cannot be acknowledged except in this way. I am grateful to Francis J. Polek for typing the manuscript; he worked at the task as though it were a labor of love and not an ill-paid job. I have tried to acknowledge my chief debts to other writers on Hawthorne as I have gone along in the body of this work, but I find that I have nowhere adequately noted my debt to Richard Fogle, whose articles I have long used and admired and whose book, *Nathaniel Hawthorne: The Light and the Dark*, is a significant landmark in the history of Hawthorne criticism. Finally, I am indebted to a number of people for making suggestions at various stages in the preparation of the manuscript, but especially, and most deeply, to Jeremy Ingalls, W. Stacy Johnson, and Randall Stewart.

Kansas City   H. H. W.

48461

CONTENTS

HAWTHORNE

THE MATERIAL OF ART

When Nathaniel Hawthorne was born in 1804 the decline of his family's fortunes was already far advanced and the decline of Salem as a seaport was beginning. His father's death at sea when Hawthorne was four later seemed to Hawthorne to have completed the personal decline. Salem's loss of trade to Boston and New York, so that it took on some of those aspects of a ghost town that are recorded in the Custom House essay attached to *The Scarlet Letter*, connected foreground and background in a picture nearly monochromatic. When Hawthorne married at the age of thirty-eight, his life was more than half over and he wavered between a feeling that the best years were already gone and a feeling that his real life had just begun. When he was not yet sixty and while his children were still young, failing health and a premonition of early death made him both physically and psychologically an old man. A dream of lost power and innocence, a memory of Arcadia and Eden, runs through his works as a dominant theme.

Yet his life was not spectacularly unfortunate. Indeed it was, judged by the usual standards, more than usually fortunate and successful. The pathos felt by most of the biographers can hardly be fully accounted for by the outward facts. Though his family had declined in wealth and prestige, and Hawthorne himself struggled for twenty-five years to become a writer without getting any substantial encouragement, he lived to know full recognition, to be acclaimed by his own contemporaries as a great writer. Though he married late, yet he married the woman of his choice and was unusually happy in his marriage. Unlike Emerson, Longfellow, and Mark Twain, he never knew the grief brought by the death of wife and children or the desolation of outliving the friends he cared for. He was remarkably handsome, even, as some said, "beautiful," and, until the last several years of his life, enjoyed unusually good health. If he was never financially "secure," his financial problems were not, at any time in his life, to be compared with the struggles with poverty endured by many of the greatest writers. His outward life was relatively uneventful, serene, and fortunate.

There is a paradox here not easily to be resolved, but it is only one of many that become apparent when one contemplates the man and his work. When Hawthorne was a boy he suffered an injury to his foot. Though there is no evidence that the injury was especially severe, his family found the incident reason enough to account for the habit of withdrawal which boy and youth developed. The earlier biographies of Hawthorne are full of such attempts to account for aspects of the man by reference to youthful events which themselves need accounting for. After her husband's death Mrs. Hawthorne devoted herself to presenting to the world a proper picture of her famous husband, carefully altering the Notebooks and suppressing the facts to do her husband the service, as she supposed, of letting him appear in the role of the ideal Victorian man of letters, cheerful, confident, pious, refined, and optimistic. Yet there cannot be much doubt that she was right in supposing that her husband would in the main have approved of what she did to retouch the portrait.

Hawthorne wrote a good deal about his sense of isolation, his loneliness. He felt, before his marriage, imprisoned in a cell to which the key had been lost. He longed to "open an intercourse with the world." And many observers, then and later, noticed the painful shyness of the man. Yet Randall Stewart, protesting against a "romanticized" picture of Hawthorne as lonely, aloof, and alienated, has underscored the evidence of his adjustment. His was a very "normal" college career, with the usual pranks and friendships and lack of distinction in most things. He liked to smoke cigars and to drink moderately with friends over cards. His best friends were politicians, sailors, journalists, all of whom he preferred to romantic poets and transcendental philosophers. His letters and notebook entries are "earthy," as realistic and occasionally "unrefined" as we should expect to find them in any normal man even in Victorian Salem and Concord. Mr. Stewart is undoubtedly justified in his correction of the picture of Hawthorne as recluse. But which is the "real" Hawthorne, the man of the self-estimate, the man Mrs. Hawthorne tried to make him, or the man Mr. Stewart presents?

There were in fact several Hawthornes and all of them are to some degree masks. There was the "man of sensibility," as sensibility was defined in the first half of the nineteenth century, the "man of feeling" who was contemporary with Irving and Longfellow. This was the Hawthorne of the tender fancies, the whimsical sentiments, the Hawthorne of some of the sketches. Now and then, in this phase, he skirts perilously close to what today seems sentimentality. This Hawthorne wrote "The Snow Image" and "Little Daffydowndilly," was properly reverent and light-hearted, had the conventional emotions in the presence of feminine purity, and created the blonde maidens who flit through the novels like sunbeams in a dark world. This Hawthorne was contemporary, correct, an approximation to the ideal of his time.

Hawthorne liked this Hawthorne and tried to encourage him.

But not very successfully. The sense of irony, the cool skepticism, the detached, sometimes cruel sense of humor collaborated with the visions that came between sleep and waking to make it difficult for this admired Hawthorne to maintain himself. He found it difficult to feel as he knew he *ought* to feel. Often he found it difficult to feel at all, even to feel the wrong emotions. Hence, if we are searching for the "real" Hawthorne, we must take account of another Hawthorne, cold, isolated, detached, watchful, skeptical. If the picture thus presented seems quite untrue to the outlines of the public Hawthorne preserved in the records of family and friends, we need only keep two things in mind to correct the distortion: this is the most persistent shape of the self-portrayal in all of Hawthorne's writing, both fiction and non-fiction; and the self-image, though we may assume that it was created out of knowledge not available to others, could not have been the whole truth, for another part of Hawthorne very much disliked *this* Hawthorne.

Hawthorne must have been to some degree, in short, the man he saw himself as being; but he was also the man who did the seeing and passed the negative judgments on what he saw. He was the young man of "The Christmas Banquet," more unfortunate than the worst of life's unfortunates, whose tragedy lay in the fact that he could feel nothing, could not respond emotionally to life. He was the cold observer who could not muster enough faith to participate in what he observed: Coverdale peeping through the window into other lives in *The Blithedale Romance*, Paul Pry, Ethan Brand searching in every heart for the unpardonable sin, the man in the steeple looking down on those in the streets from a position remote enough to make him feel wholly detached. He was the Hawthorne of parts of the Notebooks. This Hawthorne, whose reactions to people were so frequently negative, found it easier to detect a sham than to discover

a virtue in unpromising circumstances. The Hawthorne of
the Notebooks comments on the Shakers, on American visitors to the Consulate in Liverpool, on abolitionists and other
idealists, was so detached that he might easily be imagined
using other people simply as the objects of study — the sin
committed by Ethan Brand, Aylmer, Rappaccini, Westervelt.

But there was another Hawthorne too, the one who joined
the Brook Farm community, that high-minded experiment
in practical brotherhood. It was this Hawthorne, also, who
helped a certain Miss Bacon publish a book which he felt
sure would not succeed, because she needed the help and he
believed her case, even if wrong, should get a hearing; who
stood by his friend Pierce when to do so was almost tanta-
mount to being judged guilty of treason; who was more
generous with his practical aid than in his judgments, and
who was as severe in judging himself as in judging anyone
else.

And there was, after 1850, the famous man of letters who
found it increasingly difficult to write anything which he
thought worth while. In many respects this is the most
puzzling mask of all. For twenty-five years after his graduation from college Hawthorne persevered in a long apprenticeship to his craft that brought neither fame nor money.
Creating stories that we now recognize as great and being
forced to sell them for trifling sums to obscure publications,
he continued to write steadily in the face of discouragement
and poverty. But after *The Scarlet Letter* had brought him
immediate fame and more money than he had ever got from
his writing, as well as an assured public for future works,
he tended more and more to find excuses for not writing. The
publishers pressed him for new books, and he went through
stacks of old magazines and annuals, culling stories and
sketches he had done twenty years before; or satisfied them
with retelling classic legends for children; or put them off
with promises of a novel to come when conditions were more

propitious. He protested that he could not write in summer heat, or in winter cold. In the Berkshires the novelty of mountain scenery and air soon wore off and he longed for the air of the seaside and for a more luxurious home than the red farmhouse. Salem was intolerable — and he made it more so by his acid portrayal of it in the Custom House Letter — but he could never feel at home anywhere else. England, Rome, Concord, all seemed places where it was almost impossible to work.

A good deal of sympathy has been wasted on Hawthorne because he had to take political jobs to make a living. It is generally assumed that these jobs kept him from writing; this is indeed the impression that he himself had. But the adverse circumstances that kept him from writing, or that weakened his writing, were not outward but inward. Though his position in the Boston Custom House before his marriage may have been nearly as onerous as he portrayed it, his two later political jobs were of a very different character. Neither was sufficiently burdensome to have kept a different sort of man from writing. In the Salem position described in the essay prefacing *The Scarlet Letter* Hawthorne had to work only a few hours a day, and that in a manner which should have taxed neither body nor mind. But he could write nothing until after he had been fired and the need was desperate.

In the English Consulate, again, he put in at most several hours a day, with whole weeks and even months taken out entirely for sightseeing tours and other recreation. The job was essentially a sinecure in which a different sort of artist could have done voluminous writing, for the "work" — usually no more arduous than signing his name — demanded neither much time nor much thought. In the last twenty years of his life the only extensive period when Hawthorne worked continuously at his writing was in the four years before his death, when he tortured himself in the attempt to do one more novel but could produce nothing which he could complete or was willing to publish. Hawthorne worked hard at becoming a man of letters until he was recognized as being one. After that, he worked at it only when forced to by need for money or the demands of conscience.

These are only a few of the paradoxes that emerge when we contemplate the man who made an "ideal" marriage, yet who in his last miserable years found himself utterly alone in the midst of loving wife and children; who was simple in his tastes and requirements, yet contented nowhere; who longed all his life for a home, yet discovered reasons for rejecting every home he found or made; who took part in Brook Farm utopianism, yet despised reformers; who considered his Christian faith unshakable, yet never went to church, disliked theological writings, and usually was repelled by preachers of the gospel. It is perhaps partly because of the centrality of such paradoxes that all of the existing biographies are interesting and none of them wholly satisfactory. The student of Hawthorne who wishes to get a complete and rounded view of the man must read more than one biography, then supplement the biographies he has read with the Notebooks, sketches, letters, and stories, then finally understand the man, if at all, by a leap of intuitive sympathy.

If he has made the leap successfully — and there is no publicly demonstrable test of success here — he will perhaps be aware of nuances in the works that he would otherwise have missed, read them with another level of meaning in mind, or at least approach them with a sympathy not otherwise attainable. But no merely factual knowledge of the externals of Hawthorne's life will be of much use to one who is trying to understand his works. Indeed we may put the matter more strongly: the impression one is likely to get from reading the most reliable and definitive biography is that there is little connection between the man and his works.

The Taine approach to literature, through the study of the writer's environment, is of some use, perhaps, in studying

Whitman, who "expressed" his age and found his best material in the things he did and saw and felt. But it works so poorly as to be hardly worth attempting with Hawthorne, whose creative life was wholly inward, who usually wrote badly when he tried to write of the things he outwardly saw and actually did, and who was truest to himself when he wrote of others and truest to his own age when he ignored it and wrote of the past or the legendary and the mythical. This is true no doubt partly because much of his best work falls into the genre of historical fiction; but more profoundly perhaps for two other, related, reasons: because his work is concerned with the essentials of human experience and captures those essentials in art forms that have the timelessness of classic art; and because, to a peculiar degree, that which is most valuable in Hawthorne's writing springs from the depths of head and heart where newspaper headlines make no ripple.

2

A close look at Hawthorne's sketches will prepare us better for the tales and novels than any study of the externals of his life. It is fashionable at present to depreciate the sketches, and it is true that some of them come close to a kind of Irvingesque indulgence in sentiment for its own sake. But it is by no means true that there is no "thinking" in them, as some of Hawthorne's critics seem to believe. The thinking in them is casual, to be sure, even deliberately relaxed and apparently inconsecutive, masquerading as fancy and taste. This was the demand made by the genre and the time.

But it was also the kind of thinking that Hawthorne did best; and it would seem that we should know enough by this time about the processes of creative thought to know that it does not always, perhaps does not often, take the form of high-level ratiocination. The fact about the sketches that should be recognized is that, unlike both the sketches of

Irving, who excelled in sentiment, and many of the essays of Macaulay, who excelled in a kind of reasoning, they run counter to the trend toward that dissociation of thought and feeling which marked so much nineteenth-century writing.

The paraphrasable content of "The Haunted Mind," to take one of the better early sketches for an example, is very slight, but a close look at the piece will take us far toward an understanding of Hawthorne's work. The sketch provides, first of all, a unique glimpse of the characteristically romantic approach to life and to art. It shows us that Hawthorne was not only, as we shall see, at odds with his time: he was also a part of it, sharing the romantic concern for that which can only be seen out of the corner of the eye, or in a half-light, or when the mind is relaxed. This concern with the strange, the half-known, the dimly seen, coming, as it is customary in literary histories to say, as a reaction against the rigidities and apparent superficialities of the age of common sense and limited reason, this concern with the verities which are no less important because they cannot be demonstrated by the methods favored by the age of the enlightenment — this is fully adumbrated in "The Haunted Mind."

Hawthorne asks us to consider what thoughts come to the mind halfway between sleep and waking when one starts up from midnight slumber. Then the mind is passive, the dreams are close, and the revelations that come may be "truer" than those that come to the concentrated and controlled intelligence. We think, perhaps, as we read this, of the use of drugs as an aid to creation, of Keats's praise of sleep, of the romantic tendency to prefer the night to the day and the sea to the land. But even an amateur knowledge of psychoanalysis should correct any tendency we may have to dismiss this approach to experience as simply "romantic" and of only historical interest.

The sketch reveals as much of Hawthorne's special concerns and the shape of his sensibility as it does of the outlook he shared with the writers of his youth. When you first wake up, he tells us, you are very close to your dream, and for a while its vivid illusions occupy you. But then you begin to "think," though not in a very "reasonable" way. You think various things, but principally of "how the dead are lying in their cold shrouds and narrow coffins." The long paragraph in the middle of the sketch devoted to the thoughts that come at this time is concerned wholly with death and frustration. "In the depths of every heart there is a tomb and a dungeon," it begins, introducing us both to Hawthorne's most characteristic metaphors, the tomb or dungeon of the heart, and to the feeling that pervades nearly all of his work except the deliberately light-hearted sketches he sometimes contrived to write.

"The lights, the music, and the revelry above" may, Hawthorne tells us, cause us to forget the existence of these tombs and dungeons and "the buried ones, or prisoners, whom they hide," but "sometimes, and oftenest at midnight, these dark receptacles are flung wide open. In an hour like this, when the mind has a passive sensibility, but no active strength; when the imagination is a mirror, imparting vividness to all ideas, without the power of selecting or controlling them; then pray that your griefs may slumber, and the brotherhood of remorse not break their chain."

Then, with a characteristic turn to the abstract when the revelation threatens to become too personal, Hawthorne personifies the visitors who come with the "funeral train" that moves into the center of consciousness: Sorrow, Disappointment, and Fatality appear, the last "a demon to whom you subjected yourself by some error at the outset of life." On the face of another ghost you see "the writhed lip of scorn, the mockery of that living eye, the pointed finger, touching the sore place in your heart. Do you remember any act of enormous folly at which you would blush, even in the remotest cavern of the earth? Then recognize your Shame."

Though this has in part the "dated" air of the allegorical poem and the moral essay, the reader today, whether or not he submits to Hawthorne's effort to evoke in each his own "Shame," will recognize something else at any rate: the darkness that is always so much more impressive, so much more *felt*, than the light in Hawthorne's works; the artistic superiority of the dark guilty women of the tales and novels over the pale blonde innocent maidens, the Hesters and Miriams over the Phoebes and the Hildas; the shapes of all the "villains" in the works, with their features cold and mocking; the sense of fate, whether made explicit as in "Wakefield" or recognized and denied by a conscious effort to believe in freedom, as in *The House of the Seven Gables*.

But the sketch continues: "Sufficient, without such guilt, is this nightmare of the soul; this heavy, heavy sinking of the spirits; this wintry gloom about the heart; this indistinct horror of the mind, blending itself with the darkness of the chamber." Finding that the "visions" have become intolerable — as his waking vision became to Leonard Doane in "Alice Doane's Appeal" — "By a desperate effort you start upright, breaking from a sort of conscious sleep, and gazing wildly round the bed, as if the fiends were anywhere but in your haunted mind." You try to think of pleasanter subjects. You search for anything that will remind you that life is as real as death, innocence as real as guilt. Having done so more or less successfully, "With an involuntary start you seize hold on consciousness, and prove yourself but half awake, by running a doubtful parallel between human life and the hour which has now elapsed. In both you emerge from mystery, pass through a vicissitude that you can but imperfectly control, and are borne onward to another mystery."

Most of what is best in the later works is already suggested here. I shall not now elaborate the parallels between this and the best tales and sketches, but we shall certainly see again many of these visions that come to the haunted mind.

3

Judgment of Hawthorne's relation to the public questions that occupied his contemporaries has moved in the last quarter century through a ninety-degree arc, from the opinion that he was totally unconcerned with and uninformed about social problems to the more recently conventional one that he was both well informed and vitally concerned, even when, as usually was the case, he could not agree with the popular "liberal" solutions. Admirable monographs and papers have been written on his attitudes toward reform, his political opinions, his views on society in general. What has emerged from the conflicting judgments and corrections of judgments is a paradox much like that of the "lonely yet sociable" Hawthorne that emerges from the biographies. There is too much evidence for each of the two most opposed views for the paradox to be resolved, but it may be kept from appearing to be a complete antinomy if we take the trouble to understand not only Hawthorne's particular opinions on such things as politics and reform but the larger views of which these were but special applications. And the best way to do this is to read the Notebooks and the sketches, particularly the sketches. A glance at "Fancy's Show Box," "The Celestial Railroad," and "Earth's Holocaust" will take us quickly to the center of those aspects of his views on religion and ethics, politics and reform which are of primary importance to those who are interested in his work as artist.

Hawthorne subtitles "Fancy's Show Box" "A Morality," and the choice is happily descriptive, for the piece is closely akin to medieval allegory in its form and to orthodox Christianity in its content. He begins by asking the question "What is Guilt?" — a question that his contemporary and sometime neighbor Emerson would have found, had he read the sketch, both unnecessary and essentially meaningless. He answers the question with "A stain upon the soul," thus beginning

his sketch with two assumptions that may seem quaint in a
secular society: first, that there is a real difference between
right and wrong, making it worth while to ask the question
"What is guilt?" and not just "What makes me feel guilty?";
and second, that there is an immortal soul which can receive
"stains." The question that then follows is "Must the fleshly
hand and visible frame of man set its seal to the evil designs
of the soul, in order to give them their entire validity against
the sinner?" For — and here is the further assumption, re-
pugnant to Rousseauists and other believers in the innate
natural goodness of man — it is quite clear that all of us have
wished more evil than we have wrought: "In the solitude of
a midnight chamber or in a desert, afar from men or in a
church, while the body is kneeling, the soul may pollute
itself even with those crimes which we are accustomed to
deem altogether carnal. If this be true, it is a fearful truth."

Then, with a "Let us illustrate the subject by an imaginary
example," Hawthorne describes certain scenes from the past
life of an old man, scenes that show how often he was prevented from sin by mere accidents. Part of the point he
wishes to make is that Mr. Smith's "innocence" is the product
not of blamelessness of intention but of fortunate circumstances; with slightly different circumstances he might have
been a thief or a murderer. But another part of the point
qualifies this. It is not only that we cannot take much credit
for the evil that we have not done, but that we cannot even
know, until after the fact, what our "intentions" really were:
"In truth, there is no such thing in man's nature as a settled
and full resolve, either for good or evil, except at the very
moment of execution." Hawthorne knows that the qualifications made by "settled and full" must be made if he is to
avoid a fatalism that will link him more closely with his
predestinarian Puritan forebears than he wishes to be linked.
He makes the qualifying statement. But the implications of
the sketch contain a suggestion of that feeling for the power

of fate and the relative impotence of the will which we shall
find in many of his later works.

Hawthorne ends his sketch with a paragraph brief enough
to be quoted entire, and significant enough for all his works
to deserve to be remembered:

> Yet, with the slight fancy work which we have framed, some sad
> and awful truths are interwoven. Man must not disclaim his brother-
> hood, even with the guiltiest, since, though his hand be clean, his
> heart has surely been polluted by the flitting phantoms of iniquity.
> He must feel that, when he shall knock at the gate of heaven, no
> semblance of an unspotted life can entitle him to entrance there.
> Penitence must kneel, and Mercy come from the footstool of the
> throne, or that golden gate will never open!

Much, rather too much I suspect, has been written about
Hawthorne's kinship with his Puritan ancestors in his view
of life. Modern American scholars and biographers, for the
most part remote from the Christian tradition, not only themselves lacking the faith but, what is much more pertinent,
largely ignorant of what faith has meant except as they have
encountered it in the American Puritans and contemporary
"humanist" Protestant churches, have labeled Hawthorne
"Puritan" because it was clear that he was neither a modern
pragmatic liberal nor a "Christian" as that term is understood
by the local nonsectarian community church. But here in
"Fancy's Show Box," in the most explicit statement he ever
allowed himself on the subject, when he seems closest to the
Puritans he is also closest to classic Christianity as that is
defined by the Creeds and by the agreements among the
greatest theologians, from St. Paul to St. Augustine to St.
Thomas to contemporaries like Reinhold Niebuhr and Paul
Tillich. Hawthorne has some very harsh — and some unfair —
things to say about the Puritans in his writings; but where
they were central and orthodox, rather than heretical, he
agreed with them in substance.

He is agreeing in this sketch, for example, when he says

that Penitence must kneel and divine Mercy forgive. The Calvinists expressed this by denying Salvation by Works and emphasizing the role of the Atonement and Faith. Wigglesworth has some amusingly crabbed stanzas on the subject, and Edwards illustrated it at length and with frightful vividness in his "Sinners in the Hands of an Angry God." But the idea of man's sinfulness is not a peculiarly Puritan notion, though the Puritans threw a greater emphasis on it than was traditional. It is at the center of Christian orthodoxy. Its opposite is the Pelagian heresy that plagued the early church, was defeated in the early councils, but has never been forgotten: that man, being naturally or preponderantly good, can, by using his native good will and clever intelligence, save himself unaided.

Whatever this view may be called — "religious humanism," for instance — it is not historic or classic Christianity. It is clear not only from "Fancy's Show Box" but from most of the other things he wrote that Hawthorne was no Pelagian, no Rousseauist, no secular optimist. Except for the blonde maidens who appear on the scene now and then to speak a word for the "religion of the heart," and whose own hearts seem to be pure "by nature," Hawthorne thought unredeemed human nature a weak reed. When he came, toward the end of his life, to write *The Marble Faun* he showed himself more aware of the force of the optimistic view than he ever had been before. He presented it, in one of its aspects, with temporarily suspended judgment. But even then, "liberalized" by his European years and the currents of the times, he finally denied the doctrine with a vehemence that suggests its potential attractiveness to him and ended his book with his heroine speaking for orthodoxy. "Fancy's Show Box" places Hawthorne squarely in the center in the battle of Faith and Works, a position in which a part of him at least remained all his life.

But if he denies both the "total depravity" of the Puritans

and the natural goodness of the Pelagians and the moderns, preferring instead a position sometimes described by the theologians as "natural depravity" — not necessarily "complete" but universal and inevitable — his conclusion from this position is not, as some might expect, cynical or despairing. On it he bases his belief in the brotherhood of man: "Man must not disclaim his brotherhood, even with the guiltiest . . ." It might be worth while today to look into Hawthorne to see how solid a case for democratic values and democratic safeguards can be made on the basis of a belief in the reality of evil in man. Emerson admitted once in his private journal that he had never been able to make evil seem real to himself. It was very real to Hawthorne, whose politics were Jacksonian democratic, not Whig like Emerson's. Attempts today to defend democracy, against the charges of Communist and Fascist alike, on the basis of Emersonian philosophy suggest to me that the self-proclaimed "philosophers of democracy" like Emerson and Whitman are less serviceable to us than traditional conservatives like Hawthorne or skeptical conservatives like Melville.

"The Celestial Railroad" and "Earth's Holocaust" are sketches of a very different order from "Fancy's Show Box." Whether better or not, they are at least much more substantial, and both are explicit criticisms of his age, so that a complete comment on them would require a good deal of historical scholarship exercised in a long essay. If he is to get the full impact of "The Celestial Railroad," for example, the modern reader should have a first-hand knowledge of *Pilgrim's Progress* and a grasp of religious history, particularly of the way in which New England Puritanism changed into Unitarianism, and of what that change amounted to in doctrine and practice. For "Earth's Holocaust" he should have some knowledge of the reform movements of the 1830's and 1840's, including not only the specific reforms advocated — teetotalism, women's rights, vegetarianism, and abolition of capital punishment, for instance — but the assumptions of the reformers about human nature. As we shall see, Hawthorne's tales and novels do not make nearly so strong a demand for this kind of special knowledge as these sketches do; but that is not surprising, since one of the permanent and fundamental distinctions between art and social criticism is here involved.

Yet without the sort of historical documentation that they invite, the sketches can still tell us something of the directions of Hawthorne's thinking. "The Celestial Railroad" is a pastiche on *Pilgrim's Progress*, with the satire aimed not at Bunyan but at religious modernists of Hawthorne's day. The modern pilgrim has, in his own opinion, inestimable advantages over Bunyan's old-fashioned Everyman. The latest triumphs of applied science have made everything so much easier and quicker — including salvation. Nowadays the pilgrim rides on a railroad instead of journeying laboriously and perilously on foot. He checks his load of sins with the baggage man and is so much freer to enjoy himself on the way. He need no longer be disturbed by certain unpleasant facts, for the Slough of Despond has been filled in by the cheerful books of modern clergymen, philosophers convinced of the natural goodness of man, and Transcendental optimists. The Wicket Gate has been torn down and the Interpreter's House by-passed; the Valley of the Shadow of Death has been lighted by gas lamps and the mouth of Hell has been identified as merely the crater of an extinct volcano. "Giant Transcendentalist," with outlines so indistinct that no one has ever been able to describe him, has taken the place once occupied by Bunyan's very concrete and dangerous enemies, Pope and Pagan. Vanity Fair still continues, but its dangers have been done away with as it has been taken over by the Church. Here machines have been devised to manufacture individual morality, thus disposing of a vexatious problem; and though the occupants of the city have a habit of suddenly vanishing like soap bubbles, no one takes any notice of their disappearance.

"The Celestial Railroad" is I think one of the finest things of its kind ever written, on any score, whatever one's philosophic and religious orientation. No brief redaction can hope to convey a substantial part of its value. For this is a piece of writing which even those — and they are probably a majority in our time — who are in sympathy with Giant Transcendentalist rather than with Bunyan will find uniquely valuable. It is easy to see, at this distance, how shrewdly it finds the weaknesses in the liberal credo of its time. Only the most extreme of positivists, and those not the most intelligent, believe, for example, that there is *no* moral problem because science can produce better machines. Skeptics today can smile with Hawthorne — without sharing his sympathy for Bunyan — at the wishful thinking involved in the desire of religious modernism to keep heaven but to do away with hell. (Mr. Smooth-it-away is ready to prove "that Tophet has not even a metaphorical existence.") The Cyberneticists of today may talk hopefully of what may be accomplished by human engineering, but unless they are unusually obtuse they are not likely to miss the delightful irony of Hawthorne's description of what has happened in the warfare between religion and Vanity Fair. Like *The Screwtape Letters* of our day, most of whose delighted readers certainly do not share the religious convictions of C. S. Lewis, "The Celestial Railroad" can be appreciated by those who deny many of the assumptions behind it.

But of course it will be appreciated most by those who find themselves in sympathy with Bunyan and Hawthorne as against Mr. Smooth-it-away, the modernist preacher. One who, like Emerson, cannot believe in the reality of evil will scarcely be pleased by Hawthorne's ending, however much he may have enjoyed the historical satire on ideas and institutions that seem remote enough to be free of contemporary relevance. Mr. Smooth-it-away, the speaker's guide on the journey, refuses at the last moment to enter the Celestial city:

And then did my excellent friend Mr. Smooth-it-away laugh outright, in the midst of which cachinnation a smoke-wreath issued from his mouth and nostrils, while a twinkle of lurid flame darted out of either eye, proving indubitably that his heart was all of a red blaze. The impudent fiend! To deny the existence of Tophet, when he felt its fiery tortures raging within his breast. I rushed to the side of the boat, intending to fling myself on shore; but the wheels, as they began their revolutions, threw a dash of spray over me so cold — so deadly cold, with the chill that will never leave those waters until Death be drowned in his own river — that with a shiver and a heart-quake I awoke. Thank Heaven it was a Dream!

If this was a dream, it was a dream from the horned gate, true to the outlines of Hawthorne's most lasting convictions. The fundamental assumptions behind it were expressed in another "dream" that is also one of Hawthorne's major sketches, "Earth's Holocaust." This too is a sketch which invites, indeed almost demands, the kind of explication best afforded by historical scholarship, for it is a satirical comment on many of the most important trends and historical events of Hawthorne's age. The immediate inspiration for it may very likely have been Carlyle's *French Revolution*, with its frequent fire imagery and its underlying concept of the revolution as a consuming fire. Other sources have been suggested for the episode of the burning of the books, and Thoreau's talk of an Indian custom of annually burning all property preparatory to making a fresh start in life may have contributed its bit. But whatever the sources, the sketch has implications that reach out to touch the central problems of Hawthorne's and of any age — the nature and source of evil, the necessity and the failure of reform, the meaning of war, tradition, and the romantic concept of nature and man. The sketch is dense with allusions to particular men and events, so much so that full explanatory notes would bulk as large as the piece itself, but it is also timeless in the way in which it raises the particular to the universal. Hawthorne's contemporaries, from Emerson and Ellery Channing to Mrs. Bloomer, and the chief reforming movements of his time, from the French Revolution to feminism and the Oneida Colony, enter the picture; but the central concern remains with the permanent nature of man and of history.

"Once upon a time — but whether in the time past or time to come is a matter of little or no moment — this wide world had become so overburdened with an accumulation of worn-out trumpery that the inhabitants determined to rid themselves of it by a general bonfire." Hawthorne's guide to the site of the fire, on a prairie in the West, who interprets the events witnessed there, is another Virgil guiding Dante. And Hawthorne, like Dante, represents himself as bewildered, naïve, rather uncomprehending. The meaning of the sketch, then, is not to be found in the reactions of the narrator — Hawthorne — so much as in the comments of the "thoughtful observer" who guided him, and not so much in either as in the implications of the events themselves, partially summarized in the last paragraph by the narrator, who has profited by prolonged meditation on the events he witnessed so naïvely.

Neither the observer nor the narrator makes explicit some of the most important implications of the structure of the events they observe. The things that are burned in the fire as "wornout trumpery" range from the obviously vestigial remains of dead institutions and ideas to elements of tradition about which, in Hawthorne's opinion, there can be the sharpest debate. The principle of organization is to be found in his judgment of the universality of agreement; no reader, presumably, would agree with all the reformers, and each would draw at a different place the line between that which ought to be burned and that which ought to be saved. Thus the first thing the narrator sees being thrown in the flames is "the rubbish of the herald's office," which only the avowed monarchist, favoring return to the medieval system of a fixed social hierarchy, would want to save.

But if the need for this reform, and the benefits to be attained by it, are all but obvious, the reforms that follow are such as to command more and more qualified assent. The temperance reformers, for example, throw all alcoholic beverages on the flames, remarking correctly that drunkenness is an age-old evil. But it is at least questionable whether Prohibition is a good way to encourage temperance. The property of the privileged classes is destroyed by those eager to promote justice through economic equality. But the pre-Marxist socialism here alluded to does not seem as undebatable today as it did twenty years ago: it becomes increasingly doubtful whether justice will result from the organized avarice of class warfare.

Again, the restraining and stabilizing force of tradition is gladly burned while an Emersonian philosopher exclaims, "Now we shall get rid of the weight of dead men's thought, which has hitherto pressed so heavily on the living intellect that it has been incompetent to any effectual self-exertion." In later years in England Hawthorne sometimes resented the weight of tradition, but here the tone of the sketch suggests that he found this effort at reform mildly amusing.

The burning of worthless works of literature follows, with some of the most pointed comments Hawthorne ever made on his own productions and those of his contemporaries. An allusion to Emerson's advice to young men in "The American Scholar" not to be bookworms produced the comment from the narrator, "My dear sir, is not Nature better than a book?" in which the fallacies of uncreative "scholarship" and romantic "spontaneity" and nature-worship are equally balanced — and rejected. But the most debatable reform of all — in terms of the system of values implicit in the sketch — is yet to come. Religious reformers begin by burning the trappings of Popery and proceed to destroy the churches themselves. The narrator, taking the position that institutional religion is bad but "personal" religion is good, is still not disturbed, for, remembering perhaps Bryant's "Inscription for the Entrance to a Wood" and Emerson's constant advice, he believes that all that is being destroyed is finally unessential: " 'All is well,' said I, cheerfully. 'The woodpaths shall be the aisles of our cathedral, — the firmament itself shall be its ceiling. What needs an earthy roof between the Deity and his worshippers?' " When his guide remarks, "True, . . . but will they pause there?" the narrator is disturbed. He wonders whether it is an unmixed advantage that "The inhabitants of the earth had grown too enlightened to define their faith within a form of words, or to limit the spiritual by any analogy to our material existence. Truths which the heavens trembled at were now but a fable of the world's infancy."

When therefore the reformers finally burn all the religious literature of the past and a mighty wind comes roaring across the plain with a "desolate howl," the narrator grows pale and wonders whether the rage for reform will leave any value undestroyed. But he is comforted by his friend, who assures him that the truths which the enlightened reformers would destroy are too permanent to suffer destruction. "This," the narrator reflected,

was a strange assurance. Yet I felt inclined to credit it, the more especially as I beheld among the wallowing flames a copy of the Holy Scriptures, the pages of which, instead of being blackened into tinder, only assumed a more dazzling whiteness as the finger marks of human imperfection were purified away. Certain marginal notes and commentaries, it is true, yielded to the intensity of the fiery test, but without detriment to the smallest syllable that had flamed from the pen of inspiration.

Here then at last is a clear truth. Here is where Hawthorne drew the line between the probably justified and the dubiously worthwhile reforms on the one side and the plainly mistaken on the other. But we note that the crucial distinction is to be found in the description of an event witnessed, not in the interpretations offered by either the unwise narrator or the wise guide. Facts "speak for themselves," but what they say is always open to interpretation; and here the interpretation is left up to the reader.

What they said to Hawthorne becomes clear when we relate this passage to all his other expressed and implied opinions on the subject. Historical Christianity, he felt, had been and could properly still be believed with various degrees of "literalness." He was not ready to commit himself on the degree of literalness with which he himself believed it. But he was perfectly ready at all times to assert that the psychological, moral, and social truths embodied in the Christian tradition were too deeply imbedded in the nature of man and of things to be destroyed by enlightened seekers after novelty. Of the precise outlines of Hawthorne's personal religious faith I shall have more to say later. But at this point it is at least clear that, while recognizing and sympathizing with the valid claims of the Enlightenment, he was more profoundly in sympathy with the Christian tradition. Except in his last completed novel, *The Marble Faun* — and even that is only a partial exception — whenever he criticized historic Christianity it was from *within* its own system of values.

By contrast Emerson — whatever one's judgment of the validity of his position — criticized it always from the outside. The tradition was dead for Emerson, and he could not easily understand how it had ever been alive for thinking people. He thought the truth it contained had been misunderstood, and he would make it again available by suitable revisions. I do not wish to labor the point, but the tendency to blur distinctions that have unpleasant consequences is very strong in all of us. The distinction between the outlooks of Emerson, who thought that revelation was continuous and intuitive — "God is, not was" — and Hawthorne, who thought that revelation had been given in an historic event, is very sharp and as fundamental as any distinction that one is likely to be able to make. No wonder Emerson found he could not read Hawthorne and felt that his neighbor had wasted his talents writing trifles, while Hawthorne, despite the qualified praise given publicly in "The Old Manse," seems privately to have found Emerson tedious and without wisdom.

The sketch ends with a passage which should serve as a key to the way we must read all of Hawthorne's writing:

"Poh, poh, my good fellows!" said a dark-complexioned personage, who now joined the group, — his complexion was indeed fearfully dark, and his eyes glowed with a redder light than that of the bonfire; "be not so cast down, my dear friends; you shall see good days yet. There's one thing that these wiseacres have forgotten to throw into the fire, and without which all the rest of the conflagration is just nothing at all; yes, though they had burned the earth itself to a cinder."

"And what may that be?" eagerly demanded the last murderer.

"What but the human heart itself?" said the dark-visaged stranger with a portentous grin. "And unless they hit upon some method of purifying that foul cavern, forth from it will reissue all the shapes of wrong and misery — the same old shapes or worse ones — which they have taken such a vast deal of trouble to consume to ashes. I have stood by this livelong night and laughed in my sleeve at the whole business. Oh, take my word for it, it will be the old world yet!"

This brief conversation supplied me with a theme for lengthened thought. How sad a truth, if true it were, that man's agelong endeavor for perfection had served only to render him the mockery of the evil principle, from the fatal circumstance of an error at the very root of the matter! The heart, the heart, — there was the little yet boundless sphere wherein existed the original wrong of which the crime and misery of this outward world were merely types. Purify that inward sphere, and the many shapes of evil that haunt the outward, and which now seem almost our only realities, will turn to shadowy phantoms and vanish of their own accord; but if we go no deeper than the intellect, and strive, with merely that feeble instrument, to discern and rectify what is wrong, our whole accomplishment will be a dream, so unsubstantial that it matters little whether the bonfire, which I have so faithfully described, were what we choose to call a real event and a flame that would scorch the finger, or only a phosphoric radiance and a parable of my own brain.

"If we go no deeper than the intellect": if this is "romantic," it is also psychiatric; if it is Christian in its implications about the nature and role of the redemptive process, it is also, I believe most of us will agree, realistic, whatever the doctrinaire proponents of salvation through impersonal forces, "scientific" or "dialectical," may say. Here Hawthorne took his stand.

4

Among Hawthorne's notes for stories and sketches he never wrote is one for a piece "on the various kinds of death." Another suggests that "the diary of a coroner" would make a good subject. Still again he planned to write a tale in which "a figure of a gay, laughing, handsome youth, or a young lady, all at once, in a natural, unconcerned way, takes off its face like a mask, and shows the grinning, bare skeleton face beneath." These suggestions never got embodied in tales or sketches, but he did write a piece, not one of his best, on tombstones. And he turned the subject around to study the reverse side in the "elixir of life" theme that he tried repeatedly to treat successfully.

Death haunted Hawthorne, not in quite the same way that it did Poe, in terms of the horror of physical decay, but as it did Samuel Johnson and John Donne, as the most striking evidence of evanescence in a world where all was slipping and sliding into ruin. Hawthorne's love of Johnson was a love primarily of the man, not of the works. As he said in *Our Old Home* in connection with his pilgrimage to Lichfield to visit Johnson's birthplace, he did not remember "ever caring much about any of the stalwart Doctor's grandiloquent productions, except his two stern and masculine poems, 'London,' and 'The Vanity of Human Wishes.'" Like attracted like: he visited the spots where Johnson had walked and touched a balustrade that Johnson's hand must have touched. This act of devotion he could really *feel*. The Gothic cathedral, though surely "the most wonderful work which mortal man has yet achieved," left him uneasy: he could not "elevate" himself to its "spirited height." Yet, very typically, he deplored Johnson's "awful dread of death," which showed, he thought, "how much muddy imperfection was to be cleansed out of him, before he was capable of spiritual existence."

Like Johnson, who clung fiercely to classic stabilities in the face of literary and political revolutions which he understood better than some of his vehemently prejudiced utterances on them might lead us to believe, Hawthorne valued and tried to protect whatever elements of stability he could find in a world where all seemed subject to the Heraclitian flux. Like Johnson, he was a conservative and a traditionalist in this, and not in any lesser, sense. He was thoroughly aware of the danger of clinging to false stabilities, of valuing the form from which the inward meaning has gone. In *Our Old Home* — which is surely in competition only with Emerson's *English Traits* for the honor of being considered the greatest book ever written by an American on England — his remarks on English architectural and social evidences of antiquity make clear his resolute refusal to confuse the mask with the reality. But the deep longing was there, however much he wavered between patriotic praise of America as the land of the future and attraction to England and Italy, where the past was visibly present. His conservatism was a function of his sense of the pressure of time and death. It went deeper than his politics or his patriotism.

Even in his first, totally unsuccessful and immature published piece of fiction, *Fanshawe*, which he recognized almost immediately as bad and tried to destroy, Hawthorne struck the note which he never ceased for long to sound and which he returned to compulsively in the abortive romances of the last years. Fanshawe is a young scholar-recluse doomed to early death. He is able to sacrifice the girl to his rival without being unusually generous because death is more real, more present to him than life. He is of course a stereotype from the Gothic novels that Hawthorne had been reading. But he is more than that, for with some remodeling, of which the most important change was the dropping of the admiration with which he was portrayed, he served Hawthorne all through his career, sometimes as "villain," sometimes as objective self-portrait, but never again as "hero."

For Hawthorne did not admire morbidity, in himself or in others, though some of his contemporaries must have found him morbid, if we may judge anything from his family's repeated attempts to convince us that he was not. The man who saw the skeleton beneath the skin did not, like Poe and Whitman, enjoy self-dramatization. There is a world of difference between the portrayals of Roderick Usher and Coverdale or Young Goodman Brown, the difference between real morbidity and real health. Hawthorne had too much insight, too much capacity for self-criticism, to enjoy the posture of the young man in love with, or terrified by, death. If he himself felt its presence rather more strongly and frequently than he felt the reality of life, he knew that it was but one of several fundamental perceptions that man could lose sight of only at his peril. When he had occasion to, Hawthorne explained why this was so, as he had the wise guide explain in "Earth's Holocaust": "Death . . . is an idea that cannot easily be dispensed with in any condition between the primal innocence and that other purity and perfection which perchance we are destined to attain after travelling round the full circle."

5

There is frequently something a little forced about Hawthorne's "light" and cheerful sketches. He did a good many of them, and he liked to think that they were more "typical" of him than the pieces he later believed had been fashioned mostly out of "ice." Similarly, he preferred *The House of the Seven Gables*, with its "happy" ending, to *The Scarlet Letter*, though there has been very little disagreement among readers about which is the greater of the two novels. He was never entirely sure of himself when treating the "cheerful" subjects he wanted very much to treat convincingly.

Some of his sketches, particularly those that are least imaginative, remind us of another paradox of man and writer: he was a keen and accurate observer of men and events, but he seldom made any direct and extensive use of his observations in his best writing. And not because he did not care to: all of his life, and not simply in his years in England, Hawthorne filled his Notebooks with observations he hoped to use in stories. He made trips in the summers to what were then distant parts of New England, visited unusual spots, noted down the details of much that he saw. But he could usually find no way to use what he had gathered.

The often remarked barrenness of the English Notebooks when compared with the earlier American ones is related to the fact that in Hawthorne's new situation the temptation to observation was very great — or, as Hawthorne thought of it, the opportunities for gathering material were almost unlimited — while the stimulus to the functioning of his unique gift, his special kind of creative imagination, diminished. A chance like this was what he had always longed for as he sat in his little third-floor room in Salem, forced, as he thought, by the scantiness of his experience to fall back on his reading and his imagination for material for stories. There were so many castles and ruins in England, so much to see and inquire into and record. Surely what would come out of this would be a story far finer than those he had spun out of an early experience so limited that he had had little but the visions of the haunted mind to write about. But nothing came out of it, nothing at all in the way of even one completed novel or tale, nothing but frustration. Though he was in many ways an acute self-critic, especially of the limitations of his stories, Hawthorne did not fully understand the nature of his gift. He knew his weaknesses well enough but not his strength.

His sketchlike story "The Canterbury Pilgrims," on which I shall comment later in another connection, will illustrate the point. In 1831 Hawthorne took a trip with his uncle to Canterbury, New Hampshire, to visit a large Shaker community in that town. The existing American Notebooks do not begin until 1837, but C. P. Lathrop's study includes a part of a letter written in 1831 recording Hawthorne's impressions of this visit.

I walked to the Shaker village yesterday [he says], and was shown over the establishment, and dined there with a squire and a doctor, also of the world's people. On my arrival, the first thing I saw was a jolly old Shaker carrying an immense decanter of their superb cider; and as soon as I told him my business, he turned out a tumblerful and gave me. It was as much as a common head could clearly carry. Our dining-room was well furnished, the dinner excellent, and the table attended by a middle-aged Shaker lady, good looking and cheerful . . . This establishment is immensely rich. Their land extends two or three miles along the road, and there are streets of great houses painted yellow and tipt with red . . . On the whole, they lead a good and comfortable life, and, if it were not for their ridiculous ceremonies, a man could not do a wiser thing than to join them. Those whom I conversed with were intelligent, and appeared happy. I spoke to them about becoming a member of their society, but have come to no decision on that point.

We have had a pleasant journey enough . . . I make innumerable acquaintances, and sit down on the doorsteps with judges, generals, and all the potentates of the land, discoursing about the Salem murder [that of Mr. White], the cow-skinning of Isaac Hill, the price of hay, and the value of horse-flesh. The country is very uneven, and your Uncle Sam groans bitterly whenever we come to the foot of a low hill; though this ought to make me groan rather than him, as I have to get out and trudge every one of them.

When we have noted the tone of this letter, and the sorts of things Hawthorne observed and remembered — the cider, the well-furnished dining room, the rich land, the yellow and red houses — and then when we have gone back to "The Canterbury Pilgrims" to see what sort of story he made of this experience, we shall be in a position to begin to understand something of the relation of "experience" and art in Hawthorne, or, better, of the *kinds* of experiences in Hawthorne's life and the creative uses he was able to make of them. "The Canterbury Pilgrims" uses precisely three elements from this whole complex experience, and only two of them were matters of observation. Not mentioned in the letter quoted by Lathrop but undoubtedly impressive to Hawthorne after his five-mile trip from Canterbury village, was the granite watering trough, or "fountain," described in the opening of the tale and still to be seen today, though the spring which kept it full no longer flows into it. Then there was the fact, not only mentioned in the tale but used there symbolically, that the community is at the top of a hill above the spring. Finally, there is in the tale the *idea* of a Shaker settlement as a place of retreat from the world, an ascetic, an "other-worldly" community, a sort of Protestant monastery.

This is all. These are the elements of his visit to Canterbury that Hawthorne was able to use, the residuum amenable to his kind of creative shaping. The symbolic significance he attaches to the Shaker community in the tale — renunciation, asceticism, "other-worldliness" — is quite out of keeping with the impression we receive of *his* impression from his words about the cider, the jolly companions, and the excellent food, all of which tend to suggest that the Shakers have certainly not renounced the good things of the world in any very extreme way. There would seem, in short, to be a rather radical discontinuity between the impressions Hawthorne thought worth recording in his letter and the use made of the experience in the tale. If the suspicion arises that this degree of discontinuity is unusual in Hawthorne — we may think, after all, of the use of his notes on his trip to the Berkshires made in "Ethan Brand" — then we might check "The Canterbury Pilgrims" against the Notebook account of the later visit, with Melville and others, to another Shaker community. Here the divergence between the copious Notebook entry and the tale is even more striking. When toward the end of his life he tried hard to use his English and Italian notebook material in romances — and partially succeeded in *The Marble Faun* — he became involved, as we shall see, in creative problems which he never was able completely to solve. The relation between "experience" and art to be observed in a study of the genesis of "The Canterbury Pilgrims" was typical of the first two-thirds of Hawthorne's writing career, a period which saw nearly all of his greatest work produced.

Sometimes he tried so hard to write an imaginative piece based on observation that he almost succeeded. His "Buds and Bird Voices," the only "nature essay" he ever wrote, is a charming thing of its kind. It records the pleasure he and Sophia felt when spring came to the old manse, records it with attention to details like the lilac bushes under his study window and the litter on the lawn as the snow receded — "Nature is not cleanly, according to our prejudices." It is completely lacking in the gush and the attitudinizing so common in "nature appreciations." It is honest, cool, thoughtful. Yet its very virtues are the measure of its defects: it is so cool, so detached, so passionless that it is pretty clear that Hawthorne did not really care very much about the subject.

Put beside one of the many passages from Thoreau's pen on similar subjects, it suffers greatly from the comparison. It seems to be, as Hawthorne said of all his works in "Earth's Holocaust," made entirely out of ice. The very diction is icy in its impersonality and abstractness: the bird "voices" are never particularized, the "songsters" merely create a welcome "melody."

Only once does the sketch rise to Hawthorne's best level. The paragraph beginning "One of the things that strikes the attention when the white sheet of winter is withdrawn is the neglect and disarray that lay hidden beneath it" moves from the litter beneath the snow to the litter which the past has left in our own springtime, from this actual spring to springtime in Eden when the world was fresh and not littered with evidences of death and decay. On past and present, fatality and freedom, death and rebirth Hawthorne could really feel and write. He is removed from any comparison with Thoreau here, for he is writing from the center of a very different sensibility. The conscientious effort to describe is forgotten, and he is off on the track of meaning. But then the passage ends and the interest declines. Only in the final paragraph, when he returns to the experience of spring as "type" or "emblem" of a more general experience, does the essay regain something of the power of that one earlier paragraph.

His strictly autobiographical and journalistic sketches illustrate the same point. Reflections of his early experiences like the "Sketches from Memory" and "My Visit to Niagara" make interesting reading. Their veracity is so transparent, their descriptions of objects and events so patently to be trusted, that one has the sensation of being not in the presence of literature at all but of "sheer fact." And this is perhaps very nearly the case. Hawthorne's imagination was sluggish in the presence of Niagara Falls, as he himself was the first to insist. What distinguishes these descriptive pieces indeed is chiefly the amazing honesty with which they reflect not simply the thing seen — that is not after all so very rare an achievement — but the emotion with which it was seen, the aura and quality and meaning and value — or lack of it — of the seeing. Hawthorne in these pieces achieved nearly a hundred years earlier what Hemingway has said he tried to learn in the twenties: how to be true not simply to the fact but to the feeling about the fact. The other thing that distinguishes these pieces is the style, which was amazingly mature, controlled, and pure even in Hawthorne's earliest published writing.

Here then is the last paradox that I wish to underscore and that we shall have to try to understand: that the man who could observe so keenly, with so much detachment, and more than this, could note his feelings about what he saw with such perfect candor, could not do his best creative work when writing directly of his actual present experience of things and external events. This is a paradox not to be explained away by saying that Hawthorne wrote in the "romantic tradition," for his own tradition, the tradition which he accepted and felt, was compounded partly, to be sure, of the Gothic novel and Scott — himself not lacking in the ability to use the results of observation — but even more of Dante and Spenser and Bunyan and Johnson. Hawthorne, as has often been remarked, was in many respects more a man of the seventeenth and eighteenth centuries than of his own. Bunyan was more of a formative influence on him even than Scott, who was his favorite nineteenth-century writer. Surely "romanticism" did not prevent him from using the material in his Notebooks that he could not use.

If, with "Ethan Brand" as the chief exception, he could ordinarily use only the moral conceits, the snake in the stomach, the laugh which is misplaced and sinister, the man who searches around the world for the unpardonable sin, only to find it at last in himself, we must find some other explanation. Hawthorne's sensibility, I think we shall have to decide, could respond fully only to moral values. When he could see no moral significance in a fact, he could not ordinarily use the fact creatively. It followed that he could do his best work only when he was far enough from his subject so that the aspects of it to which he could not respond were not distracting. This would seem to be one of the chief reasons why his more personal sketches are generally the least satisfactory, and why in his fiction the past was so useful to him.

CHAPTER TWO

THE TALES: *The Use of the Past*

Hawthorne published *Fanshawe* in 1828 and attempted to destroy all copies of it soon afterward, convinced that it was too imperfect a work to deserve circulation. But even before *Fanshawe* was published he had begun to experiment with rather different materials from those which he had attempted unsuccessfully in *Fanshawe* to anneal into art. The two bodies of knowledge and experience that Hawthorne tried to work with when he started the novel were his recent experience at Bowdoin (perhaps *current* experience, if he began the work while in college, as may have been the case) and the convention of the Gothic romance. But deeper than these in the novel, and the source of those elements which make it possible for us to recognize even in it, conventional claptrap though it mostly is, certain ties with Hawthorne's greatest works, we find such abiding feelings and attitudes as the premonition of early death felt by the hero and the concern with the problem of isolation from normal life. Yet in writing *Fanshawe* Hawthorne could discover no adequate objective correlative for his feelings. His emotions, his recent experiences in college, and the Gothic formula for the novel could not be fused.

Meanwhile, in the earliest of the short tales, written before

Fanshawe was published, Hawthorne was beginning to find
his way. Most of the earliest short pieces are historical tales
in something very like the mode being created by Irving.
The chief impression one gets from "The Hollow of the
Three Hills," for instance, is that here Hawthorne is recreat-
ing an aspect of seventeenth-century New England for its
own sake — or for the sake of creating an American literature
based on American materials. When we think of these earliest pieces, we must think of Hawthorne and Irving together
as both attempting to accomplish what Emerson was soon to
recommend in his address to the American scholar, the creation of a truly national literature. As Irving was partly dis-
covering and partly manufacturing a folklore and a literature
for the Hudson Valley — and quickly running out of material,
so that he had to turn to England, Germany, and Spain for
fresh sources — so Hawthorne would seem, in these earliest
tales, to be concerned only with searching out the picturesque
aspects of the past of his own region in order at once to pre-
serve and create a New England legend.

Both of the two earliest surviving tales, for instance, "Alice
Doane's Appeal" and "The Hollow of the Three Hills," probably written just about the time of his graduation from college, treat that "picturesque wrong" of old New England,
witchcraft. Now that witchcraft was no longer believed in,
it offered a naturally romantic, a pleasantly thrilling, even a
"charming" subject, ideally suited to the young writer of
"sensibility" in the age of the romantic quest for the *outre*,
for it possessed the multiple advantages of being historical
and weird, a part of the not quite remote past, yet extraordinary. Here was something that would do in place of the
"storied and poetical associations" that Hawthorne and
James were later to deplore the lack of in the American scene.
When he came to write the preface to *The Marble Faun*,
Hawthorne would complain that "No author, without trial,
can conceive the difficulty of writing a romance about a

country where there is no shadow, no antiquity, no mystery, no picturesque and gloomy wrong, nor anything but a commonplace prosperity, in broad and simple daylight, as is happily the case with my dear native land." But now, just out of college and as yet neither weary nor sophisticated, Hawthorne was more easily satisfied. Witchcraft in seventeenth-century New England seemed gloomy and picturesque enough.

Yet even in these earliest tales there is more than Gothic romanticism and the exploitation of local history in the interest of sentiment. What Hawthorne discovered as he wrote his earliest tales was that material from the New England past provided the terms in which thought and sentiment, head and heart, could equally, and integrally, achieve expression. In the past of his ancestors he found the terms in which to *make sense* of his own feelings, to project them, to treat them, and to master them, as he had not found in *Fanshawe*, which had grown out of the relatively immediate present. How this is so will become clearer if we examine in some detail two of the early historical tales, one of which is interesting only as an experiment that failed, while the other is one of the finest tales Hawthorne ever wrote.

2

Some years after Hawthorne's death his surviving sister, Elizabeth, recalled that in 1825, the year of his graduation from college, Hawthorne had shown her his first work, "Seven Tales of My Native Land," later destroyed after it had been refused by publishers, and that among the tales was one called "Alice Doane." Hawthorne himself refers, in the frame of "Alice Doane's Appeal," to the fact that the tale he read to his listeners was one of "a series written years ago," most of which had "fed the flames." If his sister's memory was accurate and this internal reference can be depended upon, the inner tale must indeed be among the first that Hawthorne wrote. What we have in the present "Alice Doane's Appeal," then, is some fragments of an earlier tale incorporated in a sketch written probably not long before its publication in 1833.

If, as has been said, the late romances should have been short stories, it may with equal justice be said of this sketch that it contains material for a novel. It opens with Hawthorne describing a walk he once took with two female companions to Gallows Hill. Impressed by the tragic and terrible history of the spot, where now "everything that should nourish man or beast . . . has been destroyed" by woodwax, as though a physical curse had blasted the place, he decided to try to make his companions as aware of the past of the ground on which they stood as he himself was. Accordingly, he read to them a tale he had once written about murder and witchcraft in seventeenth-century Salem. Certain portions of the tale which he read are quoted in the sketch; the rest is incompletely summarized, with the transitions between the quoted fragments managed by such expressions as "I read on, and . . . described"; "By this fantastic piece of description . . . I intended to throw a ghostly glimmer round the reader"; and "I dare not give the remainder of the scene."

The tale thus partly quoted and partly summarized is highly complex. In main outline it runs like this: Leonard Doane, living alone with his sister since their parents were killed by Indians, and possessed by what Hawthorne calls a "morbid" affection for her, in a jealous rage kills a young stranger who has made love to her. Then he confesses his crime to a wizard, who by his sinister chuckles and smiles makes it clear that he already knows all about it and must indeed, through witchcraft, have had a hand in contriving it. Finally the brother and sister walk to the graveyard and there witness the multitude of the dead rising from their

graves and going through the actions habitual to them in life.
The fragments of the tale included in the sketch do not
justify the emphasis given by the title to Alice, who exists in
the fragments merely as a name, while the characters of her
brother and his victim are at least lightly sketched in.

Nevertheless, nearly all of Hawthorne's later themes are
implicit in the work: the secret guilt, the haunted mind,
fate, the universal sin, the curse from the past. Leonard
Doane is said to be conscious of a guilt deeper and more
terrible even than that for the murder he has committed.
He is haunted by an obscure shame and an obscure dread,
so that the world seems cold and unreal, frozen and lifeless.
He has a feeling of being *compelled* by some nameless force,
of being bewitched. These are the strands from which many
of Hawthorne's finest and most typical tales were later
woven.

But the strands are not woven in this tale, they are loosely
tangled. I have the impression as I read the tale that there
is a significant revelation of Hawthorne here, that Hawthorne
has not achieved the distance between himself and his symbols necessary for a good story, and that the tale is curiously
like the late unfinished romances. Two or three scenes are
particularly significant. First, there is that part of the inter-
view between Doane and the wizard in which Doane describes the events leading up to his murder of Walter Brome.
Brome is, as Randall Stewart has pointed out, an early and
rather mechanically contrived sketch of the typical Hawthorne villain — hard, cold, egotistical, mocking, educated
"in the cities of the old world." But the significant fact is not
his villainy but his likeness, very strongly emphasized, to
Doane, who, like that other early morbid protagonist, Fanshawe, is a sympathetic character. He was, Doane finally
realizes after he has killed him, the very "counterpart" of
Doane himself.

And the likeness is not simply or even chiefly physical.

Doane recognizes in his enemy the traits and potentialities, both good and bad, which he knows to exist in himself: "my soul had been conscious of the germ of all the fierce and deep passions, and of all the many varieties of wickedness, which accident had brought to their full maturity in him. Nor will I deny that, in the accursed one, I could see the withered blossom of every virtue, which, by a happier culture, had been made to bring forth fruit in me." If in the other passages describing him Brome is a sort of stage villain, as Professor Stewart says, he is saved from being a mere contrivance by this. In him the adequate symbol is not achieved, but the Hawthorne sensibility may be seen at work.

Hawthorne's sympathy for the darker sides of life, his intuitive knowledge of the springs and conditions of human action, his sense of what E. A. Robinson later expressed as "how little we have to do with what we are," a sense which he made the central theme of "Wakefield," prevented him from sentimentalizing his protagonists as it did from caricaturing his "villains." It was moreover an aspect of his sense of brotherhood, for he saw as a significant part of our shared fate the fact that we are all liable to the influence of conditions beyond our control. Thus though he exercised moral judgment, he condemned actions and attitudes rather than people. Hawthorne's villains are usually convincing precisely because Hawthorne understands the reasons for their villainy and distinguishes between actor and action. Thus Wakefield was not an evil man, Rappaccini loved his daughter, Chillingworth was at first a mild and unworldly scientist who had led a blameless life. We recall that Hawthorne said in "Fancy's Show Box" that "Man must not disclaim his brotherhood, even with the guiltiest, since, though his hand be clean, his heart has surely been polluted by the flitting phantoms of iniquity."

But there is another passage even more revealing than this. Doane continues to tell the wizard his tale. He tells how he

met Brome on a lonely road, how he was maddened by
Brome's revelation that Alice loved him, how he struck him
down and was terrified by what he had done and horrified
by the expression on the dead man's face, where death
looked "so life-like and so terrible." Then, as he looked at
the man he had just killed, he had a "vision." The passage
that follows is so suggestive, so revealing in its combination
of power in itself and irrelevance to the rest of the fragments,
that it must be quoted entire. If ever a competent psycho-
analytic study of Hawthorne is done, surely this will come
under consideration. Remembering the death of Hawthorne's own father when Hawthorne was four, the neuroti-
cism of his mother and his elder sister, his own years of unhappy seclusion, his feeling that he had been "saved" by his
marriage, his lifelong restlessness which, after the first year
or so, not even his marriage, happy though it was, could cure,
one can make what he wishes out of this hallucination in
which there is lacking only the explicit transference of the
guilt:

I know not what space of time I had thus stood, nor how the vision
came. But it seemed to me that the irrevocable years since childhood
had rolled back, and a scene, that had long been confused and broken
in my memory, arrayed itself with all its first distinctness. Me thought I
stood a weeping infant by my father's hearth; by the cold and blood-
stained hearth where he lay dead. I heard the childish wail of Alice,
and my own cry arose with hers, as we beheld the features of our
parent, fierce with the strife and distorted with the pain, in which his
spirit had passed away. As I gazed, a cold wind whistled by, and
waved my father's hair. Immediately I stood again in the lonesome
road, no more a sinless child, but a man of blood, whose tears were
falling fast over the face of this dead enemy. But the delusion was
not wholly gone; that face still wore a likeness of my father; and
because my soul shrank from the fixed glare of the eyes, I bore the
body to the lake, and would have buried it there. But before his icy
sepulchre was hewn, I heard the voices of two travellers and fled.

Still another scene demands special attention. Like the

brother-sister relation and the remarkable vision of the dead father who is also an enemy, it invites reading in psycho-analytic terms. But unlike them it is a persistent explicit symbol in Hawthorne's works. It is a picture of a *frozen* world. In an effort, as he says, to throw a "ghostly glimmer round the reader," Hawthorne describes Salem during an ice storm. Ice glittered everywhere in the cold darkness, and "One looked to behold inhabitants suited to such a town, glittering in icy garments, with motionless features, cold, sparkling eyes, and just sensation enough in their frozen hearts to shiver at each other's presence." Now this description of a frozen world is quite unnecessary for the fragmentary "plot" of the inner tale. It is, in fact, not even satisfactorily linked with the other fragments. Like so much of the material in *Fanshawe*, it is the projection of the experience of an immature writer who has not yet achieved impersonality. As in *Fanshawe*, Hawthorne here "worked in" something he had known just because it had been important to him. In *Fanshawe* it was the countryside around Bowdoin where he had rambled and been comparatively happy; in "Alice Doane's Appeal" it was the Salem in which he had shivered and longed to "open an intercourse with the world."

It is perhaps unnecessary to remark that this scene suggests some of Hawthorne's most persistent themes and character types in one powerful omnibus symbol that is more expressive than the phantoms in "Fancy's Show Box." Here we are close to the deep channel of the current of Hawthorne's imagination. In *Fanshawe* Hawthorne had portrayed a young man estranged from normal human relations, but in that work the strength of the Gothic tradition which he was uncritically following in an effort to write something salable had tinged his portrait of the scholar-recluse with admiration. In "Alice Doane's Appeal" the isolation is more impersonal: there is less of Gothic tradition and of conscious self-portraiture to complicate and confuse the projection. In later works he was to become more critical of the self-image, picturing isolation as the evil most to be avoided, the frozen heart as the origin of sin.

Finally, there is the climactic scene of the dead arising from their graves as Leonard and Alice Doane watch, certainly entranced, possibly bewitched, compelled in horror and fascination. When brother and sister arrive at the graveyard, graves open and the past inhabitants of the town appear. Our first impression on beginning to read the passage is that *all* the dead are here; at the end, we feel confused: are these all the dead, or merely the damned among the dead? Finally we decide that there is certainly a crucial confusion here, but that it is not in the mind of the reader.

The opening is clear enough:

> Each family tomb had given up its inhabitants . . . There was the gray ancestor, the aged mother, and all their descendants . . . There, too, were the children who went prattling to their tomb, and there the maiden who yielded her early beauty to death's embrace . . . old defenders of the infant colony . . . pastors of the church . . . ready to call the congregation to prayer . . . *All, in short, were there; the dead of other generations.* [Italics are mine.]

It comes, then, as a shock to read in the final sentence of the long paragraph that "none but souls accursed were there, and fiends counterfeiting the likeness of departed saints." Why this confusion of the damned with the dead? Is Hawthorne more Calvinistic than the Puritans themselves and condemning to perdition not only the unregenerate but all the former inhabitants of Salem? To ask such a question is to answer it. No one who knows Hawthorne's works can suppose that he believed in the doctrine of total depravity in the sense in which Jonathan Edwards did. And, of course, even if he had shared Edwards' outlook without significant difference, he could not have found in the doctrine any sanction for picturing *all* the dead as damned. No, this passage has less to do with Hawthorne's beliefs than with his feelings.

And it is just as clear that it is not structurally demanded by the rest of the tale. Nothing in the inner tale is clarified, nothing strengthened, by this radical confusion. Logically, the paragraph is simply inept.

Yet the confusion is significant. In the hideousness, the agony, the torment ascribed to all the dead, Hawthorne's deepest experience is speaking, as it is in the picture of the icy world. Only in the last, anticlimactic, and unconvincing sentence does he criticize and rationalize his feeling. In a vivid page he projects his symbol; in a sentence he guards himself against the accusation that he has been guilty of an error of judgment. None but the damned were here, but all were damned! Such a statement could not be allowed to stand, must be modified by the addition of "counterfeiting" fiends. In just the same way the strongly felt description of the frozen world had to be called, in the first sentence of the following paragraph, a "fantastic piece of description." Just so the whole tale must be framed in comments calculated to remove it to a safe distance.

There is a sense in which we may say that there is more revelation here than is intended. Hawthorne wanted to open an intercourse with the world, but he had no desire to lay bare his mind and heart to the casual reader. Of course it depends on what we mean by "expression" whether this tale is deeply expressive or not. On the psychological level I think it expresses a great deal. Artistically it expresses only certain blocks of feeling which Hawthorne afterwards learned to build together into unified structures. The later great tales are both more impersonal and finally more expressive, for in them fantasy has been transmuted into art. Not until he had achieved his full artistic stature could he, in "Young Goodman Brown," deal in universal, permanent, and fully meaningful terms with this sense of the omnipresence of guilt.

The sketch ends with a frame paragraph which serves as a key to Hawthorne's use of the past in all his works. The reading of the manuscript story had produced the desired effect, it had made the past come alive for the listeners. "I had reached the seldom trodden places of their hearts, and found the wellspring of their tears." Hawthorne had achieved the effect which any young writer in 1830 who was uncertain of his powers might be expected to desire. But the emphasis in the end is not on what Hawthorne as artist has achieved but on what his re-creation of the past has done and should do. "And now the past had done all it could." And what was that?

It was, as Hawthorne put it, "to assist the imagination in appealing to the heart." And *the heart* in Hawthorne's usage suggests both emotions and will. Perhaps in most general terms we could say that the vision of the past was intended to arouse the emotions of pity and terror, pity for the unfortunate dead and terror because they were so like ourselves. The emphasis throughout the tale is on the continuity of past and present, and the final sentence reëmphasizes the point which has been made both implicitly and explicitly throughout: "And here, in dark, funereal stone, should rise another monument, sadly commemorative of the errors of an earlier race, and not to be cast down while the human heart has one infirmity that may result in crime."

The belief in witchcraft, and the judicial murders that it led to, Hawthorne has said in symbol and statement, are fortunately things of the past, but our kinship with the persecutors and the persecuted remains and will remain. We too know the evil passions of the wizard, the emotions of the murderer and the murdered, the fear of the victims. We too tread the streets of an icy and still bewitched village. Death so terrible and so lifelike and life so helpless, so frozen, so deathlike, have appeared before us to be recognized for what they are. The past has illuminated the present and thus has helped to educate the will, which is concerned with the future.

3

On the surface, "My Kinsman, Major Molineux" is a historical tale of the disturbances occasioned by the conflict of crown and people in Massachusetts Colony. Young Robin, looking in the city for his wealthy kinsman, who will, he hopes, help him to rise in the world, finds at last, at the end of a mysteriously frustrating search, that Major Molineux is an unpopular Tory and is indeed being ridden out of town on a rail by an angry mob, whose leaders are disguised so that they may not be recognized by the authorities. Since there can be no help from this quarter, Robin is advised by a friendly stranger to return to the country and to rise in the world without the help of his kinsman.

This historical level of the tale is not merely started and then dropped,* as the corresponding level is in some of the later tales. It is carried through from beginning to end with fullness and consistency. The opening paragraph is devoted entirely to establishing the historicity of the story, even mentioning the sources on which Hawthorne had drawn. And after this historical "preface," as Hawthorne calls it, we are never allowed to forget that this is a piece of historical fiction. We see aspects of the clothing and manners of the age;

---

* For a reading of the tale which penetrates beneath the surface, yet finds historical concerns, in the form of political and social judgments, at the center of the work, see Q. D. Leavis, "Hawthorne as Poet," *Sewanee Review*, Spring and Summer 1951. Mrs. Leavis' interpretation seems to me interesting and valuable but somewhat misleading in its exclusively sociological emphasis.

An allegorical reading of a very different kind, in which Robin, growing to maturity, encounters Evil in the persons of the Devil (the two-faced stranger) and four of his assistant tempters, Sloth (the watchman), Avarice (the innkeeper), Lust (the prostitute), and Pride (the man of authoritative bearing) has been suggested to me by Mr. Richard Diesko. It seems to me that such a reading is essentially valid and could be worked out in detail.

If neither this nor Mrs. Leavis' reading requires any forcing of the text, then I think we are justified in concluding that this tale which has received hardly any critical attention is far richer than has been supposed.

we see the aroused populace preparing its triumph over the aristocracy and laughing at Robin for his innocence; we meet, with Robin, a prostitute in a back street, vivid with laughter and beckoning and scarlet petticoat. When we see the marching crowd, we understand, as at first Robin does not, the nature of the proceedings, the reasons for the disguises, and the political significance of this "democratic" mob action.

But about three pages along in the story we become aware of another set of meanings at work. When Robin is "pursued by an ill-mannered roar of laughter from the barber's shop," we begin to feel the tale taking on the texture of a dream. And this feeling continues and grows, until at last Robin falls asleep and is left wondering how much of the night's adventure he has dreamed and how much experienced waking. Laughter echoes through the tale as a dominant motive, cruel, mocking laughter, like the laughter of the wizard in "Alice Doane," laughter that bewilders and shames Robin as it pursues him through "a succession of crooked and narrow streets" in which he becomes "entangled." Caught in a maze from which there seems no escape, searching for something forever eluding him, innocent yet somehow obscurely in the wrong, Robin experiences complete frustration before sleep and the friendly stranger come to his aid and restore the sanity that had seemed to be slipping away in the ambiguity of evil and innocence.

When Robin meets the mysteriously sinister person with the twin bulges on his forehead he is simply frightened and bewildered. But the reader understands the reasons for the terror: for this leader of the mob, disguised for safety's sake, is in some sense the Devil himself, complete with scarcely concealed horns, eyes that glow "like fire in a cave," and a complexion appropriate to the lord of sin and death — "One side of the face blazed an intense red, while the other was black as midnight." No wonder that "the effect was as if two individual devils, a fiend of fire and a fiend of darkness, had united themselves to form this infernal visage."

Here then are all the ingredients of an adventure with good and evil going on beneath the surface of an apparently simple historical tale. Stretched on the frame of the archetypal journey-search plot, the dream material takes on more and more connotations as "that evening of ambiguity and weariness" proceeds. I have called attention to the laughter, but only a very close reading of the tale will disclose with what subtle and complex effects it is used. From the first roar of mirth coming from the barber's shop, to the laughter of all those in the tavern, "in which the innkeeper's voice might be distinguished, like the dropping of small stones into a kettle," to the "drowsy laughter — stealing along the solitary street," following and shaming Robin after his encounter with the woman in the scarlet petticoat, to the "sluggish merriment" of the beadle and the "peal of laughter like the ringing of silvery bells" of the saucy maid in scarlet, the laughter builds up in intensity until at the climax the laughing voices blend in one ugly roar and Robin himself, bewitched, joins in. "The contagion was spreading among the multitude, when all at once, it seized upon Robin, and he sent forth a shout of laughter that echoed through the street, — every man shook his sides, every man emptied his lungs, but Robin's shout was the loudest there." Then, after a pause when there seemed nothing left in the world but that hideous laughter, the mob moved on, "like fiends that throng in mockery around some dead potentate, mighty no more, but majestic still in his agony."

No wonder Robin felt that his mind was "vibrating between fancy and reality." No wonder he was "almost ready to believe that a spell was on him." For the laughter that never ceases throughout the tale, yet never for a moment remains the same or is without realistic justification, is as sinister as the laughter of any of Hawthorne's men of evil in any of his works: as hysterically compulsive as the laughter in "Alice Doane's Appeal," which is heard even in the voice of the wind and seen frozen on the face of the "dead enemy" that "still wore the likeness of my father"; as cold as the smiles of Chillingworth and Rappaccini; as contaminating as the laughter of Westervelt, in which Coverdale, like Robin before him, joins against his will. Hawthorne made much of laughter as a mask of evil in all his works, but nowhere did he use it with more powerful effect and more subtle and far-reaching meaning than here, where it is the dominant image throughout.

But all the while that the laughter is echoing and reëchoing as through the labyrinths of an endless cavern of the mind, other images are contributing their implications to make this the journey of Everyman. Like the "enemy" in "Alice Doane" who is recognized in dream as the father, Major Molineux embodies paternal kinship, here removed to the safer distance of father's cousin. Again, the feeling of compulsion that is given historical justification in "Alice Doane" and "Young Goodman Brown" by being externalized in "witchcraft," is here too, but less disguised, appearing as various levels of consciousness, or "degrees" of dream, from the mere feeling of "strangeness" that first overcomes Robin, to the suspicion that he has been bewitched, to the apparently waking nightmare of his laughter as the procession goes by, to the actual sleep that steals over him at some point undiscoverable either by him or by the reader, leaving in final doubtfulness the question of how much has been "real" and how much "dream," how much externally suggested and how much internally projected.

As the waking and the dream worlds become more and more confused, all distinctions lose their clarity, all certainty slips and slides into ambiguity. Robin's simple, straightforward questions become occasions for obscene mirth. The woman in scarlet, with her face "oval and pretty, her hair dark beneath the little cap," and her eyes bright, speaks so winningly that Robin "could not help doubting whether that sweet voice spoke Gospel truth." A dreadful uncertainty disturbs Robin: "What if the object of his search, which had been so often and so strangely thwarted, were all the time mouldering in his shroud?" Utterly alone despite the many he had met and been unable really to communicate with, Robin longs for the companionship of "any breathing thing" to break his terrible isolation. But when he recalls the happy domestic scenes of his childhood, he feels more desolate than ever, for now "he was excluded from his home."

Bewildered by the shifting appearances of the leader in evil, by the laughter and the shouting, Robin is enlightened by the friendly stranger whom he has encountered beside the church and who asks, "May not a man have several voices, Robin, as well as two complexions?" But the enlightenment does not go deep enough to prepare him for what happens as "the double-faced fellow" fixes his hypnotic gaze on Robin. For when Robin finally sees his kinsman, "large and majestic" but with a face as "pale as death" with the shame of his situation, his knees shake and his hair bristles with the depths of his emotion, compounded, as Hawthorne says, of "pity and terror." A "bewildering excitement . . . seizes upon his mind," he joins the evil throng in laughter at his kinsman's expense, and his innocence is lost.

" 'Well, Robin, are you dreaming?' inquired the gentleman, laying his hand on the youth's shoulder." Was Goodman Brown dreaming all those terrible revelations of his night in the forest? Does it matter? Truth, as Hawthorne often remarked, may sometimes come more clearly to the haunted mind hovering between sleep and waking than to the mind fully awake. As all the separate peals of laughter join in the mighty shout that awakens Robin at the point when his dream would have become intolerable, they reveal more about man's image of himself as the destroyer of the father — because he has wished the destruction — a destroyer bathed in guilt yet somehow justified, than do any stories in American literature in the nineteenth century, with the exception perhaps of some of Melville's. And the art here is more perfect, because less compulsive, than Melville usually achieved.

Everything in the story contributes to this perfection of embodiment. I have stressed the dominant image of laughter, but color too plays its part, from the black and red of the projected and personified evil in the leader of the mob to the scarlet seductiveness of the sweet-voiced girl who whispers of sin, from the blackness of the night in which Robin wanders to the "radiance" in the church and "golden light" in which he visualizes his father holding the Scriptures. Shapes, too, and distortions of shape, play their part in the revelation: the stone pillar to which Robin clings, the horseman with the sword, the phantasmagoria of figures half-seen before and behind but unapproachable. "Next he endeavored to define the form of distant ghostly indistinctness, just as his eye appeared to grasp them." Two objects most engage his attention toward the end, the church where he takes refuge and the mansion with the pillars and the Gothic window. But nothing, not even the seemingly solid mansion, is what it seems, or remains for long what it was in this world of shifting values: "by turns, the pillars of the balcony lengthened into the tall, bare stems of pines, dwindled down to human figures, settled once again into their true size and shape, and then commenced a new succession of changes." Out of such bewildering fluidity could come no hope of finding what he sought, until the words of the friendly stranger suggest that he accept the revealed reality and learn to do without the "kinsman." "You may rise in the world without the help of your kinsman, Major Molineux."

So ends a tale which belongs with the finest that Hawthorne produced, belongs indeed among the greatest stories in the language. What it "means" cannot be stated in any other way than by repeating the story, for it says what it means in the only way possible. But its *meanings* can be explored from a psychoanalytic, from an ethical, from a sociological, and from other points of view. It raises to the level of myth the universal search for the father and the need to redefine the terms of the search. It defines the universal involvement in guilt, as do "Alice Doane" and "Young Goodman Brown," and then it transcends the guilt without denying it, as those tales do not. It states as few stories do the theme that Emerson stated so insistently, the need for freedom from the past, a fresh start in every generation; but it shows that this is not possible until the past has really been met, seen for what it is, and accepted with all its implications of ambiguity and guilt. Passing through the stages of initial identification with the father image, rejection, and shame, Robin emerges at last with the help of the stranger into maturity. Between Leonard Doane's obsessive guilt and Robin's implied attitude at the end of the story there is a crucial difference. "Major Molineux" points both back to the tale of Alice Doane and forward to "Young Goodman Brown"; but its closer affinities are with the latter story, in which another young man discovers the universal involvement in guilt, only to have his discovery ruin his life because he absolutizes his partial insight and is unable thereafter to believe in the good ambiguously mingled with the evil. Again, we may compare Robin with Giovanni of "Rappaccini's Daughter," to the latter's disadvantage: for Giovanni, like several other naïve young men in Hawthorne's work, was unprepared for the ambiguity of the "mesh of good and evil" that he discovered in Rappaccini's garden and denied that it had any application to him.

As a psychological tale, then, "Major Molineux" tells us that the individual's growth to maturity is difficult and painful and involves a guilt which must be accepted. As an ethical allegory it suggests both that many snares lie in wait for the young man and that any simple dichotomy of good and evil is too simple to represent the facts. As a tale with philosophical implications, if we let the kinsman symbolize the past, it implies a rejection of both archaism and futurism, suggesting instead a dynamic conception of history. It thus not only looks back to the remarks on the appropriation of the past in the ending of "Alice Doane's Appeal" but forward to the treatment of history in *The House of the Seven Gables.* The story "means" all these things, and more; for its meanings are as endless as the reverberations of the myth which it produces from the depths of dream and the past and shapes creatively into art.

4

"My Kinsman, Major Molineux" was published in 1832, a year before the portions of the tale of Alice Doane and her brother that Hawthorne had managed to salvage came into print, a year after the publication of "The Wives of the Dead" and two years after "The Hollow of the Three Hills." It belongs with the stories written during the first half-dozen years of the apprenticeship, and its greatness partially justifies Hawthorne's discouraged remark made in a preface nearly a quarter of a century later that he could see little improvement in the late tales over the early ones. Yet if it is as good as the best that he could produce twenty years later, it is just as clearly in a very different category from what he was producing only a few years before. Hawthorne achieved aesthetic control of his materials in the years between 1825 and about 1831. In the twenty-year period that followed, all of his greatest work was published.

What he learned between 1825 and 1831 can be stated in many ways, in many different terms suggested by different, and valid, approaches. But I suggest that the formulation which most needs to be made at the present stage of Hawthorne criticism and scholarship will take its direction from the visible changes to be studied in Hawthorne's use of the past in his early tales. Hawthorne learned his craft as he learned what to do with the past. His often remarked transformation of the Gothic tale into the moral tale was a transformation of the terms in which he treated his material. The material itself did not change: there are as many Gothic elements in "Young Goodman Brown," published in 1835, as in "The Hollow of the Three Hills," as many in *The Scarlet Letter* and "Ethan Brand" in 1850 as in "Major Molineux," and considerably more in *Blithedale* and *The Marble Faun* and the late unfinished romances than in "Roger Malvin's Burial" or "The Wives of the Dead," both published in 1832. The material, again, does not notably change; the terms change. Hawthorne's "creativeness" lay in his invention, or discovery, of the terms in which he could treat the past in his own way.

To treat it in this way was to master it. One half of Hawthorne the man felt that, as he said in *The Scarlet Letter*, "the stern and sad truth" was that "the breach which guilt has once made into the human soul is never, in this mortal state, repaired." The other half believed, or believed he believed, that there was freedom as well as fate in life, so that a fresh start was possible, choice was real, the past not completely determinative of the future. I suspect that Hawthorne the man never resolved this crucial uncertainty. But Hawthorne the artist resolved it in his stories, in as many different ways as there are stories. The hope of "Major Molineux," the triumph of "Egotism, or the Bosom Serpent," the quiet confidence of "Young Goodman Brown," the ambiguity of *The Scarlet Letter*, the somewhat forced confidence of *The House of the Seven Gables*, the desperate questioning of *The Marble Faun*, are some of Hawthorne's ways of resolving the question of the nature and meaning of the past.

"The past" for Hawthorne extended unbroken through his own past and the past of his race and place, with no artificial boundary between what was "his own" and what was "merely history." For Hawthorne both consciously and unconsciously — as indeed for all of us, though we do not often recognize it and may even have the folly to deny it — the past was living in him, so that any boundary at all would be artificial. Hence the earliest tales in which he achieved mastery of his art are both "personal" — in that they objectify aspects of his personal past which we are tempted today to read in Freudian terms — and "historical" — in that they treat old New England. A useful approach to the problem of what Hawthorne learned between 1825 and 1831 is suggested by saying that he found in the past of New England a way of projecting and objectifying the concerns, the tensions, and the deep feelings that haunted him from the personal past of his childhood.

In "Alice Doane's Appeal" he had tried to bring to expression some of the feelings of "our secret souls." He had "rolled back," as he said, the "irrevocable years since childhood" and written compulsively of fantasies that could not be criticized in that form. The "blood-stained hearth," the guilt of the protagonist, "no more a sinless child, but a man of blood," the dead enemy-father who was yet also obscurely the self, the "unutterable crime, perpetrated . . . in madness or a dream," these symbols had to be further impersonalized before they could be treated rationally and artfully. (Not that art is necessarily perfectly rational, but in all but "automatic writing" and certain types of surrealism, the conscious mind operates, I assume, as critic and judge.) In "Major Molineux" and in many stories written in the same period and later, he achieved the necessary distance, found the way to the necessary impersonality, discovered the terms which enabled him to treat the themes that he had to treat if he was to do his best work. For Hawthorne as for James — and perhaps for any artist in proportion to his greatness — his art was his life and his life his art.

That he could not successfully, despite lifelong efforts to do so, treat "contemporary" experience does not contradict this. For Hawthorne, as for all of us, "experience" existed at different levels and had different degrees of relevance and urgency. When company called Hawthorne was often absent, even when he did not disappear out the back door on their arrival. It is certainly no exaggeration, though it may invite misinterpretation, to say that Hawthorne did not understand his current external experience as he understood his experience, through reading and memory and thought, of the past. "Sublime and beautiful facts," Hawthorne wrote in his volume of English sketches entitled *Our Old Home* — and he might have said all the facts in which he was most interested as an artist, had not the context demanded the narrowed statement — "sublime and beautiful facts are best understood when etherealized by distance." Distance was necessary that facts might be steeped long in a "powerful menstruum of thought."

The voluminous notes intended to provide authentic backgrounds for projected romances which fill his English and Italian journals were useless to him, as he suspected with increasing distinctness that they would be even while he gathered them and as proved to be the fact when he returned to America and tried to use them. "I once hoped, indeed," he wrote in 1863 in the preface to *Our Old Home*, to which he had turned after realizing that it would be impossible for him ever to complete his English romance,

that so slight a volume would not be all that I might write. These and other sketches, with which in a somewhat rougher form than I have given them here, my journal was copiously filled, were intended for the side-scenes and backgrounds and exterior adornment of a work of fiction of which the plan had imperfectly developed itself in my mind, and into which I ambitiously proposed to convey more of various modes of truth than I could have grasped by direct effort. Of course, I should not mention this abortive project, only that it has been utterly thrown aside and will never now be accomplished. The Present, the Immediate, the Actual has proved too potent for me. It takes away not only my scanty faculty, but even my desire for imaginative composition.

Though he was probably thinking in part of the Civil War and other current distractions when he blamed the Present for his failure of creative imagination, the facts of his whole career as a writer justify our assuming a far broader referent for "the Present, the Immediate, the Actual": not just the Civil War, but any experience present, immediate, and actual had always, in greater or less degree, proved "too potent" for him. He should have known when he was compiling them, as he realized later, what must happen to his notes before he could use them creatively. When he had attempted earlier to use current material in his romance about Brook Farm, the place had turned out to be not Brook Farm at all but a false Paradise, a delusive Arcadia, or the mythical Happy Valley of Imlac and Rasselas. Hawthorne's contemplation of his most recent external — and superficial — experience usually produced sketches, not tales; and when it was used in tales and romances it almost never produced his best and most typical work.

So we may say that when Hawthorne learned how to use the past, he learned how to treat the present and the future in the only way possible to him. Seeing the reflections mirrored in the well of the past, he could, in the fullest sense, understand them, and so deal with them.

CHAPTER THREE

THE TALES: *The Discovery of Meaning*

We have no proper term for the type of story Hawthorne created. The best of his tales are not quite what we usually mean by allegories, though some of them come rather close to fitting the ordinary meaning of that term. Neither are they symbolic stories of the type exemplified by "Flowering Judas," though again a few of them approach quite closely the sort of thing Miss Porter did in her famous story. At their most typical they lack something of the "illusion of reality" that characterizes the stories of Kafka, though they resemble them in the possibilities for allegorical interpretation they contain. Most obviously of all, they are not fiction of the type that fills the popular magazines today — or any day — with imaginary people and events designed to take our minds off our problems, help us to escape our boredom and our pain, or amuse us with "harmless" daydreams; in short, fiction with only one controlled level of meaning, and that the simplest, based on the most primitive of the many appeals fiction makes to us. Most of Hawthorne's best tales exist, like the stories of Conrad Aiken, in a realm somewhere between symbolism and allegory, as those terms are used today. If we are to arrive at a more precise statement than this, we shall have to analyze Hawthorne's procedure in general, and then look closely at several of his stories in particular.

One of the most valuable of Hawthorne's commentators, the late F. O. Matthiessen, put the matter in a way that may be taken to represent the usual opinion. Hawthorne started, he tells us, "with a dominant moral idea, for which [the scene he was describing], like Spenser's, was to be an illustration." Thus Pearl, in *The Scarlet Letter*, should be studied "as the purest type of Spenserian characterization, which starts with abstract qualities and hunts for their proper embodiment." * Hawthorne, according to this way of thinking, was an allegorist and his tales are allegories.

But there are several reasons why such a classification is inadequate. In the first place, Hawthorne's practice in his tales is not always the same kind of practice. "The Great Carbuncle" may profitably be studied in terms of Spenserian allegory, but "The Wives of the Dead" bears no discernible relation to that traditional form. In between these two extremes lies Hawthorne's normal practice. Though Hawthorne's debt to Spenser was very great, we should not fall into the error of trying to make a discovered relationship account for too much.

In the second place, it is significant that Matthiessen selected Pearl to illustrate Hawthorne's dependence on the Spenserian mode of creation in *The Scarlet Letter*, for though she is not his only illustration, she is certainly his best. Pearl has always struck readers as one-dimensional. Drawn "from life," from Hawthorne's memories of his daughter Una as she had been a few years before, Pearl is still the least convincing character in the book. Compared with his failure with her, Hawthorne's too early and too obvious revelation of Chillingworth's villainy is a minor flaw. But is Hester Spenserian in conception? Or Dimmes-

* *American Renaissance* (New York: Oxford University Press, 1941), pp. 301, 278.

dale? Or even Chillingworth as initially presented, before he becomes a "fiend"?

The same questions may be raised about the other novels. Phoebe in *The House of the Seven Gables* is perhaps only a "type" of maidenly health and purity, but are Hepzibah and Clifford essentially Spenserian, or allegorical, in conception? Hilda in *The Marble Faun* is an "emblematic" character in something like the Spenserian mode, but is Miriam? Hawthorne's range of character types is as wide as his range of stories. His practice cannot be so simply categorized. What we must recognize is that he wrote different kinds of stories, and created different kinds of characters, often in the same story. Recognizing the range of variation, we may then try to decide what is the typical or normal procedure.

The way Hawthorne normally proceeded in his writing may be suggested in a preliminary sort of way by the phrase, *thinking in terms of image and situation, character and action*. Adding "feeling" after "thinking," with a hyphen between the two, would make the phrase more accurately suggestive, but only at the cost of complicating an already complicated matter. Short of adding some such descriptive word as "feeling," I do not see how the awkwardness of the phrase may be kept within bounds without increasing the element of inaccuracy. The tales are not *thoughts fictionized*, but *thinking*: for *thoughts fictionized*, though perhaps a less cumbersome phrase, implies that the thought preexists in the absence of the tale, which later is "made up" to express it; or that a "thought" may be detached from the tale and leave nothing essential behind, as we take the meat from a nut after cracking the shell.

Neither of these latter ways of conceiving Hawthorne's tales is finally rewarding. For the ideas for stories which are so frequent in the Notebooks are not the "meanings" of the tales any more than the morals that Hawthorne sometimes appended are. They are simply the starting points, in situation, image, or concept, the opportunities, sometimes developed, sometimes not, for tales that had to get written for the "meanings" to exist. "A snake taken into a man's stomach and nourished there from fifteen years to thirty-five, tormenting him most horribly. A type of envy or some other evil passion." This is the Notebook idea which later developed into "Egotism, or the Bosom Serpent." But "Egotism" does not mean that Roderick Elliston has a snake in his stomach, nor is its meaning equivalent to "envy or some other evil passion," of which the snake, or the snake in the stomach, is a "type." What it does mean we can find out only by reading the story.

But if a change of "thinking" to "thoughts" would tend to imply an abstract and static and inorganic set of meanings, and particularly that the idea exists complete before the tale expresses it, neither will it do to say something like *tales with emphatic themes*. For this suggests that the tale preëxists and the theme is an additional, perhaps an optional, attachment, like the frosting that can be added only after the cake is baked. Hawthorne's tales were not conceived first and then found to have meaning later. Rather, they grew out of the work his mind, consciously and unconsciously, did on material which only he would have found promising.

Of these two approaches to an understanding of Hawthorne's procedure in his tales, the temptation is greater, perhaps, because of the existence of the suggestions for stories in the Notebooks, to say that he found his moral first and invented his story later to fit it. And if this description is used only to point the contrast between Hawthorne's way of working and that of many other writers of fiction, the distortion involved is probably justifiable. For Hawthorne's stories were relatively abstract in conception, just as they lend themselves with relative ease often to paraphrase in abstract terms. But one must not overlook the word "relatively" in this proposition. It is truer to say that Hawthorne's stories are fictional thinking — or processes of insight conceived and structured in narrative terms — than it is to say that the narratives *originate* in thoughts, ideas, or insights. The Notebooks have misled many into conceiving of the tales as though they were clothes draped loosely over already created skeletons of abstract thought. But of all the Notebooks jottings that Hawthorne used in existing stories, I know of none that can serve as an even approximately adequate statement of the meaning of the story to which it finally led, or in which it got embodied.

If this were not so, we should be able to measure the conceptual value of Hawthorne's tales by applying a yardstick — subjective, presumably — to the value of his "philosophy," his ideas as he expressed them outside his tales, for example in his Notebooks. But when we do so, we find — by my yardstick, at least, and it is applied sympathetically — that Hawthorne's thinking outside his tales is much less impressive than his thinking in his tales. It is, to be sure, instinct with the realism that made him unable to read Emerson or Emerson him. It is attractive in the quality of absolute honesty that shines through it, and the shrewdness that so often deflated the pompous and redefined the stereotyped. But still I suppose the most sympathetic commentator would not claim for Hawthorne a place among the world's — or even America's — great philosophers or "thinkers." Yet his tales are generally held to be among America's great short stories, and their greatness has been conceived by nearly all critics to be a product of their depth and complexity of meaning.

One way of resolving this seeming paradox is to recall Hawthorne's words, already quoted, on what he had hoped to accomplish in his English romance. In his fiction, he said, he could apprehend "more of various modes of truth" than he could grasp by "direct effort." What we have to recognize is that in some sense the story *is* the meaning, and the meaning the story. Sometimes this is very clear, indeed almost obvious when we stop to think of it, even if we are not used to thinking in terms of the critical concept of embodiment. "Wakefield," for example, which is in some of the most important respects typical of Hawthorne's procedure (though a failure of development, a failure of creative energy, keeps it from being one of the great tales) begins like this:

> In some old magazine or newspaper I recollect a story, told as truth, of a man — let us call him Wakefield — who absented himself for a long time from his wife. The fact, thus abstractly stated, is not very uncommon, nor — without a proper distinction of circumstances — to be condemned either as naughty or nonsensical.

The fact "thus abstractly stated" is not meaningful, though it is the starting point of the story, the stimulus, in contact with Hawthorne's sensibility, to meaning. But the tale that Hawthorne developed from it has all kinds of meanings, including some that Hawthorne tried to state for us. It means, among other things, what Hawthorne said abstractly in his final sentences, though we shall not fully understand these words unless we know their context:

> Amid the seeming confusion of our mysterious world, individuals are so nicely adjusted to a system, and systems to one another and to a whole, that, by stepping aside for a moment, a man exposes himself to a fearful risk of losing his place forever. Like Wakefield, he may become, as it were, the Outcast of the Universe.

It means, then, that we must not break what Hawthorne called in "Ethan Brand" the "magnetic chain" of organic relationships that bind us to society. Or it means that individualistic isolation, complete independence if you will, is possible only at the price of death. Or it means that our lives are only partially under our control, so that we are not the masters of our fate, the captains of our souls. Hawthorne interrupts his tale at one point to express his wish that he might "exemplify how an influence beyond our control lays

its strong hand on every deed which we do, and weaves its
consequences into an iron tissue of necessity." The tale
"means" all these things, and more.

And these meanings which it has are discovered, as Hawthorne makes clear in his introductory paragraphs, in the
course and structure of the tale itself — discovered by Hawthorne as well as by the reader. Hawthorne's own words
should be quoted at this point:

> This outline is all that I remember. But the incident, though of the
> purest originality, unexampled, and probably never to be repeated,
> is one, I think, which appeals to the generous sympathies of mankind.
> We know, each for himself, that none of us would perpetrate such a
> folly, yet feel as if some other might. To my own contemplations, at
> least, it has often recurred, always exciting wonder, but with a sense
> that the story must be true, and a conception of its hero's character.
> Whenever any subject so forcibly affects the mind, time is well spent
> in thinking of it. If the reader choose, let him do his own meditation;
> or if he prefer to ramble with me through the twenty years of
> Wakefield's vagary, I bid him welcome; trusting that there will be a
> pervading spirit and a moral, even should we fail to find them, done
> up neatly, and condensed into the final sentence. Thought has always
> its efficacy, and every striking incident its moral.

In "The Canterbury Pilgrims" and "Roger Malvin's Burial"
Hawthorne did not even attempt to abstract and condense
the moral "neatly" in the final sentences, but they are stories
in which everything is dominated by what we may call their
"moral meaning." They will serve better than some of the
more famous tales — partly because we can approach them
with fewer preconceptions — to illustrate the kind of "efficacy" which "thought" has in Hawthorne, and the way in
which the "moral" is discovered through the "incident."

2

"The Canterbury Pilgrims" is one of the less well-known
tales, and there is a sense in which its obscurity is justified:
it is surely not among the greatest tales by any standard. It

is quite abstract, its characters are mere types, there is almost
no action in it, and when the characters speak they tend to
speak in artificial "set speeches." It is more like a pageant
than a story, a *tableau vivant* with actors posed in emblematic
attitudes against a picturesque and expressive backdrop. Yet
all this does not mean that the tale is without value, however
far it may be from the sort of thing we naturally tend to like
today.

We have seen something of the nature of Hawthorne's
actual experience in his first visit to a Shaker village. But
when he came to write the tale prompted by the visit, he
ignored the cider and the good food and jolly company:
these did not fit into any meaning that he could grasp. He
began instead with the settlement as viewed from a distance:
from a distance great enough to enable him to see its whole
outline, its significance, its meaning. He began with a description of the spring at the bottom of the hill below the
community. He began with the *Gestalt* of the Canterbury
Shakers.

Reading the accounts of the actual visit and then reading
the story, it is easy enough to see the kinds of questions
prompted by this *Gestalt*. The Shaker community was a form
of Protestant monasticism. Though it might serve excellent
food, it was essentially ascetic in its orientation, as was evi-
denced by its vow of chastity. It believed in giving up the
world. Was its otherworldly ideal of renunciation justified
by the nature of experience? Quite apart from theological
problems, was the possibility of fulfillment in life so slight
as to justify, on what we may call pragmatic grounds, the
Shaker preference for security, both here and hereafter, at
the price of experience?

But before these questions could be meaningfully asked
they had to be conceived in dramatic terms. If a young
Shaker couple leaving the establishment to marry and try
life together in "the world" were to meet a group of the

world's embittered failures on their way into this retreat, what would the effect be on the lovers? Would this sight of the frustration and disillusionment that come with experience make them want to turn back? What should their attitude be toward the suffering and evil in the world? So the story which grew out of Hawthorne's pleasant visit with the Shakers has nothing to do with any of the details he recorded in his letter. It is built instead around the dramatic meeting on a moonlit night of two groups traveling together in opposite directions, Josiah and Miriam leaving the community and a group of converts on their way in to this refuge from the world. The painting of this emblematic scene, and the stories told by the incoming travelers, make up the substance of the tale. Almost the only action is the arrival and final departure of the two groups, and the characters are too lightly sketched in to develop as characters. But the theme develops, and meanings that arise from and are discovered in the technique are many and far from obvious.

The first sentence introduces a note of ironic blending of romance and reality, wish and fact, which is to be one of the main motives. "The summer moon, which shines in so many a tale, was beaming over a broad extent of uneven country." The summer moon, romance, is immediately qualified by the memory of the false moonshine of the popular romantic tale. The statement without the qualification would be, as Hawthorne recognizes, flat and banal: "The summer moon . . . beams." But the qualification is not an apology for an inept sentence, for the rest of the tale develops, qualifies, and enlarges the tension developed by the incongruity of the statement and modifier of the opening sentence: dreams exist (though they are moonshine without the facts) and facts exist (though they do not fully exist without the dreams that complete them and give them meaning). And the relation between them is not disjunctive but inclusive. Or again, from a different point of view, the first sentence tells us that this tale will be written within the popular romantic tradition, but its attitudes will be partly antiromantic. All the commonplaces of romantic fiction will be here — summer moonlight, a rural setting full of "the beauty of nature," a modest young couple very much in love, a final decision to dare all for love — yet used with a difference.

The opening statement is expanded, the ironical qualification dropped, in the remainder of the first paragraph. Hawthorne describes, in a more intimate and personal tone than he ordinarily adopted, a spring that has been made to flow into a hand-hewn granite trough placed beside the road leading up the hill to the Shaker settlement. Now the spring in its primary aspect, the sparkling water itself, is natural and beautiful; it reinforces the primary, or unqualified, meaning of the moon symbol. We have then a moon–spring combination, of which the paraphrasable content might perhaps be inadequately stated as *the beauty, innocence, and purity of nature*. But this meaning, already challenged by the irony attached to "moon," and later to be further modified by being associated with the complementary beauty, innocence, and purity of ascetic renunciation, is immediately qualified by being juxtaposed with the value achieved not by nature but by man, particularly by man as artist. The narrator is pleased to note that here nature has been modified by man's hand in the shaping of the granite receptacle for the water: "The work of neat hands and considerate art was visible about this blessed fountain."

The paragraph ends on what appears to be a note of whimsy. The spring seemed not to overflow, yet the water bubbled up into the basin continuously. Could this mean that nature could not afford "to lavish so pure a liquid, as she does the waters of all meaner fountains"? Here we have, I think, the key to the chief symbolic significance of the spring, which is so strongly emphasized that it would be surprising to find it not wholly functional. Here "nature" and "art" are nicely balanced, held in equilibrium, like the water which maintained its constant level. (A glance at the now dry granite basin today will show how the Shakers contrived this: the intake and outlet pipes were close together at the bottom of the "fountain," where they would be difficult to see.) If we keep in mind the distinction thus suggested between the natural and the artful or human, we shall see at the end of the story that it parallels other contrasts set up and explored. And if we remember the unqualified approval with which Hawthorne describes this "blessed fountain" which so nicely unites such contrasts as nature and art and the eternal and the temporal, achieving what seems if not a miraculous unity at least an ideal equilibrium, we shall, I think, come to realize that the paragraph Hawthorne devotes to this spring or fountain is not a wasteful bit of added "nature description."

Now two lovers come down the road from the buildings on the hill. They stop at the spring to drink and rest before continuing their "flight" — for, Shakers from early childhood, they dare not face the elders of the community, avow their "carnal" passion, and announce their intention of leaving, even though Shaker rules did not forbid a member's leaving at any time. Though they are breaking no law, they have feelings of guilt and anxiety mingled with their yearning for each other and their dreams of happiness together. And not only guilt and anxiety but reluctance to leave a familiar and dear spot — "and this may be the last time we shall ever taste of this water." Their decision has already been a difficult one, and its reaffirmation will be made yet more difficult.

For now some travelers come toiling up the road and stop at the spring to rest. Worn and dirty from their journey afoot and with an as yet mysterious gloom in their aspect, they are depressing even before they begin to talk. Here is an inauspicious beginning for an elopement. And the tales they tell are calculated to disillusion the young couple if anything

could. They confront romantic idealism with the hard facts
of life.

The first of the travelers to tell his story is a disappointed
poet. " 'In me,' said he, with a certain majesty of utterance,
'in me, you behold a poet.' " Now the burden of the poet's
story is that the world does not reward true merit, that the
bad and the vulgar in art are more widely praised than the
fine; that, in short, the world is gross, practical, and insensitive: it positively prefers the second-rate. We remember
Hawthorne's impatience with that "damned mob of scribbling
women" who, in his day, were so popular, while his own
earlier works went comparatively unread. We think of the
aging Melville collecting customs duties and of Poe in his
barren cottage and we think we know what Hawthorne
means: genius must starve in a garret or enter a Shaker
community while mediocrity rules the day.

But such a reading is closer to being the opposite of the
meaning intended than to representing it. The poet speaks
"with a certain majesty," and there is much truth in what he
says of the public; but as he continues to talk, his words make
him a ridiculous as well as a pitiable character. He is a cari-
cature of a romantic poet. Conceiving himself as a brave,
lofty, and suffering soul, he wears his hair long and arranged
to emphasize the height of his forehead. With "an intelligent
eye" and striking features, he enjoys his role of nobility in
exile, genius unappreciated. He revels in self-pity. He dwells
upon the loftiness of his gifts — he is a poet of the soul, not
a mere versifier — and upon his suffering. A *poseur* enjoying
martyrdom, he is sensitive to the moonlight, likes the word
"etherial," and composes "effusions." He is Shelley and Byron
combined into a type for which Hawthorne evidently had
little sympathy. Little — but some; for though it is strikingly
apparent that the poet is treated with less sympathy than
the other pilgrims receive, it is also apparent that he is more
like Hawthorne himself than are the others — a merchant,

a farmer, and a farmer's wife — for he too is, or wants to be, "an artist of the beautiful." Hawthorne's most cutting irony is reserved for the type most like himself — the dreamer, the artist, the seeker after significance, the writer who believes he has great gifts, but who is unappreciated by the public.

The second refugee from the world's ills to tell his story is a merchant who has failed in business and lost his fortune. Too old and too discouraged to begin again, he joins the poet in seeking haven from a world which has frustrated his ambitions. Like the poet, too, he is vain. Like the poet, finally, he is embittered by experience. But he is unlike the poet in all other respects. The poet was a misfit from the beginning. The merchant is practical and worldly; he has always accepted the world's standards and lived by them. By them he became a great success, and by them he now knows himself a failure. There was a touch of nobility, however pitiable, in the vain and deluded poet; there is nothing but ignobility in the merchant. "A small man, of quick and unquiet gestures, about fifty years old, with a narrow forehead, all wrinkled and drawn together," he hopes to find a place for himself in the Shaker community by becoming their business manager and increasing their wealth through shrewd management. The only questions he addresses to the lovers concern the extent of the community's holdings.

Yet the merchant is treated with less irony than the poet. Why? Partly, perhaps, as I have already suggested, because Hawthorne's strongest irony was usually reserved for himself. But for another reason too, certainly: as the merchant is less vain than the poet, less consumed and dominated by pride, so he is more nearly "true." With lower standards and potentialities than those of the poet, he is yet less of the dissimulator, less the fraud. The tone of the passage that presents him is serious and unambiguous for the most part. The only notes of irony are reserved for the emphasis on his worldly motives for entering an ascetic religious society and on the absurd pride that coexists with evident failure as he comforts himself and attempts to impress others with the memory of his former great riches.

Since Josiah and Miriam have no wish either to be poets or to gain riches, they are not discouraged by these reports of the vicissitudes to which those who live "in the world's way" are liable:

"I will not turn back for this," replied Josiah calmly, "any more than for the advice of the varse-maker, between whom and thee, friend, I see a sort of likeness, though I can't justly say where it lies."

But the confidence which has not yet been shaken is about to receive a jolt, for now the farmer speaks. From the first sentence introducing him, it is evident that he is more worthy of our respect than the poet or the merchant. He is no fop, like the poet, nor is there any apparent vanity in his behavior. He is not pinched, nervous, and mean, like the merchant. All he has asked has been a simple livelihood, earned with his own hands, and a chance to rear his family in peace and love. He has asked, that is, what Josiah and Miriam hope for. But he has been crushed by repeated failures brought on by no fault of his own, neither by vain and inordinate ambition nor by a too mercenary view of what constitutes success and failure. Now, sullen and despondent, he tells how years ago he married "just such a neat and pretty young woman as Miriam," and how he has failed.

"I have labored hard for years; and my means have been growing narrower, and my living poorer, and my heart colder and heavier, all the time; till at last I could bear it no longer. I set myself down to calculate whether I had best go on the Oregon expedition, or come here to the Shaker village; but I had not hope enough left in me to begin the world over again; and, to make my story short, here I am. And now, youngster, take my advice, and turn back; or else some few years hence, you'll have to climb this hill, with as heavy a heart as mine."

This story, unlike the other two, affects the young couple

deeply. Here, after all, is a simple person like themselves, a person who has asked for little and received nothing, who has had no delusions, unless justice be a delusion. ("I thought it a matter of course that the Lord would help me, because I was willing to help myself.") But their greatest shock is yet to come. The farmer had referred to his bride at the beginning of his story but has made no further reference to her as his story has progressed. Miriam thinks that both the wife and the children must be dead. Now we learn that the tired, dispirited, unhappy woman in the party is the farmer's wife, and that the two children asleep on the ground are theirs, two others having died. The wife's expression and tone of voice mingle "fretfulness," "irritability," and "sadness." It is she who tells that part of the tale that "makes all the rest so hard to bear":

> "If you and your sweetheart marry, you'll be kind and pleasant to each other for a year or two, and while that's the case, you never will repent; but, by and by, he'll grow gloomy, rough, and hard to please, and you'll be peevish, and full of little angry fits, and apt to be complaining by the fireside, when he comes to rest himself from his troubles out of doors; so your love will wear away by little and little, and leave you miserable at last."

This last revelation of the nature of experience shakes the lovers profoundly. Their experience has given them no basis for judging whether the experience of the unhappy couple is rare, typical, or inevitable. But Hawthorne makes sure that the reader knows more than Josiah and Miriam. The tone in which these last two tales, especially the wife's, is told is one of utter seriousness: there is real pathos in their story, more moving than the frustration of the poet or the failure of the merchant. If this be true of the world, then it may well be given up.

Still Hawthorne is not through with his unhappy couple. There is more to their stories than can be revealed simply by a tone which implies that tragedy is real. Action, and an author's comment (the only intrusion of the author after the introductory paragraph) are needed for the final revelation:

As she ceased, the yeoman and his wife exchanged a glance, in which there was more and warmer affection than they had supposed to have escaped the frost of a wintry fate, in either of their breasts. At that moment, when they stood on the utmost verge of married life, one word fitly spoken, or perhaps one peculiar look, had they had mutual confidence enough to reciprocate it, might have renewed all their old feelings, and sent them back, resolved to sustain each other amid the struggles of the world. But the crisis passed, and never came again. Just then, also, the children, roused by their mother's voice, looked up, and added their wailing accents to the testimony borne by all Canterbury pilgrims against the world from which they fled.

Now that the last of the pilgrims has told her tale, Hawthorne returns our attention to the young lovers. Each succeeding story has affected them more than the preceding one, and now they are deeply disturbed. These tales have come to seem "omens" of the "disappointed hope, and unavailing toil, domestic grief, and estranged affection" which they too may well expect. But they do not hesitate for long. Embracing, they declare that they will not go back. "The world can never be dark for us, for we will always love one another."

This statement of the lovers, which is also the last bit of dialogue in the story, must seem, in the context of the summary that I have given thus far, to be quite unjustified by the revelations of the nature of the world that have preceded it. The story, which has opened with moonlight and the beauty of nature, closes with young love reaffirmed. More moonlight? Has the tension between the irony and the "romance" disappeared, to leave this just another romantic tale after all, despite the qualifications? Before we attempt to decide, we must turn back to look more closely at certain implications of the nature of the travelers and of the arrangement of the tales they tell.

First, we remember that the pilgrims are presented in a

climactic order of increasing sympathy for them on the part
of the author and the reader, of increasing pathos, and of increasing relevance to the situation of the lovers. Second, we
recall that Josiah sees something in common between the
poet and the merchant. What the two have in common is
plainly vanity or pride and the false values that spring from
that vice. The poet lives for fame, the merchant for wealth
and power; each has striven in vain for a vain end, an end
calculated, if achieved, to magnify the self in the way peculiar to that self. But is there any relationship between these
two and the farmer and his wife? That there is Hawthorne
has suggested in his presentation of the death of their love
and of their missed opportunity for the beginning of a renewal of it. The farm couple have once felt the "romantic
love" which Josiah and Miriam now feel, but worry, disappointment, hardships, and the natural lessening of desire
with the years have destroyed that romantic love. Their
troubles, as they have hardened and embittered the couple,
have driven both man and wife into self-absorption, so that
finally the two are isolated from each other and from the
world. They too, like the poet and the merchant, are victims
of pride.

The story, then, indirectly suggests the theme of pride that
is so often present in Hawthorne's work. For the opposite
of the pride of poet, merchant, and the farm couple is love.
But *love* is a peculiarly ambiguous word. The Shaker couple
are already "in love," but the implication of the story is that
"the world" will deal harshly with this sort of love. Unless
their love survives the attrition or death of desire, unless
to some degree *eros* changes to *agape*, they will surely not
"always love one another." * Whether they will continue to

* That Hawthorne was a realist about the normal course of married love
is just what we should expect, unless our views of him have been formed not
from his works but from Mrs. Hawthorne's re-creation of her husband in her
Passages from the American Note-Books. Once, after describing a display of
affection by a newly wed couple whom he had observed in a stage-coach,

love after they have ceased to be "in love" we cannot know, and fortunately for the effect of the story, Hawthorne does not try to tell us. If their love does survive it will become more conspicuously an aspect and a manifestation of Christian *caritas*. This too is a part of the meaning of the tale.

But this question of the meaning of the climactic statement has led us away from the broader theme, which, as we have seen, is whether the nature of life is such as to justify, or even to require, extreme renunciation. In "The Shaker Bridal" and elsewhere Hawthorne expressed himself on the Shakers, and his attitude was one of disapproval.† Like Melville, he was much interested in this remnant of an earlier day lingering on in bustling, secular nineteenth-century America. But his religious outlook was not ascetic. Interested in the fulfillment rather than the extinction of the human creature, with completion rather than substitution as the goal, he was willing to follow reason as far as reason would carry him and to explore the full implications of the concept of incarnation. He decided that asceticism was more of a distortion than a fulfillment. When the "world's people" continued up the hill at the close of the story to enter the Shaker society, they "sought a home where all former ties of nature or society would be sundered, and all old distinctions leveled, and a cold and passionless security be substituted for mortal hope and fear, as in that other refuge of the world's weary outcasts, the grave." Hawthorne's sympathies went with the lovers as, "with chastened hopes, but more confiding affections, [they] went on to mingle in an untried life."

Hawthorne added the comment, "It would be pleasant to meet them again next summer, and note the change." See Randall Stewart, ed., *The American Notebooks* (New Haven: Yale University Press, 1932), pp. 33–34.

† See *The American Notebooks*, pp. 229–230. On the occasion of his visit with Melville to a Shaker community in the Berkshires, Hawthorne wrote of "these foolish Shakers" that "the sooner the sect is extinct the better."

They went down the road, *down* from the pure and noble but inhumanly lofty Shaker community to the middle world. Both the Shaker ideal and the world of nature, the story suggests, have a beauty and a purity not exhibited in man's experience. As the Shaker community is the symbol of all religious renunciation, so the water and the moon are symbols of that morally neutral beauty of nature which often seemed to Thoreau a more than adequate substitute for human companionship. And since the two "escapes" from man's humanity, the one above, the other below, have much in common, it is interesting that they should be linked together at the beginning of the tale, and then that the one should be rejected and the other left behind as the tale proceeds.

So the tale that begins in light and develops in darkness emerges at last into the light again. But the shadows have not been totally dispelled at the end. Ominous destructive agents at first, they have become the accepted circumference of the shrunken but clearer core of light. The summer moon, which opens the tale like the statement of the theme in the first bars of a quartet, is immediately so qualified that as a symbol it points both to lasting value and to delusive hopes. Perhaps the only unambiguous symbol in the whole tale is the fountain. Young love, introduced, like the moonlight, at first idyllically, is quickly confronted by the harsh reality that would destroy it. Even the hill, with its religious ideal at the top and the world of sordid experience below, is an ambiguous symbol.

But the story does not end in unresolved antinomy. Moonlight and moonshine, romance and fact, noble ideal and ignoble reality, each has been modified by the presence of its opposite. So that when the young couple decide to go on into "untried life" they embody an idea which is significantly different from that which they suggested at the beginning. Something has been achieved, some new meaning created, by the antinomies that have been explored. Out of the contrasts of the height of the hill and the depth of the world below, the excessive sensibility of the poet and the callousness of the merchant, the naïve idealism of the lovers and the hopeless frustration of the married couple, a meaning has emerged which we now recognize as faintly foreshadowed at the very beginning in the "blessed fountain." For here too "opposites" were brought together and reconciled by some "secret charm," so that the narrator was struck by the fancy that here was some almost impossible ideal actually achieved. Nature and "the work of neat hands and considerate art" had coöperated to achieve this ideal: nature and human craft, or art, together had made it possible. The fountain, both natural and artful, suggests, as we now are in a position to see, a middle ground between the merely "natural" lives of "the world's people," lives ultimately defeated by the world's contingencies, and the unnatural, "ideal" renunciations of the Shakers.

"The Canterbury Pilgrims" is, then, a tale literally built out of progressively complex explorations of contrasted themes. The whole meaning and value of the tale are products of the tension thus produced. And when hindsight enables us to see that the resolution achieved out of discord at the end was already foreshadowed in the opening paragraph, we realize that Hawthorne has here written a tale very like a beautifully constructed piece of music. If nevertheless it is not one of the really great tales, it is easy to see why. It is intricately balanced and harmonious in structure but relatively thin in texture. It has, at best perhaps, only half the value of "My Kinsman, Major Molineux," for its values remain, comparatively, mere ideas — musical ideas of the highest order, but only lightly sketched in, as in a preliminary plan rather than in a developed work. The characters are very nearly allegorical figures, their tales little more than summaries of significant action. The value that the story has — and it has considerable value in my judgment — is a function very largely of what we may call its structure. And its structure is a structure of meanings fictionally, or dramatically and pictorially, discovered and conceived.

3

If "The Canterbury Pilgrims" suggests a scale up and down which the meaning moves like a melody stated and elaborated with classic artistry, "Roger Malvin's Burial" is more likely to suggest to most readers a dream, with more than the usual dream's depths visible beneath the limpid surface. The immense difference between these two tales suggests the range of Hawthorne's artistry, but the two are alike in one respect: in both, the burden of meaning carried by structure is relatively greater than it is in some of the better-known later tales such as "Rappaccini's Daughter."

Like "My Kinsman, Major Molineux," "Roger Malvin's Burial" opens with a paragraph of historical background, not properly a part of the tale itself but a preparation for it. "The fate of the few combatants who were in a condition to retreat after 'Lovell's Fight' " in the border wars of 1725 will provide the subject for a tale which will play "the moonlight of romance" over a page of Colonial history. The tale that follows provides further evidence of what Hawthorne meant by "romance" and of the use to which he put history, but what chiefly concerns us now is the way in which the structure of the tale expresses the meaning.

In summary, the situation is this. Two of Lovell's men, one old and the other young, have escaped the destruction of their force and are making their way back to the settlements. The older of the two, however, has been severely wounded in the fight, and as the story opens he is resting beneath a rock in a forest glade, unable to go farther. He urges the young man to go on and save himself if possible, pointing out that staying with him will mean that two lives will be lost instead of one. Finally the younger man decides to do so, comforting himself with the thought that he may thus be able to send back help for the older. Later as he is about to die of his own severe wounds he is found near the edge of the settlement and nursed back to health by the girl whom he later marries, the daughter of the friend he left to die in the forest. Although he intends to tell of the circumstances of the older man's death, he never actually does so. He marries the daughter of his friend, keeps his secret to himself, and rears a son who grows to adolescence. But a feeling of guilt increases within him until he can bear it no longer, and he sets out with his family for new land to the west. Journeying through the forest, he finds himself drawn continually away from the planned course and in the direction of the place where years before he had left his friend to die alone. Arrived at the spot without the man's recognizing it at first, the family makes camp, and father and son go into the woods separately. Hearing a sound near him, the father fires blindly, killing his son, who has been his only comfort in the unhappy isolation that has grown on him through the years.

Even a bare summary of this sort suffices to suggest some of the overtones of the tale. Here, most clearly, is the usual preoccupation with secret guilt, with the resulting isolation, and with a sense of compulsion. The young man who grows old in bitterness is another Goodman Brown, introduced to the evil in the world by his own participation in it. He is Robin of "My Kinsman, Major Molineux," in later years compelled to return to the spot where he had joined in laughter at his kinsman's expense. He is Abraham sacrificing Isaac: compelled as it seemed to him by a "supernatural power," he kills his son. The plot of the tale is as elemental and suggestive as any that Hawthorne ever wrote.

The deepening and strengthening of the suggestions implicit in the basic situation is accomplished with great economy, without the profusion of imagery common in the later tales. The rock against which the dying old man leaned and beneath which the child is later killed is explicitly a gravestone and implicitly an altar like those in the Old Testament on which sacrifice was offered. The two key scenes of the story take place deep in the *heart* of the dark forest, in a glade which Reuben is unable to forget as he is unable to cast out the secret that lies in "the sepulchre of his heart." The branch around which he had tied his handkerchief upon leaving his older friend so that he might find the spot again has been withered by time ("Whose guilt had blasted it?") and falls in "soft light fragments upon the rock, upon the leaves, upon Reuben, upon his wife and child, and upon Roger Malvin's bones" after the son has been sacrificed. These few are the outstanding symbolic devices in this tale rich in its depths and deceptively plain on its surface.

For the rest, the implications are developed in the contours of the situations. Did Reuben do wrong in leaving the dying man? He himself was gravely wounded, and staying, though it could be conceived as a religious duty, could certainly have no practical benefits. Where would the right lie in a situation like this? Surely one's duty to others should not require self-sacrifice when the sacrifice would almost certainly be useless to the other person. It is not at all certain that Reuben did any wrong in leaving the dying man.

Why then was he consumed by a sense of guilt thereafter until he had killed what was most dear to him? Hawthorne suggests that, in the first place, it was not so much the overt act of desertion as the conditions under which it took place that justified the feeling of guilt. When Roger Malvin urges his "son" to leave him, he plays shrewdly upon the capacity of man to rationalize his interests. He points out that if Reuben leaves he will be able to look after the daughter he is to marry, he may get help to come, and that at any rate it is his duty to obey the one who has loved him like a father and who "should have something of a father's authority."

Thus in the conflict between the claims of opposed duties it is possible for Reuben to follow self-interest without admitting to himself that he has done so. Malvin's words

reminded him that there were other and less questionable duties than that of sharing the fate of a man whom his death could not benefit. Nor can it be affirmed that no selfish feeling strove to enter Reuben's heart, though the consciousness made him more earnestly resist his companion's entreaties . . . No merely selfish motive, nor even the desolate condition of Dorcas, could have induced him to desert his companion at such a moment — but his wishes seized on the thought that Malvin's life might be preserved, and his sanguine nature heightened almost to certainty the remote possibility of procuring human aid.

The moral complexity of the original situation, in short, amounts to almost complete ambiguity. In a situation so opaque with conflicting rights, no clear judgment can be brought against Reuben for his action. But the state of mind and heart which permitted and prompted the action is another matter. Reuben was not honest with himself about his motives. Here if anywhere lay a clear reason for the feeling of guilt that came to torment him.

And this original failure of honesty was compounded by another act of rationalization that was likewise almost, if not entirely, justifiable: he did not tell Dorcas and the others that he had left her father to die alone. Circumstances conspired to make it easy for him to keep this to himself. He was near death when he was discovered near the settlement. He found that everyone assumed that he had heroically remained with the dying man, to do what he could for him at the end and to bury his body. When, once, he tried to tell the truth he found that his words were interpreted according to the preconceptions of his hearers. The thought occurred to him that to tell the truth would inflict upon his wife useless suffering which he would like to spare her. So he allowed the untruth to be believed. Again, whose motives are so perfect that he can safely, as Hawthorne puts it, "impute blame"?

But the actions which thus far had seemed so natural, so justifiable, involved a consequence which Reuben could not escape or justify to himself. When he had left Roger Malvin to die, he had promised that he would return to give the bones of his friend Christian burial. Now he was unable to keep that vow without revealing that he had permitted a lie to be believed. Here at last was a great and perfectly clear wrong: a promise to a dying man, and especially to a "father," must surely be kept. But what would once have been easy was now impossible without an intolerable sacrifice. Thus Reuben Bourne was guilty without ever having committed any clear overt wrong. His "sin," indeed, lay not so much in anything he had done as in what he had failed to do. But the end of ambiguity was not there, for the only unambiguous wrong of which he was guilty — failing to keep his promise — was itself the necessary result not of a clear-cut present choice but of previous choices made in ambiguous situations without full knowledge of the consequences.

The story then is concerned not with the obvious guilt of recognized sinners but with the complex and obscure guilt in which one who "means well" and is as good as the next man gets involved. Like Original Sin, Reuben's guilt is at once, and paradoxically, the result of a chain of previous wrong choices and the consequence of a "fatal necessity." Like Original Sin too, it required a dramatic and extraordinary sacrifice for the undoing of its consequences.

Nothing in the tale clarifies the "simple" and "obvious" question of how much if any wrong Reuben did in leaving the dying man. Indeed the answer to the abstract ethical question of the degree of self-sacrifice demanded by Christian ethics is deliberately obscured. In terms of purely rational ethics the only implication of the surface level of the story would be the same as the explicit moral of *The Scarlet*

Letter, "Be true! Be true! Show freely to the world, if not your worst, yet some trait whereby the worst may be inferred." Reuben was not true. From one point of view not sin but refusal to acknowledge sin drove him to his doom.

Although this theme of the effects of concealment — so common in Hawthorne that there is a temptation to call it *the* meaning once we have discovered it — is surely developed, the central meaning of the story is not to be found here either, but equally, and alternatively, on the levels of myth and of the unconscious. In our day, when readings of stories in these terms are being overdone with the enthusiasm of fresh discovery, it may be natural to suspect that at this point we are overreading, seeing too much in a simple tale. But Hawthorne himself has answered this objection: he has made it impossible to disregard the mythical and the unconscious in reading the story.

In the first place, his emphasis on Reuben's motives in his two "guilty" acts prepares us for what is to follow. Hawthorne understood consciously and thoroughly the process we now call rationalization, and he described the process as it took place in Reuben's mind. To discern the motives of thinking is to penetrate some little way below the level of what is normally in the consciousness. But more significantly, he makes Reuben's return to the place of his first "guilt" compulsive. From the route which had been consciously selected to take them to their new home Reuben continually strays, though he is an excellent woodsman, and his straying takes always the same direction. Corrected by his son, who notices the strange "mistake," Reuben agrees and changes his direction, only to turn again and again in the way he was obscurely compelled to take. "Cyrus, perceiving that his father gradually resumed the old direction, forbore to interfere; nor, though something began to weigh upon his heart, did his adventurous nature permit him to regret the increased length and mystery of their way."

And it was indeed a mysterious journey which they were undertaking. After they have arrived near the place of Roger Malvin's death, Reuben leaves Dorcas at the fire to follow Cyrus into the woods in search of game. I have said that Hawthorne underscores the "mystery" here, but the precise emphasis he gives to the mystery deserves to be noted. Reuben, wholly preoccupied with the "strange reflections" arising from his feeling of guilt, which has lately come so much to the foreground as to destroy the man Dorcas had loved and married, "strays" through the woods "rather like a sleepwalker than a hunter," circling the camp and approaching without realizing it the nearby great rock in the glade.

He was musing on the strange influence that had led him away from his premeditated course, and so far into the depths of the wilderness. Unable to penetrate the secret place of his soul where his motives lay hidden, he believed that a supernatural voice had called him onward, and that a supernatural power had obstructed his retreat. He trusted that it was Heaven's intent to afford him an opportunity of expiating his sin; he hoped that he might find the bones so long unburied; and that, having laid the earth over them, peace would throw its sunlight into the sepulchre of his heart. From these thoughts he was aroused by a rustling in the forest at some distance from the spot to which he had wandered. Perceiving the motion of some object behind a thick veil of undergrowth, he fired, with the instinct of a hunter and the aim of a practiced marksman. A low moan, which told of his success, and by which even animals can express their dying agony, was unheeded by Reuben Bourne. What were the recollections now breaking upon him?

I suppose Hawthorne could not have made the element of unconscious compulsion in the return to the spot and the shooting of the son more explicit than he has without dropping entirely the surface level of the story. But there is another aspect of the situation that Hawthorne merely hints. As he has been ridden by his feeling of guilt through the years, Reuben has grown away from Dorcas until there is a wall of separation between them. But he does not lose his love for his son. "The boy was loved by his father with a deep and silent strength, as if whatever was good and happy in his own nature had been transferred to his child, carrying his affections with it." When he kills the child, then, he is killing what he most loved, but he is doing more than that: he is killing the symbolic extension of himself. A feeling of guilt arising out of one's relation to the father may lead, the psychologist might say, to the need to destroy or mutilate the guilty self. What the psychologist would know and document systematically, Hawthorne knew in his creative mind in this story and wrought into a structure of relationships that involve archetypal patterns.

The relation between this tale and the stories of Leonard Doane, who suffered from the fantasy that he had killed his father, and Robin, who laughed cruelly at the man he hoped would be like a father to him, should by now be clear enough. But there are other aspects of the story that deserve mention. In all of Hawthorne's tales there is perhaps no subtler presentation of certain aspects of the nature of secret guilt — its springs, its nature, and its effects. Reuben Bourne is guilty, in so far as his guilt can be related to the objective moral world and is not merely "psychological," of what Hawthorne calls "moral cowardice": he cannot bring himself first to face the truth about himself and then to share it with others, even those he loves. "Unable to penetrate to the secret place of his soul where his motives lay hidden," he is prevented from knowing himself, and so from changing himself constructively. A psychologist might say that he lacked "insight." A theologian would say that his blindness and cowardice spring, like Dimmesdale's, from a very subtle, quite unconscious, pride. He is unable to humble himself to the extent that would be required by a recognition of his true motives and nature and by subsequent confession of sin. He suffers but, like Dimmesdale again, does not really repent until he is driven by his suffering to the self-sacrificial act which brings his release. Then "His sin was expiated, — the curse was gone from him; and in the hour when he had shed blood dearer to him than his own, a prayer, the first for years, went up to Heaven from the lips of Reuben Bourne."

These closing words of the story, like the Biblical allusions throughout, make it clear that a reading of the tale in terms of both primitive religious myth and the historical and theological aspects of creedal Christianity are as clearly justified as the psychological reading is. Oedipus and the sacrificial savior loom in the background of this tale whose foreground is fashioned out of Colonial history and the nature and effects of concealed guilt. Original Sin and the Atonement are as clearly involved in Reuben Bourne's story as are the psychology of guilt and the demands of the unconscious.

And all these meanings are embodied in structure — in situation and character and action, in motive to action and result of action. The tale is not as rich in texture as the greatest of Hawthorne's later stories; not so much of the meaning is carried by image and symbol. But it is one of Hawthorne's greatest tales nevertheless, for there is no part of its structure which is not instinct with meaning, and no meaning in the tale which is not embodied in its structure. In it we see exemplified the structure of meaning as Hawthorne created it.

4

Hawthorne's weaker tales make it clear that the danger he constantly faced was that he would over-intellectualize his material. "Wakefield" carries too great a burden of thought for so slight a framework: what stimulated Hawthorne here was the initial situation of a man who willfully isolates himself. Between Wakefield's departure from his wife and his return, Hawthorne merely summarizes the actions of twenty years. The story never expands much beyond anecdote.

"The Canterbury Pilgrims" is stronger, I think — though that has not been the usual opinion, if we may judge by frequency of inclusion in the anthologies. In it we have more immediacy, more life, more concreteness. Even so the characters are rather abstractly conceived: the romantic young couple, the vain little poet, the embittered merchant, the defeated farm couple. These are descendants of the Virtues and the Vices of the medieval morality plays. Josiah is Everyman, young and in love and wondering whether his dreams will be fulfilled. With "The Christmas Banquet," "The Man of Adamant," "The Great Carbuncle," "Lady Eleanor's Mantle," and a half dozen or so others, "The Canterbury Pilgrims" seems almost to justify the description of Hawthorne as an allegorist.

Yet even in these tales there is a significant difference between Hawthorne's practice and allegory as we see it in Spenser and Bunyan. Hawthorne does not start with a wholly preconceived, an abstract and external, set of meanings and then embody them, even in his most allegorical tales. We may say that a system of values and beliefs such as Bunyan knew was not available to him; or at any rate, that he could not accept whatever was available. But whatever explanation we may give of the fact, the fact remains that Hawthorne's "allegories" are more subjective, more complex, and more ambiguous than anything in *Pilgrim's Progress* or *The Faerie Queene*. If these tales are allegory, they are allegory in a new mode, a mode which it might be less misleading to call a highly intellectualized form of symbolism.

Hawthorne's besetting danger of over-intellectualization was only the misuse of his greatest strength. "Roger Malvin's Burial" is certainly one of his best tales, but it too has very little action and its characters are only sufficiently sketched in to make them credible. Its illusion of reality is slight by comparison with contemporary practice, and its burden of meaning great by any standard. Any reader wholly insensitive to its meanings as they develop would surely find it something less than compelling. It does not invite us so much to share Reuben Bourne's experience as to contemplate it. The experience it affords is highly intellectual, but it is experience conceived and structured in aesthetic, not in philosophic, terms.

Like "Wakefield," "The Canterbury Pilgrims," and "Roger Malvin's Burial," most of Hawthorne's tales contain very little overt action, but what action there is, is symbolic. In the greater tales this economy helps to produce the effect of concentrated brilliance. In the weaker ones, it contributes to our impression that the tales are not fiction at all, but sketches. Lack of action is characteristic of both the weaker sketchlike takes and the very best among both the tales and the novels. It has often been noted that *The Scarlet Letter* begins after the actions that would provide the plot of most novels; and the subsequent "actions" it does treat take place almost entirely within the minds and hearts of the characters. *The Marble Faun*, in contrast, which has a great deal more overt action, is clearly an inferior novel. "Young Goodman Brown," one of the very finest of the tales, contains so little and such simple overt action that a summary concerned with its plot alone could be adequately given in an uncrowded sentence. "Mr. Higginbotham's Catastrophe," on the other hand, has a rather full and complicated plot, but it is surely not one of Hawthorne's best works.

The action is not only relatively little in proportion to the length of the tales but is usually of the simplest character. One form that plot commonly takes is the journey. "My Kinsman, Major Molineux" is built around Robin's trip to and through, and implied later departure from, Boston. We see him arrive and wander through the streets, receiving the revelations that lead to his departure. The physical action in "Roger Malvin's Burial" is limited to Reuben's preparing to leave his friend and his later return to the same spot, the events of the intervening years being chiefly summarized rather than presented as they happen. In "The Canterbury Pilgrims" travelers going in opposite directions meet, talk, and depart on their different ways; that is all the action there is. Wakefield leaves his home and later returns. The searchers for the great carbuncle, once they have been introduced in their camp, set out on their quest; what they discover on the way is the essence of the story. The man of adamant journeys to his cave and there receives a visitor from across the sea; since he does not depart with her, he is lost. Ethan Brand searches far and wide for the Unpardonable Sin, returns to his lime kiln, and throws himself into the flames because he has at last found, in an unexpected place, that for which he has sought. Goodman Brown journeys into and returns from the forest, bringing back with him the revelations he has gained there. This journey-plot is so frequent in Hawthorne that sketches like "The Procession of Life" and "Main Street" differ from the tales not so much in "lacking plot" as in failing to develop character: the casual reflections of the narrator, clearly in these pieces Hawthorne himself, are not an adequate substitute for the creation of a Goodman Brown, or even of a Reverend Mr. Hooper with his veil.

From these very simple patterns of action Hawthorne developed designs of great complexity. Once he had seen the general meanings implicit in his basic situation, he saw reflections and qualifications of them everywhere. The *Gestalt* once perceived came to dominate everything, even the style. Everything fell into place in the pattern. Actions, characters, and scenes fell naturally into pairs, or into groups of three or four. Sometimes of course he overdid it, especially when "imagination" failed and "fancy" took over. He liked to bring balance out of apparently random arrangements, or to experiment with unbalance when balance was too strongly expected. Leland Schubert has commented on many of these features of Hawthorne's tales adequately so far as the mere existence of rhythmically balanced "artistic" patterns is concerned. What he does not adequately explore is the functional aspect of the devices he notes. The subject contains material for a monograph; I shall give only two examples of the sort of thing that should be looked for in the tales.

"The Canterbury Pilgrims" is wrought in terms of duality. Everything comes in pairs. The incoming travelers balance the outgoing pair — in circumstances as well as in the direction and intent of their journey. The community on the hill balances the world in the valley — in its nature as well as in its location. The incoming group of six travelers may be divided into two groups of two and four persons, with the four divisible into two and two: the poet and the merchant who speak first and are united by the "likeness" Josiah sees between them; the farmer and his wife, whose tales follow and complement each other, and their two sleeping children. At the end of the story, when the two contrasting groups prepare to continue each in its own direction, even the style is affected by the strength of the controlling pattern. "The Shaker youth and maiden," Hawthorne writes,

looked mournfully into each other's eyes. They had stepped across the threshold of their homes, when lo! the dark array of cares and sorrows that rose up to warn them back. The varied narratives of the strangers had arranged themselves into a parable; they seemed not merely instances of woeful fate that had befallen others, but shadowy omens of disappointed hope and unavailing toil, domestic grief and estranged affection, that would cloud the onward path of these poor fugitives. But after one instant's hesitation, they opened their arms, and sealed their resolve with as pure and fond an embrace as ever youthful love had hallowed.

Everything here — and on through the next two paragraphs to the final sentence of the tale — is in twos: *youth* and *maiden*; *had but stepped* when *cares and sorrows rose*; not merely *instances* but *shadowy omens*; *disappointed hope* and *unavailing toil*; *domestic grief* and *estranged affection*; they *opened their arms* and *sealed their resolve*; *pure* and *fond*. Even the rhythm is a reminder of the basic dualisms in the tale. Lightly suggested in the passage I have quoted, it comes out more strongly as we move toward the final sentence: "The lovers drank at the Shaker spring, and then, with chastened hopes, but more confiding affections, went on to mingle in an untried life." At the risk of seeming to some overobvious and to others arbitrary, I shall arrange this sentence to emphasize the sound patterns as they appear to me:

The lovers drank (and then)	at the Shaker spring,
with chastened hopes,	but more confiding affections,
went on to mingle	in an untried life.

This sort of thing is much too common in Hawthorne to require extended comment or emphasis.* What needs to be said, and what may be said briefly since it must be obvious, is that the passage I have analyzed for its rhythm is evidence that even the sound of this tale is expressive. Rhythm, sentence structure, image and symbol, structure in its larger aspects as patterns of action and character and situation — all are subdued to the demands of the "subject," with its contrasts of the world and the spirit, pride and love, the life of full experience and the life of renunciation, pessimism

---

* Compare, for example, the ending of "Young Goodman Brown," where rhythm and euphony, including alliteration and assonance, combine to add their emotional intensities to the tale: "And when he had lived long, and was borne to his grave a hoary corpse, followed by Faith, an aged woman, and children and grandchildren, a goodly procession, besides neighbors not a few, they carved no hopeful verse upon his tombstone, for his dying hour was gloom."

and optimism, despair and hope, past and future, death and life. (It is equally true, of course, to say that we do not know what this "subject" comprises until we see its various aspects grow out of the structures which embody and express them.)

If the number two permeates "The Canterbury Pilgrims," three is no less prominent in "Roger Malvin's Burial." The action, as we have seen, falls into three parts: Reuben's leaving Roger Malvin, living with the secret guilt, and returning to expiate the sin. (This may of course also be thought of as journeys in opposite directions over the same route, from and then to the place of guilt, with a pause in between, during which the effects of the wrongful departure accumulate to require the expiating return.) The characters, too, are a part of the pattern. For though there are four chief characters in all, they do not exist at the same time, so that effectively there are first one set of three, then another set of three: father-in-law to be, son-in-law to be, and wife to be; then father, wife, and son.

The persons making up the pattern change, but the pattern remains. Roger dies and Reuben becomes a father, thus taking his place in the pattern, while Cyrus moves into the place formerly occupied by Reuben. Only Dorcas does not move or develop, either in terms of this pattern or in terms of her status as a fictional character, as a person with recognizable traits. She is static because, like Rosina in "Egotism," she embodies a truth which does not change. Reuben "kills" his father-in-law, then is driven by his guilt to kill his symbolic self, his son. He develops through the stages of blindness, guilt, and redemption. But Dorcas is first and last perfect love, which knows no change.

With this triadic design dominant throughout the tale, as it is, we should not be surprised to find that the last sentence catches up all these suggestions and expresses them in one final pattern in which sound, grammar, and rational content all work together to express what is at once and alternatively the "matter" and the "manner," the subject and the vehicle, the theme and the expression, of one of the great tales in the language:

His sin was expiated, — the curse was gone from him; and in the hour when he had shed blood dearer to him than his own, a prayer, the first for years, went up to Heaven from the lips of Reuben Bourne.

CHAPTER FOUR

THE TALES: *The Texture of Meaning*

One of the most rewarding critical examinations of Hawthorne's work is entitled "Hawthorne as Poet."[*] Though Mrs. Leavis's title is apt, Hawthorne does not seem to have cared much for the poetry of his own century, or for the work of the lesser poets of any period. Shakespeare, Milton, Spenser, especially Spenser, he loved, but except for these he seems for the most part to have found prose more to his liking. Yet at least once, writing to Longfellow, he called himself a poet, and his own works in prose are a kind of poetry.

Even his pieces that come closest to being pure history or pure allegory are ordinarily enriched by that kind of texture that we have come to expect to find in verse. The usual contrast between "realistic" and "romantic" fiction, in which Hawthorne is assigned a place at the far end of the romantic side of the spectrum, is less useful for an attempt to understand Hawthorne's fiction than has been supposed. His fiction is "romantic" enough, to be sure, whatever meanings such a statement may carry; but it is more significant to note that it is completely *made*, as the poet, the maker, makes his poems. The more helpful contrast is between fiction as

[*] Q. D. Leavis, in *Sewanee Review*, Spring and Summer 1951.

report, as a branch of journalism or of the writing of history, and fiction as Hawthorne conceived it, as a formal aesthetic structure wrought from whatever materials, whether the visions of the haunted mind or ideas or the data of history or a little of all of these.

Hawthorne, in short, was an artist, not a reporter and not a historian, despite his extensive use of the material of history. He conceived of himself as, and was, "an artist of the beautiful," even when he wrote what he sometimes thought of as his "blasted allegories." His "allegories of the heart" introduce a new element into the traditional mode. Neither Spenser's nor Bunyan's work is in any significant sense allegory of the "heart": Spenser and Bunyan allegorized "Truth," public, accepted, external truth; and the texture they gave it was incidental. In Hawthorne's work the texture is decisive, the "truth" dubious, ambiguous, indecisive. The evidence of this can be found as easily in "The Minister's Black Veil" as in "Roger Malvin's Burial," in "The Man of Adamant" as in "Rappaccini's Daughter." In all of Hawthorne's successful tales the texture is rich. The images become symbols, and the symbols and allusions expand to myth.

2

"The human heart to be allegorized as a cavern," Hawthorne jotted in his Notebook as an idea for a story. "The Man of Adamant" comes as close, I think, to being pure allegory as any tale that Hawthorne ever wrote. A comparison of it with "Roger Malvin's Burial" will suggest two of the limits within which the tales exist. Yet even here, where the symbolism is so clear and the general structure so obviously an embodiment of an abstract judgment, or set of judgments, the texture enriches the theme. Though Hawthorne calls his tale an "apologue" and it is tempting to dismiss it as an allegorized sermon on the dangers of spiritual pride, the

piece turns out to be a work of art and not merely a statement of doctrine.

With "The Gentle Boy," "The Maypole of Merrymount,"
and "Main Street," the "Man of Adamant" is one of the clearest revelations of Hawthorne's attitude toward the Puritanism of his ancestors. Indeed the theme, in all but its largest
outlines, is directly concerned with a judgment of the kind
of religiousness of which Hawthorne always saw the Puritans
as "types," and we shall understand *The Scarlet Letter* more
fully if we know the judgments made here. The whole situation is outlined, and the outcome foreshadowed, in the opening paragraph.

> In the old times of religious gloom and intolerance, lived Richard
> Digby, the gloomiest and most intolerant of a stern brotherhood. His
> plan of salvation was so narrow that, like a plank in a tempestuous
> sea, it could avail no sinner but himself, who bestrode it triumphantly,
> and hurled anathemas against the wretches whom he saw struggling
> with the billows of eternal death. In his view of the matter, it was a
> most abominable crime — as, indeed, it is a great folly — for men to
> trust to their own strength, or even to grapple to any other fragment
> of the wreck, save this narrow plank, which, moreover, he took special
> care to keep out of their reach. In other words, as his creed was like
> no man's else, and being well pleased that Providence had intrusted
> him alone, of mortals, with the treasure of a true faith, Richard Digby
> determined to seclude himself to the sole and constant enjoyment of
> his happy fortune.

In his first sentence Hawthorne sets up the historical boundaries of his theme, justifying our seeing this tale as his
judgment of the errors not of an individual but of an era.
For Richard Digby is unlike his fellow Puritans only in carrying their traits to an extreme: he is "the gloomiest and most
intolerant" in a time of "religious gloom and intolerance."
The tale anatomizes a "stern brotherhood."

But the negative judgment of the first paragraph is qualified as soon as it is made. If it is uncharitable and intolerant
of Richard Digby to consider it "a most abominable crime"

for men to "trust to their own strength," it is not doctrinally mistaken or foolish to do so. Hawthorne's "as, indeed, it is a great folly" establishes the limits of Digby's error: not wrong doctrine but hardness of heart, not a mistaken faith but a failure of charity. In the same way Hawthorne later characterized the Puritan populace in *The Scarlet Letter*: not that adultery was not a sin — not that it was, as it seems to many in our day, merely a mistake or an inconvenience or a violation of a taboo — but that condemnation of the sin must not preclude charity toward the sinner.

The second paragraph of the tale establishes a parallel, at once historically accurate in its reflections of Puritan thought and symbolically suggestive in its context, between Digby and the Chosen People of the Old Testament. To keep his unique religion uncontaminated, he decides not to "tarry longer in the tents of Kedar." The third paragraph continues to enforce the parallel as it pictures his departure from the settlement in order to build himself "a tabernacle in the wilderness." The Old Testament overtones, suggesting the Chosen People's devotion to the true God, remind us that such action may sometimes be necessary. Though the irony in the suggestion that he will "smite and slay any intruder upon his hallowed seclusion" is strong, memories of the righteous smiting and slaying done by the Chosen People act as counter agents to the negative judgment. In short, Digby is clearly established as a man like Aylmer in "The Birthmark," who does the wrong thing from a motive not in itself wrong, indeed in isolation high and noble; like him also in falling into sin because of too perfect a trust in his own powers; like him finally in being a paradoxical figure the depth of whose error is a measure of the strength of his devotion to what seemed an "ideal" cause.

What follows may be considered a commentary on the words of St. Paul, "And now abideth faith, hope, charity, these three, but the greatest of these is charity." Digby's faith was intense but he had no charity; lacking this, his faith too became false. Concerned only to keep his faith pure, he took the steps which inevitably corrupted it. He who had had no sympathy for the "poor wretches whom he saw struggling with the billows of eternal death," when he reaches a cave reminiscent of "Elijah's cave at Horeb, though perhaps it more resembled Abraham's sepulchral cave at Machpelah," is unable in its dim light even to read his Bible correctly. Naturally, then, when the vision of Mary Goffe appears to him, begging him to return with her to those who need his help, he turns her away. Since it is clear that the vision of Mary Goffe is a heavenly influence offering him a last chance to escape his self-imposed doom ("What else but faith and love united could have sustained so delicate a creature . . .?"), it is likewise clear, as St. Paul said, that "If ye have not charity" ye have nothing, not even faith. Richard Digby is lost in his dark cave, lost from the very thing it had been his supreme purpose to guard and cultivate. The tale expresses the depth and centrality of Hawthorne's understanding of Christianity.

As in the first paragraph Hawthorne qualified his condemnation of Digby by expressing his own agreement with the doctrine that there is no salvation by good works alone — for if there were, then men might safely "trust to their own strength" — so he uses Biblical allusions throughout to enrich his tale. The denunciations Digby hurls at those whose faith he judges corrupted are like those of the prophets who recalled their people from worship of false gods. His cave, like Elijah's and Abraham's, is a sacred place in the wilderness. He remembers that strait is the gate and narrow the way that leads to salvation, and few there be that find it: "Of a truth, the only way to heaven leadeth through the narrow entrance of this cave, — and I alone have found it." He shares the conviction and the dedication of the prophets and saints who have corrected the errors of their times.

He forgets that the entrance to heaven is through a gate, not a cave. The cave in which he sits until he is calcified is at once the cavern of the heart's isolation and the entrance to the underworld. If it is like Elijah's retreat, it is even more like Abraham's place of death. The initial tentative suggestion of this is at once a foreshadowing of the outcome of the plot and a suggestion of the way in which the tension between the "hallowed seclusion" and the "dreariest depths of the forest," both initially applied to the place of Digby's retreat, is to be resolved. We have been prepared then for the discovery that the feet of Mary Goffe bear the wounds of thorns. Denying his brotherhood with sinful and wretched mankind, rejecting the sunlight for the darkness of his cave and the pure water of the spring that bubbled near the entrance for the drippings from the roof — that he might not be interrupted in the reading of his Bible, so intense was his devotion — Digby rejects likewise the sacramental cup of "hallowed water" which Mary Goffe offers. A cavern, clearly, is a most unsuitable spot in which to worship God. Refusing to come out of it, Digby rejected what Hawthorne tells us is "pure Religion."

For "pure Religion" not only does not forget that "the greatest of these is charity," it does not reject the natural light of the sun or the pure water of the natural spring in which Mary Goffe dipped her "birchen cup." The imagery of light and water and cave in the apologue of Richard Digby takes us into areas of meaning at once historical, theological, and psychological, though the tale remains an almost pure allegory on the nature and effects of bigotry. The Puritan flight into the wilderness across the sea that they might practice their Biblical faith, their great emphasis on the Old Testament and their conviction that they were the new Chosen People, their intolerance and their cruelty in persecuting dissenters from what was itself dissent, their rejection of general opinion embodied in tradition — all these aspects of the history of Hawthorne's forebears are here symbolized. The Puritan doctrine of total depravity is likewise a part of the background of this tale of a man who, like Jonathan Edwards in "Sinners in the Hands of an Angry God," predicted "vengeance and unutterable woe" for all but the elect; but so is the sense of isolation from which Hawthorne suffered before his marriage helped him to "open an intercourse with the world"; and so are the dreadful specters that spring from the heart in vision or in dream in "Alice Doane's Appeal" and "My Kinsman, Major Molineux." Digby rejected the corrective influences of nature — the Natural Revelation offered to Reason in the spring and the sunlight — and of love, and so was lost, as Roderick Elliston, intent upon the serpent in his bosom, would have been if he had not been saved by Rosina and his friend, by the voices of love and reason.

Abstractly allegorical as it is, then, in comparison with most of Hawthorne's better-known tales, "The Man of Adamant" can take us, through the implications of its imagery and its allusions, into meanings richer than those we should expect in an "apologue." Though its value is largely conceptual, it can tell us much of the nature of imagery and symbolism in the tales, for both its difference from and its similarities to such stories as those of Roger Malvin and Major Molineux are instructive. It defines one end of the scale of Hawthorne's practice, which includes "The Wives of the Dead" and "The Hollow of the Three Hills" at one extreme and "Dr. Heidegger's Experiment," "The Minister's Black Veil," "The Great Carbuncle," and "The Man of Adamant" at the other.

But a tale more centrally located, more nearly in Hawthorne's middle ground between symbolism and allegory, will disclose aspects of his practice which none of the tales we have examined so far have shown us. Such a tale is "Rappaccini's Daughter."

3

We are almost certain to approach "Rappaccini's Daughter" with preconceptions. We are likely to have read it at least once, if we have read any of Hawthorne, and we think we "know what it means." The frequency with which it has been reprinted in the anthologies, selected for special comment in the histories of literature, and dramatized on radio and television, shows that it has commonly been held to be one of the finest of Hawthorne's tales. Only Austin Warren, with his belief that the symbolism of the tale is false because "the physical and the psychic do not correspond,"* seems to have entered a strong objection to this opinion. Yet a survey of the remarks that scholars and critics have made on the story — and almost everyone who has ever treated Hawthorne, the short story, or the history of American literature has mentioned it — suggests either that the story's reputation is quite unjustified or that, though just, it has little to do with the story's real meaning and nature, is, in fact, only an indication that the tale may be used as a convenient illustration of many Hawthornesque themes and devices.

Ordinarily comment on the tale is limited to the statement that it illustrates one simple abstract idea, or theme, usually the *libido sciendi*, or lust for knowledge. Just how this can be (for the scientist in the tale is a minor character, which poses the problem of why, if the tale is about the *libido sciendi*, Hawthorne did not write about Rappaccini instead of about his daughter) is usually explained, not by any analysis, even of the briefest sort, of the tale itself, but by reference to some other story. Thus for example the tale is seen as a "companion-piece" to "The Birthmark" and "Ethan Brand," as a statement of the theme of isolation that is found in almost all the other Hawthorne stories, or even as a counterpart of "Lady Elea-

---

* *Hawthorne: Representative Selections* (New York, American Book Company, 1934), p. 367.

nor's Mantle." We are told that when we read of Beatrice,
experimentally poisoned by her scientific father, we should
think of Georgiana, of Lady Eleanor, and even of Chillingworth. Though no other Hawthorne story has excited more
comment, most of the treatments of it are not very helpful,
and some of them are positively misleading. The story has its
difficulties, especially if it is approached as allegory.

It opens with Giovanni Guasconti, a young student who
has come from Southern Italy to study in Padua, taking lodg-
ings in a gloomy old mansion. The young man is in no way
remarkable. Even in his homesickness he is merely typical,
the natural man. Looking out of his window, however, he
soon discovers something that is remarkable and that immediately arouses his — and the reader's — interest: a garden,
belonging, he is told, to the famous Dr. Rappaccini, who
distills potent medicines from its rare herbs. Looking now
with increased interest, Giovanni studies the garden with
care, and Hawthorne devotes a page to telling us what he
saw.

This garden, then, is the first high point of the story, and
since it will continue as a prime symbol we must see what
it is that merits so much emphasis. The first particular item
of this "botanic garden" to catch Giovanni's eye is a ruined
fountain in the center. The water that gushes from the fountain sparkles in the sunlight. Its loveliness cheers Giovanni
and makes him feel "as if the fountain were an immortal
spirit that sung its song unceasingly." Here is beauty in the
midst of ruin and gloom and — it will soon become evident —
evil. We shall see this symbolic representation of the inter-
mingling of good and evil repeated in the plant, in the
garden as a whole, in Beatrice, and finally in the total structure of the tale. Meanwhile, however, Giovanni's attention
has turned from the fountain itself to a striking plant that
grows beside it. "There was one shrub in particular," we
read, that, set in a marble vase and bearing a profusion of

purple blossoms, "seemed to illuminate the garden." The plant, we soon learn, is poisonous; it is the vehicle of the evil in the story. Yet it draws its nourishment from the pure water of the fountain and illuminates the garden with its beauty even while it contaminates the air with its sweet but deadly fragrance. Here in the beautiful but deadly shrub we see the fountain symbol again in more complex, because organic rather than inorganic, form.

From the cluster of garden images the tale now shifts to the father in the garden. Giovanni becomes aware of "a tall, emaciated, sallow, and sickly-looking man, dressed in a scholar's garb of black." Old and somewhat infirm, the man is especially distinguished, Giovanni thinks, by "a face singularly marked with intellect and cultivation, but which could never, even in his more youthful days, have expressed much warmth of heart." At this point the temptation is strong to stop reading, to underline this passage, and to decide that the tale is simply a companion-piece to some other tale, for the portrait is so familiar: a scientist, coldly intellectual, consumed by the *libido sciendi*, with a heart as stony as Ethan Brand's. But let us not go too fast. The portrait of the father in the garden is not complete, nor do we yet know what part he is to play in the tale.

Giovanni watches the old man inspect his garden and notes one very peculiar, indeed obscurely frightening, aspect of the scene: "the man's demeanor was that of one walking among malignant influences, such as savage beasts, or deadly snakes, or evil spirits." This peculiar behavior of the old man is the strangest thing in the tale so far. It is the first explicit revelation of the fact that we have here to do with no ordinary garden and no ordinary old man pottering around it, that here we shall encounter magic and myth. "It was strangely frightful," Hawthorne tells us, "to the young man's imagination to see this air of insecurity in a person cultivating a garden, that most simple and innocent of human toils, and which had been alike the joy and labor of the unfallen parents of the race." The words "that most simple and innocent of human toils" serve, one sees, both to reëmphasize the theme of the mixture and deceptiveness of good and evil and to prepare for the striking transposition of the theme into another key in the clause that follows. Is it not clear that we are moving from a garden in Padua to an older garden, from the father of Beatrice to a universal father, from fact to myth? "Was this garden, then, the Eden of the present world? And this man, with such perception of harm in what his own hands caused to grow, — was he the Adam?"

This is the end of the first part of the story, the first scene that prepares for the drama. All but one of the important symbols and characters have now been presented, and that one, Beatrice, is the most important of all, the Hamlet who does not enter until scene two. We do not need to go beyond this first part to see the direction the story is taking. Though the familiar Hawthorne theme of the *libido sciendi* has appeared, we should not emphasize it at the expense of what Hawthorne has himself emphasized. What we have here so far is an observer, a magic garden, a mythical father, and an obscure evil somehow wrought by him.

The rest of the tale develops the situation which has been created before Beatrice appears — which does not, of course, mean that she is not the main character and the chief symbol, but only that she has been properly prepared for. Rappaccini calls for his daughter. Giovanni, watching from his window, is immediately struck by her beauty as she comes through the garden. Her voice before he sees her ("as rich as a tropical sunset") and her clothes after he sees her ("beautiful as the day") suggest to him the strange luxuriant beauty of the flowers in the garden. "She looked radiant with life, health, and energy." Like Rima as she is first glimpsed in her green mansions, Beatrice seems perfectly a part of nature. Thus far we see Beatrice chiefly as an extension of the garden imagery. If this were the complete Beatrice we might be justified in concluding that the tale is not one of Hawthorne's best because the analogy between the girl and the flower, between human nature and subhuman nature, is false. The physical and the psychic certainly do not perfectly correspond. But the story does not finally suggest that they do. We have not seen Beatrice as a person yet, only as a figure in the garden.

If Beatrice reminds Giovanni of the flowers, and if the flowers seem both beautiful and obscurely evil, then the first paradox associated with Beatrice has already been established. It simply extends and deepens the paradox of the garden itself, the fountain, and the special plant: intermingled beauty and ruin, health and death, good and evil. This correspondence of the several symbols — inorganic, vegetable, and animal — has yet to be further emphasized before there can be any significant modification. For it is so obvious to "common sense" that girl and plant are not the same that Hawthorne must first establish his analogy before he can reveal a further insight by altering it. To do so he is forced again, as in the suggestion of obscure evil in the garden, to turn from the "realistic" to the magical. The father commits the special plant to his daughter's sole charge. She accepts gladly, calls the plant "sister," expresses love of it, and exclaims that its fragrance is to her "as the breath of life." Giovanni watches her as she tends the plant with loving care. Darkness falls and he closes his window. When he goes to bed he dreams "of a rich flower and a beautiful girl. Flower and maiden were different, and yet the same, and fraught with some strange peril in either shape." Intermingled good and evil in nature has been established, on all levels. This is the first meaning which the tale as a symbolic structure creates. It is not the last. To take an analogy from the drama, we have here the end of the first act of the play, not the play. In *Hamlet* too the basic situation is clear by the end of the first act but the final meaning of the play is not.

The development during the middle portion of the story may be summarized briefly. Giovanni is consumed with curiosity about the garden and its inhabitants. He looks out of his window whenever possible. He rationalizes his interest, explaining to himself his prying curiosity with the thought that here in this strange northern city the garden will serve "as a symbolic language to keep him in communion with Nature." He learns from Professor Baglioni that Dr. Rappaccini is marvelously skilled in science but that his reputation is bad. When he presses for other details, he learns that the particular evil imputed to Dr. Rappaccini is that he "cares infinitely more for science than for mankind. His patients are interesting to him only as subjects for some new experiment." Giovanni concludes that Rappaccini must be an "awful man indeed."

Now since this *libido sciendi* characterization of Rappaccini has so often been taken to be *the* meaning of the tale, I should like to pause at this point and suggest some of the reasons why it cannot be more than one of several meanings and not the chief of them. First, Beatrice is the chief character, the center of interest, and the primary symbol throughout, from the title to her death at the end.* Rappaccini, from the time when we first see him inspecting the garden until, at the end, he steps forward again to join Giovanni and Beatrice, is nearly always in the background, a sinister but shadowy figure. Once Giovanni sees him in a crowd. The doctor seems to be studying the young man with cold curiosity, and Baglioni warns that he may be performing a "new experiment" — that is, planning to let Giovanni come in contact with Beatrice so that he may study the result. But of

---

* It is perhaps worth noting that in his playful preface Hawthorne, pretending that he is merely editing the works of an obscure French author, supplies a French title for the tale that emphasizes the centrality of Beatrice: *Beatrice; ou la Belle Empoisonneuse.*

course this "experiment" would involve no significant new act on the doctor's part: he would simply allow the young people to have their way while he watched the spreading effects of his poison. Neither the significance of Rappaccini as a symbol nor his position in the story as a background character is changed by this or by Giovanni's suspicion that it may have been Rappaccini who prompted Dame Lisabetta to reveal the gate to the garden.

To repeat: Rappaccini and his black magic must be ever present to make the story literally possible and symbolically meaningful, but it is present evil, a woman poisoned, that is the chief subject of the story. Black magic is assumed here as witchcraft is in "Young Goodman Brown." It is not the father, whose cold intellectuality has been established before the tale is one-fifth completed, but the evil which he has wrought which here chiefly concerns us.

Returning to the summary of the action, we find Giovanni's interest in the garden and its inhabitants becoming fascination and the fascination centering on the person of Beatrice. He is attracted first of all by her physical beauty, but he soon notes also the "sweetness" and "simplicity" of her face. When flowers seem to wilt at her touch, when a lizard dies after the juice of the plant is dropped on him, when a butterfly dies after it comes too close to her, he is forced to think of the apparent affinity between Beatrice and the beautiful but obscurely dangerous plant. He tries to believe that his eyes have deceived him. A simple, unaware man without, as Hawthorne tells us, a "deep heart," he rationalizes easily and quiets his fears while his passion takes more and more complete possession of him. Warned by Baglioni against becoming further involved in Rappaccini's experiment, he experiences new doubts and fears but manages to push them into the back of his mind. But when, in the garden at last and alone, he examines the flowers closely, he is further disturbed by noting that "their gorgeousness seemed fierce, passionate, and even unnatural." It begins to seem to him that they are not truly "of God's making, but the monstrous offspring of man's depraved fancy, glowing with only an evil mockery of beauty."

Giovanni's perception that there is something unnatural about the plants, and so, by the analogy which has been established, about Beatrice as well, does not modify the identity of garden and girl of which Giovanni has been aware all along, but it does alter the shared content of that identity. It throws into an ironical light Giovanni's early desire to "commune with nature" through the medium of the garden. Can there be two natures, one original and one corrupt? But this is a complication on which Giovanni has no time to ponder, for Beatrice appears and he is once more lost in the fascination which her beauty holds for him.

The only new revelations in the remainder of the middle part of the story concern Beatrice. They make her a person, not simply, as she has chiefly been when viewed only from the distance of the window, a symbol of man's involvement in nature. (Again, they make her a person, not simply a behavioristic automaton, as anyone may appear to be when studied for certain purposes from the outside.) When she first finds Giovanni in the garden she is of course surprised, but the surprise in her face was "brightened by a simple and kind expression of pleasure." We should not expect this of an evil person. Hawthorne's normal practice would lead us to expect some suggestion of cunning, some hint that this "simple and kind expression" is only a mask of evil designs if she were really evil. F. O. Matthiessen has said that Giovanni was wrong in supposing that he could save her, that he was wrong because she has been made really evil. But of course she is evil only in so far as she shares the poison of the plant. It may turn out that the poison is ineradicable as long as she lives: but she has a spirit which can choose death. She is both evil and not evil. She is the victim of an original sin but she has not committed any actual sin nor is she guilty of any of the capital vices. From the point of view of the Christian frame of reference within which the tale is written, the distinction is an important one.

Again, when she becomes aware of Giovanni's doubts and fears concerning her, she protests her innocence and says that she is not, as is reputed, skilled in science, that she knows nothing of the lore of her father. Her appearance is deceptive but her words come from the depths of her heart: "Those you may believe." She seems, Hawthorne tells us, as she says this to be more radiant than ever, to radiate "the light of truth itself." Once more we must say that if Hawthorne meant Beatrice to be wholly evil he has written ineptly. For unlike the many ideas that are the productions of Giovanni's fancy, these suggestions of the essential purity of Beatrice are directly stated by Hawthorne: not that it seemed to Giovanni that she was kind and simple but that she *was*. On the other hand, when he looked into her eyes and saw the beauty of her soul, it *seemed* to him that there was no more danger. Hawthorne is distinguishing carefully between conceptions which he presents as justified and those which are the products of poor Giovanni's ability to delude himself. There was danger, more danger than Beatrice herself knew, though everything she said was true. Giovanni's "mistake" was like that of young Goodman Brown: he had not the wit to see her as other than simply good or simply bad.

Only two more revelations of the nature of Beatrice are needed to complete this central part of the story. First, she falls in love with Giovanni. She watches daily for his appearance and flies to his side "with confidence as unreserved as if they had been playmates from infancy." Second, as her love for Giovanni grows her dependence on the plant lessens. Even after their first meeting, though she still addresses the plant as before, she notes that "For the first time in my life . . . I had forgotten thee." Now her former "sisterhood" with the plant saddens her. She warns Giovanni not to touch it or to touch her. Her great happiness at their meetings is punctuated by an increasingly "desolate" awareness of her "separation." One need not stress the point that love has brought her to a full awareness of her situation, to a realization of the plant as evil and of herself as not after all simply a sister of the plant, and finally to both greater despair and greater joy than she had ever known before. The plant–girl analogy, which seemed complete earlier in the tale partly because we knew Beatrice only incompletely, as an "appearance," as a creature in nature, and partly because she had not yet been awakened by love, is now broken. What remains of it is only the fact that Beatrice has been poisoned by the plant as the result of an experiment by her father. But the analogy had to be established before the breaking of it could come as a revelation.

The final act of the story begins when Giovanni, hearing from Baglioni the story of the terrible result of Rappaccini's "insane zeal for science" and being warned that he too may become a victim of it, decides to take a powerful antidote that Baglioni has distilled, get Beatrice to drink it, and thus see if he cannot work a radical cure. Buying Beatrice a bouquet to take to her with the medicine, he finds to his horror that the flowers wither at his touch. Angry and frightened, with all his love, which has never been of the same quality as Beatrice's love for him, changed to fear and hatred, he rushes into the garden to stand before "the bright and loving eyes of Beatrice." Again the sight of her beauty and the memory of her apparent sweetness and purity move him. But he is as blind in his fright as he had been in his infatuation. He bursts out with questions and accusations. She tells him all she knows of her "awful doom," of the plant that her father created, and of its obscure connection with her own being. Giovanni responds to her frank statements with contempt and loathing. He speaks of his "unutterable hatred" of her and mocks her broken prayer with "fiendish scorn."

In thus reacting as though he were the only one who had lost something, Giovanni is behaving as we had expected. For we have seen his foolishness and Hawthorne has remarked on his "vanity" and his "shallowness of feeling and insincerity of character." His shallow love turns quickly to hatred. Though he has felt, in his happy moments, that "There is something truer and more real than what we can see with the eyes and touch with the finger," he is not able, now that he fears for his own safety, to see anything in Beatrice but a threat to himself.

Beatrice, now fully aware of the situation and its meaning, desperately hurt by his cruelty, asserts again her innocence of intention: "Not for a world of bliss would I have done it!" To Giovanni's suggestion that they both drink the antidote, she says that she alone will drink it and he must await the result. As she does so, her father approaches and tells her that she is no longer alone, that she now has a companion in her isolation. Addressing her as "daughter of my pride and triumph," he denies that he has inflicted great misery on her: has he not given her greater power over others than any woman has ever had before, power even to kill at a touch?

She replies that she would be loved, not feared. "But now it matters not," for she is going where the evil which her father has striven to mingle with her being will pass away. The pain of Giovanni's "words of hatred" will fall away too in a moment. She wonders whether there was not always more evil in Giovanni's nature than in her own. Then she dies, "a poor victim of man's ingenuity and of thwarted nature, and of the fatality that attends all such efforts of perverted wisdom." Her "earthly part," Hawthorne tells us, could not throw off the poison her father had implanted, so that "the powerful antidote was death." Baglioni, appearing with rather improbable timeliness, observes the scene in the garden and taunts Rappaccini with the unforeseen "upshot" of his experiment.

Several comments are necessary on this ending, which may seem to ring several false notes. First, the emphasis in the end is where it has been all along: on Rappaccini's daughter, her poisonousness and innocence, her awful doom, her awareness, her acceptance of death as the antidote, her escape from the poison. If the note about her "ascending" seems a flaw to the modern mind, it is at least consistent with the frame of ideas within which the entire story is told, though it must be noted that she, not Hawthorne, uses this physical imagery.

Second, as the tale has progressed Hawthorne has made us increasingly aware of Giovanni's unadmirable character. He is not actively bad, he is only "natural"; but the natural man of the orthodox theologians lacks spiritual insight until it is given him. There were signs, Hawthorne has told us, in Beatrice's behavior which, "had Giovanni known how to estimate them, would have assured him that all this ugly mystery was but an earthly illusion." But Giovanni did not have Beatrice's "quick spiritual sense"; he was "incapable . . . of such high faith." In short, we know so much about Giovanni that we do not care what happens to him at the end, partially poisoned though he is. We know that all are poisoned and that he is less deserving of our interest than are many. We are content that he should be forgotten. Finally, Rappaccini's evil nature we have known from the beginning. He has been lurking in the shadows throughout the tale while our interest has been fixed on Beatrice, and his brief participation in the action at the end does nothing to change our estimate of him.

But Beatrice we have not known fully until the end. It has been her story all along, her tragedy, her doom. And we now know that she is not at all like Chillingworth, not at all like Lady Eleanor. She does remind us of Georgiana in

"The Birthmark," but "Rappaccini's Daughter" and "The Birthmark" are not "companion-pieces" unless we mean by that term only that they supplement each other with their different revelations of Hawthorne's attitudes. "The Birthmark" is concerned with man's search for perfection and with the impossibility of attaining it. The title of the story points to the flaw, not to the woman in whom the flaw appears, and Georgiana is seen in the tale only as flawed beauty. The plot is built around Aylmer's growing obsession with the birthmark and his fatal attempt to remove it. Aylmer himself is portrayed not only as a scientist but, and particularly, as a perfectionist, a misguided idealist who, inspired by pure motives, would accomplish good, not harm, if the world were different. Centered as it is on Aylmer rather than on Georgiana, the tale assumes man's inherent imperfection and develops the tragic folly of supposing that things may be otherwise.

Compare all this with the situation in "Rappaccini's Daughter." This tale concerns the origin, the nature, and the cure of man's radically mixed, his good-and-evil being. The title points to the daughter, not to her imperfection, and Beatrice is portrayed as a human being, a tragic figure, so that she is the center of interest throughout the tale. The plot consists of a controlled revelation of her full character. Rappaccini is like Aylmer only in being a scientist with great confidence in his scientific powers: he acts from a very different kind of pride from Aylmer's. Holding consciously to diabolic values, he is evil rather than deluded. Power is his end and science but his means to it. Finally, while the preparation and use of the antidote are central in "The Birthmark," here the antidote is only accessory, a subordinate symbol completing the structure built by the others. If the two stories contain similarities — a scientist who cares more for science than for people, a mark of man's imperfection (the hand in both stories), a death as a result of an attempt to remove this imperfection — they involve as many or more dissimilarities. And these dissimilarities are the keys to their significance as unique works of art. To discuss them in common terms is to concentrate on Hawthorne as "thinker" and to ignore him as artist.

If we can now agree on what the tale is not about, perhaps we are ready to attend to the implications of the images and symbols that give this tale a texture as rich as any that Hawthorne ever created. We have seen that the garden and the flowers and plants in it form a cluster of symbols pointing in three directions: first toward nature; then, as Hawthorne explicitly broadens the area of significance, toward Eden; and finally, in a revelation that comes to the reader but not, until it is too late and then without real understanding, to Giovanni, toward nature corrupted by man's depravity. The fountain, with its marble vase in the midst of the pool, suggests, in its setting, another world in ruins, the world of classical civilization and its Renaissance revival. But if the beauty and vitality of nature are not to be taken as implying the Romantic conception of nature as "the great Mother of us all," wholly beneficent in its power and edifying in its "moral lessons," and if classical civilization is in ruins with the fountain which typifies it, we are left with a pair of ambiguous values disappointing to humanist and romantic naturalist alike. What of the nature and destiny of human beings in such a world?

All the lines of symbolic implication in the tale converge and join with the implications of the larger elements of structure to define human nature as just as ambiguous and paradoxical as nonhuman nature and the fountain. Like the flowers, and particularly like her special flower, Beatrice is lovely but poisonous, innocent but corrupt. As we see it in her, human nature is in ruins, like the fountain. As the fountain's statue of Vertumnus, the classical god of vegetation, growth, the natural cycles of the seasons, is wreathed by "serpent-like" creepers, so her nature has been corrupted by evil, ruined by the work of the father with the snake-like eyes. Beatrice typifies the condition of man since the Fall, as that condition is defined by historic Christianity. And what we know of Giovanni and Rappaccini strengthens the conclusions about human nature we have drawn from Beatrice. Giovanni is not a "bad" young man as men go, but there is more evil in him than meets the eye; and Rappaccini has made evil his good.

Color images support the implications we have seen in the garden, flower, fountain, and serpent imagery. There are three gradations of color in the tale, and they are much emphasized. First there is the pure sunshine, corresponding to the illusions of "unspoiled nature" attributed to Giovanni, who has known nature only in the sunny southern parts of Italy, a land lost or unattainable to him in Padua, the "present world." The sunshine makes the water of the fountain sparkle cheerfully and gives the garden the appearance of perfect innocence. But the chief flower in the garden is purple, a color ambiguous in its associations with royalty and death and disturbing in its emotional effects. And Beatrice, though we are told of her dress only that she was "arrayed with as much richness of taste as the most splendid of the flowers," is associated with her "sister" flower not only because both are beautiful and sinister, and because this flower requires her special care, but in terms of color: when Giovanni first hears her voice it makes him think of "deep hues of purple or crimson and of perfumes heavily delectable." Finally, there is the black constantly associated with Rappaccini. If the sunlight suggests a positive value and red and purple an ambiguous value, black here is unambiguously negative. Together with the imagery of snakes and cold, it defines Rappaccini as an evil force in the story.

The temptation at this point is to try to make a completely allegorical reading. But the tale will not yield a satisfactory allegory. In a sense Rappaccini "created" the garden and Beatrice, but he is surely not a symbol of an evil God. So far as the garden is "nature," it would be more accurate to say that he "corrupted" than that he "created" it. To Beatrice he stands more nearly in the situation of Adam than of God. Though he is associated with serpent imagery, he is not Satan either, despite the evil which he throws around him like a shadow, though he may have become an agent of the prince of evil. He is not even a "type" of mankind, for that role is assigned to Beatrice and, less clearly, to Giovanni. If his garden is indeed "the Eden of the present world," as Hawthorne suggests, it does not correspond precisely to the Eden from which "our first parents" were driven out. Though Beatrice suggests the present condition of man, she is not to be taken as suggesting that man is simply a victim, not personally guilty of any actual sin, as she is not. Finally, Dr. Baglioni has so far proved completely resistant to any attempt to place him in an allegorical scheme.

"Rappaccini's Daughter" is a symbolic tale of the type Hawthorne made peculiarly his own, a symbolic tale with allegorical elements but without the fixed and systematic identifications proper to allegory. Its meaning is very largely the function of its texture. As its images become symbols and its symbols expand to suggest myth, the simple anecdote of the poisoned girl takes on that density of meaning that we have come to expect of Hawthorne's tales at their best.

4

"The Man of Adamant" has considerably more literary value than we should expect of an apologue, and "Rappaccini's Daughter" has the kind of value we do not find in pure allegory. In both, the texture supplies a complexity that qualifies and deepens the meanings implied in the anecdotal structure. In both, the degree of aesthetic distance is great and the illusion of reality slight by contemporary standards;

the appeal is to the contemplative side of the aesthetic experience. Yet even "The Man of Adamant" provides material for contemplation that a philosophic statement on the nature and effects of bigotry could hardly provide.

As for "Rappaccini's Daughter," it is like "Roger Malvin's Burial" in moving from the literal to the symbolic and finally to the mythic. If it seems less a product of the passive sensibility than "Roger Malvin's Burial" and "My Kinsman, Major Molineux" its texture is more intricately wrought. In this it is more nearly like *The House of the Seven Gables* than like *The Scarlet Letter*; it may be used to define one of the modes of Hawthorne's fiction. That he preferred this mode to that which sprang more directly from the type of sensibility he described in "The Haunted Mind" is not surprising in view of what we have seen of the visions that so often haunted him between sleep and waking.

All the best of Hawthorne's tales exist in the area bounded by allegory and history, archetype and myth. They convey the kind of knowledge poetry conveys, in symbolic terms not essentially different from those poetry uses. The less successful tales fall short of greatness as "The Great Carbuncle" falls short, by not establishing firmly enough the concrete, the actual, the historical; or they fail as some of the "Legends of the Province House" do, by not infusing history with sufficient meaning. "The Great Carbuncle" and "Howe's Masquerade" are both memorable stories in their different ways, but they are not in the same category of greatness with "Roger Malvin's Burial" and "Young Goodman Brown" and "Rappaccini's Daughter." The difference between the lesser and the greater seems to lie in this: that the greater, whether they spring from the depths or the top of the mind, have both the universality of "The Man of Adamant" and the historicity of "Howe's Masquerade." Hawthorne's best tales have as much illusion of reality as they need to set up significances we cannot easily exhaust.

pragmatic - practical approach to problems or affairs.

CHAPTER FIVE

THE SCARLET LETTER

It is an interesting fact that Hawthorne's most widely read and admired novel is also the one that has inspired the most inconclusive debate about its meaning. *The Scarlet Letter* has been read as evidence of Hawthorne's "transcendentalism" and of his "Puritanism." It has been interpreted as a declaration in favor of feminism and as a half-hearted, and to that extent defective, statement of pragmatic modernism. Since Hawthorne was not a transcendentalist, a Puritan, or a feminist by any interpretation, however broad, of these terms, as even a slight acquaintance with his life and work is sufficient to show, the best thing to do with the first three of these interpretations is to dismiss them as clearly on the wrong track. As for the pragmatic reading, it is perhaps politic to wait and see. But it might be remarked now that it is hardly to be considered surprising that a reading conducted in terms of the variety of pragmatic liberalism fathered by Emerson, nourished by James, and matured by Dewey should find the novel worth only an A-minus.

Yet the very variety of the critical interpretations points to several conclusions, one of which surely is that if *The Scarlet Letter* is allegory at all, it cannot be allegory of the older mode, with its clear-cut abstractions, for if it were, surely there would not be so much disagreement about its meaning. If it is rather a work of symbolism of the type Hawthorne made his own in the best of the tales, then we should expect that paraphrase will not be easy, and hasty paraphrase will not be rewarding.

2

* In the three paragraphs of his opening chapter Hawthorne introduces the three chief symbols that will serve to give structure to the story on the thematic level, hints at the fourth, and starts two of the chief lines of imagery. The opening sentence suggests the darkness ("sad-colored," "gray"), the rigidity ("oak," "iron"), and the aspiration ("steeple-crowned") of the people "amongst whom religion and law were almost identical." Later sentences add "weatherstains," "a yet darker aspect," and "gloomy" to the suggestions already begun through color imagery. The closing words of the chapter make the metaphorical use of color explicit: Hawthorne hopes that a wild rose beside the prison door may serve "to symbolize some sweet moral blossom, that may be found along the track, or relieve the darkening close of a tale of human frailty and sorrow."

A large part of the opening chapter is allotted to this rosebush and to some weeds that also grow beside the prison. Having learned to respect the economy with which Hawthorne worked in his tales, we should guess, even if we had not read beyond this first chapter, that these will turn out not to be merely "realistic" or "atmospheric" details. We should expect to meet them again, with expanded connotations. Actually, the flower and weed imagery is second in importance only to the color imagery in the novel. The more than thirty occasions on which it is subsequently found are not, like the even more frequent heart images, casual, or partly to be accounted for as stylistic mannerisms, the reflexes as it were of Hawhorne's style, but chief keys to the symbolic structure and intention of this work.

Finally, in addition to the Puritans themselves, the jail before which they stand, and the weeds and the rose, one other object, and only one, is mentioned in this first chapter. In the only generalized comment in a chapter otherwise devoted to objective description, Hawthorne tells us that "The founders of a new colony, whatever Utopia of human virtue and happiness they might originally project, have invariably recognized it among their earliest practical necessities to allot a portion of the virgin soil as a cemetery, and another as the site of a prison." The three climactic scenes of the novel take place before the scaffold in front of the prison. The cemetery, by contrast, remains in the background. We are not allowed to forget it, we learn that Chillingworth has a special interest in it, but we are not encouraged to make it the center of our attention until the end, when it moves into the foreground as the site of the tombstone with the strange inscription.

The cemetery, the prison, and the rose, with their associated values and the extensions of suggestion given them by the image patterns that intersect them, as the ugliest weeds are later discovered growing out of graves, suggest a symbolic pattern within which nearly everything that is most important in the novel may be placed. The cemetery and the prison are negative values, in some sense evils. The rose is a positive value, beautiful, in some sense a good. But the cemetery and the prison are not negative in the same sense: death, "the last great enemy," is a natural evil, resulting as some theologies would have it from moral evil but distinguished by coming to saint and sinner alike; the prison is a reminder of the present actuality of moral evil. Natural and moral evil, then, death and sin, are here suggested. The rose is "good" in the same sense in which the cemetery is an "evil": its beauty is neither moral nor immoral but is certainly a positive value. Like the beauty of a healthy child or an animal, it is the product not of choice but of necessity, of the laws of its being, so that it can be admired but not judged. Pearl, later in the story, is similarly immune from judgment. There is no strong suggestion of moral goodness in this first chapter, nor will there be in what is to follow. The cemetery and the weeds contrast with the rose, but only the suggestions of worship in the shape of the hats of the Puritans contrast with the prison, and those steeple-crowned hats are gray, a color which later takes on strongly negative associations.

Among the ideas implicit in the opening chapter, then, are, first, that the novel is to be concerned with the relationships of good and evil; second, that it will distinguish between two types of good and evil; and, third, that moral good will be less strongly felt than moral and natural evil. A symmetrical pattern is theoretically suggested here, and as we shall see, in the rest of the novel. But what is actually felt is an asymmetrical pattern, an imbalance, in which the shapes of moral and natural evil loom so large as to make it difficult to discern, or to "believe in" once we have discerned, the reality of moral goodness or redemption. The rose, in short, is finally not sufficient to relieve "the darkening close of a tale of human frailty and sorrow." The celestial radiance later seen gleaming from the white hair of Mr. Wilson is not sufficient either, nor the snowy innocence said to exist in the bosoms of certain maidens. In writing *The Scarlet Letter* Hawthorne let his genius takes its course, and death and sin turned out to be more convincing than life and goodness.

3

The extremes of Mr. Wilson's "light" and Chillingworth's "blackness" meet not only in the gray of Hester's dress and

the Puritan hats, and in the indeterminate drabness of the
Puritan clothing, but also in the ambiguous suggestions of
red. Images of color, and of light and shade, are more numerous than any other images in the novel. Readers have always
been aware that Hawthorne has used these images "artistically," and sometimes that he has used them "expressively";
yet precisely what they express and how they express it have
never, even in the extended treatments of the subject, been
adequately analyzed. Some of them Hawthorne makes explicitly symbolic, others seem obscurely to be so, while still
others resist every effort at translation into abstract terms.
Faced with this profusion and complexity of evidence, most
commentators have wavered between the opinion that the
color images are used "allegorically" and the even less dis-
cerning opinion that they are only in the vaguest sense, as
realistic background, functional. Here, as on a number of
other aspects of Hawthorne's work, criticism is forced to
make something like a fresh start. I think it will prove useful
as a preliminary to later analysis to distinguish among three
ways in which images of color and light and shade appear
in the novel.

There is, first, the pure sensory image used literally, not
figuratively, though the literalness of its use will not destroy
whatever intrinsic symbolic value it may have. Second, there
is the color or shade of light or darkness that must be taken
literally but that also has explicit symbolic value. Finally,
there is the image that has only, or chiefly, symbolic value,
so that it cannot be taken literally. I shall call these pure,
mixed, and drained images. It will be clear that this sort
of classification cuts across other types of analysis, such as
that which distinguishes between emphatic and casual imagery and that which seeks to isolate implicit paradox or distinguish types of ambiguity. The strategy here is intended
to bring out the degree of "literalness" with which Hawthorne writes, and this matter in turn has an important bear-

ing on the question of whether *The Scarlet Letter* is symbolism or allegory.

But first it must be clear that there is a real basis in the novel for making such distinctions — or that the data will lend themselves to such manipulation without forcing. A look at the first several chapters will be enough I think to give us an answer. Thus on the first page the grayness of the hats and the "weatherstains" of the jail are pure images, sense impressions to be taken quite literally. Only after we have become conscious of the part played by color in the tale are we apt to be aware of the appropriateness of these colors, though to be sure they may have had their effect on us before we became conscious of that effect. So likewise the "bright" morning sun and the "ruddy" cheeks of the spectators in the next chapter are first of all, and always fundamentally, to be understood in a perfectly literal sense. Again, the first time the scarlet letter is mentioned, the color image is pure: "On the breast of her gown, in fine red cloth, surrounded with an elaborate embroidery and fantastic flourishes of gold-thread, appeared the letter *A*."

Mixed images, on the other hand, have more than that suggestion of figurative extension that any image, however pure, will have: they may be said to *denote* both literal and figurative colors, so that in them the natural symbolism of color becomes explicit. The jail is "gloomy," that is, both physically and emotionally dark. The second time the letter is mentioned, its color has acquired a moral connotation from its context: Hester stood before the crowd with "desperate recklessness" while everyone looked at the sign of her ignominy, "that SCARLET LETTER." More clearly an example of this mixed type of image is the beadle's statement that here in this righteous colony "iniquity is dragged out into the sunshine": for Hester has just been brought from the literal darkness of the jail into the literal sunshine of the square, and this action is an example of "iniquity" which has been hidden or unknown being made public, brought into the (figurative) light. The speaker has meant his remark as a figure of speech, while the reader sees that it is literally appropriate too; there is a two-way movement, from the literal to the figurative, and from the figurative back to the literal, going on here and elsewhere in the color images in the novel. One final example in this preliminary survey of the mixed type of image: "his face darkened with some powerful emotion." Now powerful emotion may literally darken the face by flushing it, but here the symbolic effect of darkness, as that which is feared and evil, is also clear. This is the first reference to the "darkness" of Chillingworth.

The third or drained type of image is much less frequent than the other two. (There are ten times as many pure images as drained, and about twice as many mixed, according to my count.) On the first page we hear of the "black flower" of civilized society, a prison, and we realize that "black" is here figurative, for though the jail has been described as dark and weatherstained, it is not black in any literal sense. Again, in the last sentence of the first chapter we hear of the "darkening close" of the tale, and we read "darkening" to mean gloomy (in the emotional sense), sad. Finally, when the Reverend Mr. Wilson speaks to Hester of the "blackness" of her sin, the primary significance of the word, both for Hester and for the reader, is intensive and qualitative in a moral sense; the residue of literal meaning merely adds to the emotional overtones. Here, as in the "smile of dark and self-relying intelligence" displayed by Chillingworth, there is hardly any literal meaning left.

The colors presented in these three types of images are associated with natural good (beauty, health), moral and spiritual good (holiness), natural evil (ugliness, death), and moral evil (sin). With the exception of the yellow starch on the linen of Mistress Hibbens, in which I can discern only historical verisimilitude, all the colors in the novel, including yellow as used elsewhere, are associated with one or more natural or moral values, positive or negative. The most frequent colors are red in its several shades and black, pure or mixed, as in "gray" "shadowy," and "darksome." Red is ambiguous throughout, suggesting both sunlight and roses, on the one hand, and the traditional associations called up by "the scarlet woman" on the other. Pearl, a "natural" child, is dressed in red, Hester's letter is red, the roses are red, the bloom on healthy cheeks is red, and the glow in Chillingworth's eyes is thought to be red with the light of infernal fires. Black, dark gray, brown, all the darker shades, ordinarily suggest both natural and moral evil. Green and yellow are associated with natural good, with life and beauty.

Light is of various kinds. Sunlight suggests both truth and health. It is analogous to the spiritual Light of Revelation, which in Hawthorne's scheme of values should "illumine" nature, and to the light of grace. But there are also the "false light" of meteors and the "red light" of evil. Mr. Wilson, the most saintly of the Puritan ministers and the most sympathetic of the lesser characters, has "white" hair and light-colored ("gray") eyes, in marked contrast to the only colors assigned to Governor Bellingham, who has a "dark" feather and a "black" tunic. Thus too Dimmesdale, a mixed figure of lofty aspirations and base conduct, is seen as having a "white," lofty, and impending brow and "brown," melancholy eyes. Dressed in "black," he walks by choice in the "shadowy" bypaths. Hester is seen as red (her letter and her vivid complexion), gray (her dress), and black (her hair and eyes), the first two ambiguous in their associations, the last saved from being wholly negative by the glints of sunlight often seen in her hair. Pearl, though she has her mother's black hair and eyes, is usually seen as a flash of red and light: the "deep and vivid tints" of her "bright" complexion and "gorgeous robes" often throw an absolute circle of "radiance" around her. Chillingworth is compounded of shades of "darkness," except for the red, or reddish blue, glow thought to be seen in his eyes.

The relationships between the three types of images, the several colors, and their associated moral and natural values are highly complex, but I shall risk a few generalizations, the first of which is the most obvious. The use of colors in the novel is, as Leland Schubert has said, rhythmic, but it is more than that, for the rhythm is functional and expressive. In "The Interior of a Heart," for instance, there are twenty-two color images, all but two of which are black or white. The heart is Dimmesdale's, and Dimmesdale wavers between good and evil, we might almost say between the supernatural and the unnatural. It is conceptually right that he should be associated with both the radiance of Wilson and the darkness of Chillingworth. He is never associated with the greens and yellows and reds of sunlit nature.

Again, the chapter called "Hester at Her Needle" has eighteen color images, eleven of them red, seven black, dark, and white. Hester stands in an ambiguous position between Chillingworth and the white maidens, as Dimmesdale does between Chillingworth and Wilson, but she differs from him in her relation to nature. For a final example, on one page of "The Minister's Vigil," when the approach of Mr. Wilson and the threat of disclosure coincide, there are nine color images, eight of which are of light or whiteness. Recalling the beadle's earlier remark about the Puritan effort to drag iniquity out into the sunshine, in which light was associated with an uncharitable violation of the human heart, we become aware of what is sometimes obscured in discussions of Hawthorne: that color imagery is functional *in context*.

The most significant use of color in the novel is in the three key scenes, Hester on the scaffold with the infant Pearl, Dimmesdale with Hester and Pearl on the scaffold at midnight, and the three on the scaffold again at the end. In the first, Hester is dragged into the light and stands there "with the hot, mid-day sun burning down upon her face and lighting up its shame; with the scarlet letter of infamy on her breast. . ." In the second there is at first only the darkness of the "obscure night," which renders Dimmesdale's gesture ineffectual. Then two kinds of light appear. First there is the gleam of the lantern of the saintly Mr. Wilson, who appeared in his illuminated circle to be radiant with the "distant shine of the celestial city"; but Mr. Wilson's light does not reach Dimmesdale, who is thus "saved" by a narrow margin from disclosure. After Mr. Wilson's light recedes in the darkness, a meteor flames in the sky, making all visible, but in a "false" light, so that what Chillingworth sees by its aid is not true. Neither light in this scene accomplishes the necessary revelation. That is left for the final climactic scaffold scene, in which the three come together voluntarily in the light of the sun.

The second generalization I should like to suggest about the light and color images is this: their significance is enriched by the relations between the three types of images. In the first place, the pure images are so much the most numerous that they tend to establish, by sheer weight of repetition, the reading of the others. Where there is so much blackness, "gloomy" is bound to carry its physical as well as its emotional denotation. This becomes clearer when we compare the use of darkness in, say, *Dr. Grimshawe's Secret* with its use here. When in the later novel Redclyffe is said to exist in a darkened dream, we do not know quite what to make of it, for darkness has not been established as a motif in the novel. But when Governor Bellingham says that Pearl is "in the dark" concerning her soul, the expression means far more to the reader than that she is not, in the opinion of the governor, properly instructed: it calls up the whole range of colors, and the moral and other values attached to them, which the reader has absorbed by this time.

We have another of those sudden expansions from image to symbol that is so conspicuous a feature of the novel.

In short, the marked predominance of pure images keeps the mixed and drained ones from losing force by becoming abstractly figurative, and this in turn is one of the reasons why the novel never becomes allegory. Though we must say that there is a struggle going on in the novel between the forces of darkness and of light, the preponderance of pure images keeps this struggle from becoming neatly dichotomous. When we read that Chillingworth had conceived "a new purpose, dark, it is true, if not guilty," we do not read this as a pleonasm, for darkness has acquired many associations beyond the guilt it may hide. Again, the "light" of the church is saved from being a mere figure for "the teaching of the church" by the fact that light has become associated with a cluster of positive values, both natural and moral, that cannot be translated adequately as "doctrine."

Finally, two drained images will illustrate the point. "The holy whiteness of the clergyman's good fame," in reference to Dimmesdale, draws a part of its meaning from the light constantly associated with Mr. Wilson and Christian Revelation, but another part from the false light of the meteor, which has only recently ceased to cast its distorting glare over the scene. And the smile that "flickered" over Chillingworth's face "so derisively" that the spectator could see his "blackness" "all the better for it" is also a false light which nevertheless may reveal some things truly, as the light of the meteor had revealed "the black, freshly turned earth" of the garden plots near the scaffold.

But the movement flows in another direction too, for the presence of the mixed and drained images underlines the symbolic value of the pure images. When Pearl, inspired by her mother's example, makes a letter out of eelgrass for her own breast, and Hester says that "the green letter, and on thy childish bosom, has no purport," we realize that the statement is true in several different senses: from Hester's point of view, the green letter has none of the "purport" that her own letter has, and she, of course, is preoccupied with just that kind of meaning; but from the reader's point of view, the greenness of the letter is an appropriate reminder of Pearl's association with nature. And when we see the Indians in the square on Election Day, the predominant reds and yellows of their barbaric finery and the black of their "snake-like" eyes carry associations with nature and with evil, but none at all with "celestial illumination." Like the weathered wood of the jail, the Indian costumes gather meaning from their context.

The point of my third generalization about the three types of images has perhaps already become sufficiently clear from what has been said, but it is so important that I should not like to let it rest on implication. The movement of the different colors back and forth between pure and drained images helps to keep what Hawthorne calls his "mesh of good and evil" a true mesh, with the strands intricately interwoven. Hawthorne usually presents a pure image first, establishing the sensed color, then expands it into a mixed image, exploring its connotations, then at last uses the color in a drained image that out of the total context of the novel would be bare and lifeless, or merely whimsical, but that in context is rich in the associations it has acquired along the way. But sometimes he reverses this process, and sometimes he jumbles the order, so that the colors are never completely fixed in the degree of their literalness or the extension of their symbolic values. When we read, for instance, of the "radiant halo" surrounding the head of Mr. Wilson as he walked through a "gloomy night of sin," the image that we should expect to be merely figurative, the "halo" of sanctity, turns out to be literal as well, for the light is shed by Mr. Wilson's lantern; and the one that we should at first expect to be literal — for we already know that it is a dark night, and as we start reading "this gloomy night . . ." we think we are getting a mere restatement of the darkness — turns out to be also figurative, forcing us to revise the reaction we had prepared.

The relations between the light and color images and their symbolic values are, then, neither static and schematized nor wholly free and arbitrary, but contextual within a general framework supplied by traditional patterns of color symbolism. The traditional associations of light and dark, for example, are apparently archetypal. Literature is filled with the darkness of death and sin and the light of life and goodness; and the common speech allows us to "throw light" upon a problem as often as we "explain" or "clarify" it. Perhaps the most nearly fixed in its symbolic values of all the colors in the novel is black. Yet even it is sometimes used ambiguously. Hester's black hair, that glistened so often in the sunlight before she covered it with a cap, and Pearl's "dark, glistening curls," so well set off by her scarlet costume, are examples. On the other hand, the red that runs through the book as a motif is almost always used ambiguously. Only a few examples, like the "red glare" in Chillingworth's eyes, are wholly clear, with one set of suggestions canceled out and another emphasized. The wild roses and the scarlet letter, Pearl's costume and her mother's complexion do not exhaust the possibilities. Chillingworth's light is thought to be a reflection of the infernal fires, but Pearl is also said to be a flame. When the forest, seeming to recognize a kindred spirit in Pearl, offers her partridgeberries "red as drops of blood" the gift carries with it memories not only of the rose bush but of the scarlet letter.

In short, red, black, gray, sunlight, firelight, and the less frequent green, yellow, blue, and purple are not simply descriptive of the setting and characters. In a very real sense they are themselves actors in the story that moves through and behind the story. Even in their absence they help to tell the tale. When we find that the most strongly and frequently presented colors are those most commonly associated with negative or ambiguous moral values, or with positive natural values, and that the light of positive moral and spiritual values is both less vivid and less frequent, we are not surprised. The first chapter prepared us for this, and Hawthorne's tales prepared us before that. Perhaps the largest generalization we may draw from a study of the approximately 425 light and color images is that Hawthorne conceived, but did not strongly feel, the possibility of escape from evil and the past.

4

The "burdock, pigweed, apple-peru, and such unsightly vegetation" growing beside the prison, that "black flower of civilized society," where grass should have been, begin the flower and weed imagery, which, in some thirty images and extended analogies, reinforces and extends the implications of the imagery of color and light. Since these implications have already been drawn out, I shall simply call attention briefly to four relationships Hawthorne has set up.

First, and most clearly, the unnatural flowers and unsightly vegetation are aligned with moral evil, and with Chillingworth in particular. He too with his deformity is "unsightly." Low, dark, and ugly, he suggests to some people the notion that his step must wither the grass wherever he walks. The sun seems not to fall on him but to create "a circle of ominous shadow moving along with his deformity." It is natural enough then to find him explicitly associated with "deadly nightshade" and other types of "vegetable wickedness," to see him displaying a "dark, flabby leaf" found growing out of a grave, and to hear that prominent among the herbs he has gathered are some "black weeds" that have "sprung up out of a buried heart." When his evil work was done "he positively withered up, shriveled away . . . like an uprooted weed that lies wilting in the sun." Flower and weed imagery unites with light and color imagery to define Chillingworth's position as that of the chief sinner.

But Chillingworth is not the only one so aligned. Less emphatically, the Puritans themselves are associated with weeds and black flowers. The implications of color imagery first set up the association: as their "Puritanic gloom" increases in the second generation to "the blackest shade of Puritanism," we begin to see them as cousins to the "nightshade" and so are prepared for Pearl's pretense that the weeds she attacks in her solitary games are Puritan children. Accustomed to her apparently infallible instinct for the truth, we see in her game something more than childish imagination.

The second relationship deserving of note also starts in the first chapter. We recall Hawthorne's saying of the wild rose-bush in bloom beside the prison that he hoped it might "relieve the darkening close" of his tale. No "sweet moral blossom" plays any significant part in the main story, but the happy fortune of Pearl, related in the concluding chapter, does offer a contrast with the "frailty and sorrow" of the tale proper. Thus Pearl's final role is foreshadowed in the first chapter. But Hawthorne does not wait until the end to make this apparent. He constantly associates her not only with the scarlet letter on her mother's dress but with the red rose. The rose bears "delicate gems" and Pearl is the red-clad "gem" of her mother's bosom. Her flowerlike beauty is frequently underscored. And naturally so, for we are told that she had sprung, "a lovely and immortal flower," out of the "rank luxuriance" of a guilty passion.

The position thus defined is repeatedly emphasized. Pearl cries for a red rose in the governor's garden. She answers the catechetical question who made her by declaring that she had not been made at all but "had been plucked by her mother off the bush of wild roses that grew by the prison door." She decorates her hair with flowers, which are said to become her perfectly. She is reflected in the pool in "all the brilliant picturesqueness of her beauty, in its adornment of flowers." Her "flower-girdled and sunny image" has all the glory of a "bright flower." Pearl is a difficult child, capricious, unintentionally cruel, unfeeling in her demand for truth, but she has both the "naturalness" and the beauty of the rose, and like the rose she is a symbol of love and promise.

These are the associations Hawthorne most carefully elaborates, but there are two others worth noting briefly. Weeds or "black flowers" are on several occasions associated with Hester. The most striking instance of this occurs when Pearl pauses in the graveyard to pick "burrs" and arrange them "along the lines of the scarlet letter that decorated the maternal bosom, to which the burrs, as their nature was, tenaciously adhered." The burrs are like Pearl in acting according to nature, and what they suggest in their clinging cannot be wholly false. Hester implicitly acknowledges the truth of what the burrs have revealed when she suggests to Dimmesdale that they let the "black flower" of their love "blossom as it may."

But a more frequent and impressive association is set up between Hester and normal flowers. Even the badge of her shame, the token of her "guilty" love, is thus associated with natural beauty. The scarlet letter is related to the red rose from the very beginning. As Hester stands before her judges in the opening scenes, the sun shines on just two spots of vivid color in all that massed black, brown, and gray: on the rose and the letter, both red. The embroidery with which she decorates the letter further emphasizes the likeness, so that when Pearl throws flowers at her mother's badge and they hit the mark, we share her sense that this is appropriate. Burrs and flowers seem to have an affinity for Hester's letter. Hawthorne was too much of a Protestant to share the Catholic attitude toward "natural law": the imagery here suggests that moral law and nature's ways do not perfectly coincide, or run parallel on different levels; they cross, perhaps at something less than a right angle. At the point of their crossing the lovers' fate is determined. No reversal of the implied moral judgment is suggested when nature seems to rejoice at the reaffirmed love of the pair in the forest: "Such was the sympathy of Nature — that wild, heathen Nature of the forest, never subjugated to human law, nor illumined by higher truth — with the bliss of these two spirits! Love, whether newly born, or aroused from a death-like slumber, must always create a sunshine."

Hester's emblem, then, points to a love both good and bad. The ambiguity of her gray robes and dark glistening hair, her black eyes and bright complexion, is thus emphasized by the flower and weed imagery. As Chillingworth is associated with weeds, Pearl with flowers, and Dimmesdale with no natural growing thing at all, so Hester walks her ambiguous way between burdock and rose, neither of which is alone sufficient to define her nature and her position.

5

There are nearly twice as many heart images as there are flower and weed images, but with one exception Hawthorne insists upon them less. If they are in some respects even more revealing, we may guess that that is because they spring from Hawthorne's deepest concerns and most abiding insights, not from the top of his head but from his own heart. It is even more difficult to imagine Hawthorne's style stripped of its heart images than to picture Dimmesdale without his hand over his heart. The minister's gesture is both consciously emblematic and a stylistic reflex.

But the heart imagery begins before we meet the minister. When Hester brings Pearl out of the dark "dungeon or . . .

prison" we have veiled heart imagery, for the heart in Hawthorne is nearly as often a dungeon as it is a cavern or tomb.
But this bringing out of the heart's secrets into the light is
not voluntary, it is forced. It cannot then in Hawthorne's
scheme of values be beneficial. One must "be true," but one
cannot force others to be true. When the Puritans insist on
"dragging" Hester into the public gaze — and get, clearly, a
good deal of pleasure out of so doing — and then try to extort
her secret from her, what they are doing constitutes an attempt at what Hawthorne calls elsewhere "a violation of
the human heart" — the sin of Brand, Chillingworth, and
other Hawthorne villains. To those who might be inclined
to think that society has a right to do what the individual
should not, Hawthorne has an answer, given in his comment
on the stocks, that more common Puritan instrument for
punishing by making the culprit publicly display his shame:
"There can be no outrage, methinks, against our common
nature, — whatever be the delinquencies of the individual, —
no outrage more flagrant than to forbid the culprit to hide
his face for shame."

The judges then stand in need of judgment. The Puritan
people are here playing the role later played by Chillingworth. The heart imagery of the opening scenes establishes
a tension that continues throughout the novel and is central
to its meaning. That this interpretation does not constitute
an overreading is suggested by the way light imagery reinforces heart imagery at this point: when we first see her,
Hester's beauty shines out and makes a "halo," and Hawthorne says that to some she might have suggested an "image
of the Divine Maternity." "The people's victim and life-long
bond-slave," as Hawthorne calls her, is not sinless, but neither
is she a sinner among the righteous. She is involved in a
mesh of good and evil.

Many of the other uses of heart imagery are, as we should
expect them to be, casual, almost incidental. They serve

chiefly to keep us aware that we are here concerned finally
with nothing less significant or permanent than the truths
of the heart. Running reminders of the central heart images,
they deepen and extend the reverberations of the action,
sometimes into areas that defy analysis. The governor's mansion, for example, seems obscurely to be the heart of the
Puritan rulers: behind a façade that glitters with fragments
of broken glass, there is a suit of armor that reflects Hester's
badge in magnified and distorted form. Despite the sunshine
on the stucco walls, there would seem to be in this mansion
an exaggerated consciousness of sin and almost no awareness
of goodness, so that if we read this passage as a heart image
we are reminded of "Young Goodman Brown."

Many of the others among the running heart images are
clearer. The heart is a grave, in which corpses are buried.
The heart is a chamber, in which the minister keeps his
vigils in utter darkness; when Chillingworth enters the
chamber, he is violating the heart. The heart is a hearth,
in which one is wise to keep a fire. The heart is tomblike,
or a niche in which images are set up and surrounded by
curtains. The heart (or breast or bosom) is the place where
the devil is most apt to set his mark. Of the fifty or so distinct
heart images I have noted in the novel, most are of this order.

But those associated with Chillingworth are of special interest, for, along with the imagery of light and color and
of weeds and flowers, they are the chief indications of his
place in the scheme of values in the novel. What they do
principally, of course, is once again to counter the judgment
implied by the overt situation. Chillingworth, the "wronged"
husband, does not cease to be the victim of injury when he
strives "to go deep into his patient's bosom . . . like a treas-
ure seeker in a dark cavern," but he makes it necessary to
ask who is more greatly injured, he or the man who has
"wronged" him. As the images continue the implication becomes clearer, so that, long before Dimmesdale has risen

through his final act of honesty and courage, Chillingworth is seen as more sinning than sinned against, as more sinful even than the minister. "He now dug into the poor clergyman's heart, like a miner searching for gold; or rather, like a sexton delving into a grave. . ." He stole into the chamber of the heart like a thief and there turned over, without valuing, "many precious materials, in the shape of high aspirations for the welfare of his race, warm love of souls, pure sentiments, natural piety, strengthened by thought and study, and illuminated by revelation." As he does so he imagines that his interest in what he finds is purely objective and disinterested, even scientific: "He had begun an investigation, as he imagined, with the severe and equal integrity of a judge, desirous only of truth, even as if the question involved no more than the air-drawn lines and figures of a geometrical problem, instead of human passions, and wrongs inflicted on himself." He is aided in his rationalization by the fact that his own heart is like a "cheerless habitation," cold in the absence of any household fire. But all the while it is becoming clearer that he is like Ethan Brand, who with "cold and remorseless purpose" conducted a psychological experiment on the heart of a young girl and "wasted, absorbed, and perhaps annihilated her soul, in the process."

Partly then as a result of the impact of the heart imagery, the reader feels his principal concern altered once again. First he was in suspense about the identity of Hester's partner in sin. Then, as that question begins to be answered, he wonders whether the minister will be publicly exposed and justice be done. But almost immediately, in "The Leech" and "The Leech and His Patient," he becomes concerned to have the minister escape somehow the persecutions of his tormentor. The central chapter on the relation between the two men, "The Leech and His Patient," begins and ends in heart imagery.

The most extended heart image is the forest scene. The

forest in which Hester and Pearl take their walk has all the
attributes common to normal human hearts in Hawthorne's
work. It is black, mysterious, dismal, dim, gloomy, shadowy,
obscure, and dreary. It is thought by the public to be where
the Black Man meets his accomplices. It has in its depths a
stream which as it mirrors the truth whispers "tales out of
the heart of the old forest." But when Hester and Dimmesdale decide to follow the dictates of their hearts and, escap-
ing man's law, live by nature, then "the wood's heart of
mystery" becomes a "mystery of joy" and sunshine lights up
the gloomy spot. In the four chapters concerned with this
meeting, heart imagery plays a leading part, so that no analysis of the incident is likely to be adequate which does not
take it into account.

6

Probably the symbolism of the names of the characters
is more important than the remaining patterns of imagery.
Pearl, of course, gets her name from the "pearl of great price"
used in St. Matthew to suggest the incomparable value of the
hope of heaven. Hester's initial mood of bitter rebellion
against her situation is clear in the naming of her child.
And the other chief characters too have significant names.
"Hester" is a modern form of "Esther"; and the Old Testament Esther is gifted with beauty, strength, and dignity.
Courageous and loyal, she defends a weak and oppressed
people. The obvious parallel between the two women contributes one more implication that Hester is to be seen as
finally "in the right." And it offers another bit of evidence
to those who like to stress the feminist implications of the
novel, for we may see the "weaker sex" defended by Hester
as but a variant of the weak people defended by Esther.

The minister's first name, Arthur, tends to suggest that
devotion to a high ideal associated with King Arthur. It is

at once descriptive and ironic as the name of Hester's partner in adultery. His last name falls naturally into two parts, with the root of the first part, "dim," suggesting both weakness and darkness, and the second part, "dale," suggesting, in its meaning of valley, the heart, of which Hawthorne is so frequently reminded by any hollow, opening, or cavity.

Finally, "Chillingworth" is also made up of two parts, the first of which suggests coldness and the second merit or worthiness. It is a name more transparently descriptive of this man than Dimmesdale is of the minister. For Chillingworth has, as he acknowledges to Hester, a cold heart, and his sin is one of the cold sins. Yet he was once a worthy man: decent, self-controlled, law-abiding, scholarly, "good" as the world tends to measure goodness, with nothing lacking except the most important thing of all, charity.

Names, then, are symbolic here, as they so frequently are in Hawthorne. There may be more name symbolism in the novel than I have indicated; there is certainly not less.

Of the other image patterns one of the most prominent is that of circles and chains. Considering the two as making up one pattern, since Hawthorne seems to think of them together, we find that each of the five times a circle or chain appears, it has the effect of increasing the guilt of the Puritan people and decreasing, or qualifying, Hester's. In the first few pages, for instance, we learn that the letter "had the effect of a spell, taking her out of the ordinary relations with humanity, and enclosing her in a sphere by herself." Hester then is in something like the position of Wakefield, who also was outside all "ordinary relations with humanity." But she has not chosen her fate, she has had it imposed upon her. The Puritan people who imposed it must be guilty of a very grave wrong indeed in Hawthorne's catalogue of sins. She is guilty of adultery, they of lack of charity. And since they had created "a sort of magic circle" around her, so that even in the crowd she was always alone, the reader can hardly blame her for casting away "the fragments of a broken chain" and thinking that "the world's law was no law for her mind." She had been literally forced into practicing Emerson's greatest virtue, self-reliance, in the isolation of her "magic circle of ignominy." No less excuse, in Hawthorne's world, would have exonerated her for breaking the connections in the "electric chain" of mutual sympathy and interdependence that should bind us together.

As circle and chain imagery is associated with Hester and helps to define her position, serpent imagery is associated with Chillingworth. At his first appearance we see a "writhing" horror "twisting" itself across his features. We are asked to visualize his figure as "low," a strange adjective surely if it means only "short," but appropriate to one who is said to "creep" along the ground. His ultimate transformation into a fiend should not take us by surprise if we have noted the snake imagery associated with him.

Another of Hawthorne's favorite image patterns, that of mirrors and pools that reflect, is used in the novel more prominently than the snake imagery, but with scattered rather than concentrated effect. The most telling instance is one we have already noted in passing in another connection: the reflection of Hester's letter in the polished suit of armor in the governor's house. The convex surface so magnifies and distorts the letter that she is quite obliterated by it: she is changed from a person to an abstraction, a walking sin.* Again the imagery connects the Puritan people and Chillingworth: compare his detached, "scientific" interest in Dimmesdale, not as a unique person but as an object to be investigated, with the Puritan view of Hester.

Unlike the curved mirror made by the armor, suited only to distort, natural mirrors, and especially those formed by water, whether of pools, streams, or fountains, normally tell

---

* See Yvor Winters, "Maule's Curse," *In Defense of Reason* (New York: William Morrow, 1947).

the truth in Hawthorne, especially the hidden truth of the heart.* We may presume that Dimmesdale saw something of the truth of his heart when for protracted periods he stared at himself in the mirror under the strongest possible light. And we may be sure that the brook in the forest mirrors truths otherwise hidden as well as the flowery beauty of Pearl. (Three chapters later it *becomes* a heart.) Thus, whether distorted or "true," the revelations of the mirrors in the novel are significant.

Finally, geometrical forms and patterns, the *shapes* of things, seem to me to be quite consistently functional throughout. Clearest are the images of the pointed arch, which draws the eye upward, or the less concrete images of height, suggesting aspiration, piety, or loftiness of purpose, and the low and twisted, suggesting evil. We note the "steeple-crowned" hats in the first sentence, and Hawthorne reminds us of them again. They suggest, not only in their obvious association with churches and so with worship but in the intrinsic character of their shape, the lofty aspirations and devotion to what was taken to be religious duty that conceived and created the New England theocracy. Again, Dimmesdale is so presented that the reader pictures him as tall and thin, in marked contrast with Chillingworth, who is seen as "low," "twisted," and "deformed."

With these hints that whenever shape is prominent it is significant, we may be justified in seeing in the scarlet letter itself something more than the first letter of *adultery*, something more than the first letter of the alternative reading *angel* preferred finally by some of the people: a design like that of steeples and the pointed arches of Gothic "cathedrals," a shape leading the eye upward toward heavenly things: all nature seemed to rejoice when the lovers reaffirmed in the forest a love that under different circumstances

* See Hawthorne's essay "Monsieur du Miroir" and Malcolm Cowley's "Hawthorne in the Looking Glass," *Sewanee Review*, October 1948.

would have taken a place very high among positive moral values. That these implications do not "justify" adultery is clear. Hester's scarlet letter remains as ambiguous in its implications as her social position as outcast and sister of mercy, adulteress and light of the sickroom. Hester remains, as Hawthorne might have said, a "type" of those paradoxes of human nature that we have seen earlier in Rappaccini's daughter.

7

The Scarlet Letter is the most nearly static of all Hawthorne's novels. There is very little external action. We can see one of the evidences for this, and perhaps also one of the reasons for it, when we compare the amount of space Hawthorne devotes to exposition and description with the amount he devotes to narration. It is likewise true, in a sense not yet fully explored, that on the deepest level of meaning the novel has only an ambiguous movement. But in between the surface and the depths movement is constant and complex, and it is in this middle area that the principal value of the work lies.

The movement may be conceived as being up and down the lines of natural and moral value, lines which, if they were to be represented in a diagram, should be conceived as crossing to form an *X*. Thus, most obviously, Hester's rise takes her from low on the line of moral value, a "scarlet woman" guilty of a sin black in the eyes of the Puritans, to a position not too remote from Mr. Wilson's, as she becomes a sister of mercy and the light of the sickroom: this when we measure by the yardstick of community approval. When we apply a standard of measurement less relativistic — and all but the most consistent ethical relativists will do so, consciously or unconsciously, thoughtfully or unthoughtfully — we are also likely to find that there has been a "rise." I suppose most of us will agree, whatever our religion or philosophy may be, that Hester has gained in stature and dignity by enduring and transcending suffering, and that she has grown in awareness of social responsibility. Like all tragic protagonists, she has demonstrated the dignity and potentialities of man, even in her defeat.

Dimmesdale is a more complicated, though less admirable and sympathetic, figure. He first descends from his original position as the saintly guide and inspiration of the godly to the position he occupies during the greater part of the novel as very nearly the worst of the sinners in his hypocrisy and cowardice, then reascends by his final act of courageous honesty to a position somewhere in between his reputation for light and his reality of darkness. He emerges at last, that is, into the light of day, if only dubiously into that shining from the celestial city. We cannot help feeling, I think, that if he had had any help he might have emerged from the darkness much sooner.

As for Chillingworth, he of course descends, but not to reascend. As in his injured pride and inhuman curiosity he devotes himself to prying into the minister's heart, whatever goodness had been his — which had always been negative, the mere absence of overt evil — disappears and pride moves into what had been a merely cold heart, prompting to revenge and displacing intellectual curiosity, which continues only as a rationalization, a "good" reason serving to distract attention from the real one. He becomes a moral monster who feeds only on another's torment, divorced wholly from the sources of life and goodness. He is eloquent testimony to the belief that Hawthorne shared with Shakespeare and Melville, among others: that it is possible for man to make evil his good.

Thus the three principal characters move up and down the scale of moral values in a kind of counterpoint: Chillingworth clearly down, Hester ambiguously up, Dimmesdale in both directions, first down, then up, to end somewhere in the center. But this is not the end of the matter. Because there are obscure but real relationships, if only of analogy, between the moral and the natural (I am using "natural" in the sense of those aspects of existence studied by the natural sciences, which do not include the concept of freedom of choice among their working principles or their assumptions), because there are relations between the moral and the natural, the movements of the characters up and down the scale of moral values involve them in symbolic movements on the scale of natural values. The moral journeys are, in fact, as we have abundantly seen, largely suggested by physical imagery. Chillingworth becomes blacker and more twisted as he becomes more evil. Hester's beauty withers under the scorching brand, then momentarily reasserts itself in the forest scene, then disappears again. Dimmesdale becomes paler and walks more frequently in the shadow as his torment increases and his sin is multiplied.

But the moral changes are not simply made visible by the changes in the imagery: in their turn they require the visible changes and determine their direction. The outstanding example of this is of course Chillingworth's transformation. As we infer the potential evil in him from the snake imagery, the deformity, and the darkness associated with him when we first see him, so later his dedication to evil as his good suggests the "fancy" of the lurid flame in his eyes and the "notion" that it would be appropriate if he blasted the beauty of nature wherever he walked. So too the minister's moral journey suggests to the minds of the people both the red stigma which some think they see over his heart and the red A in the sky, with its ambiguous significance of angel or adultery. The total structure of the novel implies that the relation between fact and value is never simple: that neither is reducible to the other, yet that they are never wholly distinct.

All three of the chief characters, in short, exist on both of our crossed lines, the moral and the natural. They are seen in two perspectives, not identical but obscurely related. Pearl's situation, however, is somewhat different. She seems not to exist on the moral line at all. She is an object of natural beauty, a flower, a gem, instinctively trusted by the wild creatures of the forest. She is as incapable of deceit or dishonesty as nature itself, and at times as unsympathetic. She is not good or bad, because she is not responsible. Like the letter on her mother's breast, she is an emblem of sin. Like the red spot over the minister's heart, she is also a result of sin. But she is not herself a moral agent. Even when she torments her mother with her demands for the truth, or refuses to acknowledge the minister until he acknowledges them, she is not bad, she is merely natural. She is capricious with an animal's, or a small child's, lack of understanding of the human situation and consequent lack of responsiveness to emotions which it cannot understand.

Pearl is more than a picture of an intelligent and willful child drawn in part from Hawthorne's observations of his daughter Una: she is a symbol of what the human being would be if his situation were simplified by his existing on the natural plane only, as a creature. Hawthorne tells us that Pearl is potentially an immortal soul, but actually, at least before the "Conclusion," she seems more nearly a bird, a flower, or a ray of sunlight. Because of this "naturalness," this simplification, she can reach the patches of sunlight in the forest when Hester cannot: she is first cousin to the sunlight in moral neutrality as well as in brightness. From one point of view it seems curious that most readers find it harder to "believe in" Pearl than in any other major character in the book except perhaps in Chillingworth in his last stages, for Pearl is the only character drawn from Hawthorne's immediate experience with a living person. If the naturalistic aesthetic of the late nineteenth century were a

correct description of the nature and processes of art, we
should expect to find Pearl Hawthorne's most "real" character. That she is not (though it is easy to exaggerate her "un-
reality") is I suspect partly the result of the drastic simplification of life Hawthorne has here indulged in, in giving
Pearl existence only on the natural plane. He has surely exaggerated a child's incapacity for moral action, its lack of
involvement in the demands of right and wrong, and so has
produced in Pearl the only important character in the book
who constantly comes close to being an abstraction. In creating Pearl, Hawthorne wrote partly out of the currents of
primitivism of his age, suppressing or refusing to extend his
normal insights, much as he made an exception to his convictions about the nature of the human heart when he created
his blonde maidens, who are equally hard to "believe in,"
and for rather similar reasons. Oversimplified conceptions of
experience cannot be made convincing.

Since "history" is created by the interaction of natural
conditions and human choice, there is a significant sense in
which Pearl has no history in the story. She moves in and
out of the foreground, a bright spot of color in a gloomy
scene, serving to remind Hester of her sin and the reader of
the human condition by the absence of one of its two poles
in her being, but never becoming herself fully human. In
the final scaffold scene Hawthorne shows us Pearl weeping
for the first time and tells us that her tears "were the pledge
that she would grow up amid human joy and sorrow, nor
forever do battle with the world, but be a woman in it." In
the "Conclusion," when Hawthorne gives us a glimpse of
the years following the real end of his tale in the minister's
confession, he suggests that Pearl grew to happy womanhood
abroad. If so, she must have taken her place with Hester
and Dimmesdale and Chillingworth in the realm of moral
values, making her history and being made by it.

But the others, including the Puritan populace, have histories and are involved in the larger movements of history created by all of them together existing in nature as creatures and moral beings. Hester might not have committed adultery had Chillingworth had a warmer heart, or perhaps even had he been younger or less deformed. He might not have fallen from a decent moral neutrality to positive vice had she not first fallen. Hester is forced to become stronger because the minister is so weak, and he gains strength by contact with her strength when they meet again in the forest. Chillingworth is stimulated by his victim's helplessness to greater excesses of torment and sin, and the Puritan women around the scaffold are stirred by Hester's youth and beauty to greater cruelty than was implicit in their inquisition anyway. History as conceived in *The Scarlet Letter* is complex, dynamic, ambiguous; it is never static or abstractly linear, as both simple materialism and simple moralism tend to picture it. St. Paul's "We are members one of another" could be taken as a text to be illustrated by the histories of human hearts recounted in the novel.

Yet with all this complex movement on two planes, with all this richness, this density, of history, when we ask ourselves the final questions of meaning and value we find the movement indecisive or arrested in one direction, continuing clearly only in the other. The Puritan people and Chillingworth are condemned, but are Hester and Dimmesdale redeemed? It is significant in this connection that Pearl's growth into womanhood takes place after the end of the story proper. It is also significant that though Hester bore her suffering nobly, it is not clear that she ever repented; and that, though he indulged in several kinds of penance, it is possible to doubt that the minister ever did. The redemptive love and knowledge that worked the cure of Roderick Elliston in "Egotism" do not enter the picture here — though, to be sure, Elliston's was a less complicated case than Hester's and Dimmesdale's.

There is, then, despite Hester's rise, no certainty of final release from evil or of the kind of meaning to be found in tragedy, no well-grounded hope of escape from their sin for the sinners. The minister's dying words and the legend engraved on the tombstone both seem to me to make this clear. We recall the scene of the dance on the graves in "Alice Doane's Appeal." Here is a vision of history containing judgment but not mercy, condemnation but not forgiveness, sin and suffering but no remission, no "newness of life." If, as someone has suggested, the heraldic wording of the gravestone's inscription contains the possible suggestion that, just as the stigma of bastardy was wiped out by being emblazoned as the bar sinister on the noble escutcheon, so the sinfulness of the adultery was removed by being thus permanently acknowledged, the suggestion is surely not strongly supported by what has preceded. Hawthorne, in this respect a man of his age, never formulated his religious feelings and attitudes into any clear-cut theology. If he had done so, he might have been puzzled by the question of how central and significant a place to give to the Atonement.

In this final theological sense then the work is static. On the natural plane, beauty and ugliness, red rose and pigweed, equally exist with indisputable reality. But on the moral plane, only evil and suffering are really vivid and indisputable. Hawthorne's constant exception to his ordinary characterization of the human heart, the spotless, lily-like hearts of pure maidens, will hardly bear looking into. The light around Mr. Wilson's head shines too weakly to penetrate far into the surrounding gloom. And the only light into which Dimmesdale certainly emerges is the light of common day. The novel is structured around the metaphor of bringing the guilty secret from the black depths of the heart out into the light. But it is suggestive not only of what went on in his own heart but of the poverty both of the Puritanism of which he wrote and of the Unitarianism which Puritanism

became and which Hawthorne knew at first hand that Hawthorne could conceive of the need but not the existence or
the nature of any further step. After confession, what then?
"No great wrong is ever undone." Surely being "true," the
one moral among many, as Hawthorne tells us, that he chose
to underscore, is not enough. *The Scarlet Letter* sprang from
Hawthorne's heart, not from his head.

The dominant symbols, to return to the first chapter once
more, are the cemetery, the prison, and the rose. The religious idealism suggested by the steeple-crowned hats is
ineffective, positively perverted even, as the man of adamant's sincere piety was perverted by his fanaticism. The
clearest tones in the book are the black of the prison and
the weeds and the grave, and the redness of the letter and
the rose, suggesting moral and natural evil and natural goodness, but not moral goodness. "On a field, sable, the letter A,
gules." Of the literal and figurative light, one, the sunlight,
is strong and positive, while the other, shining, as St. John
tells us, from the Light of the World, falls fitfully and dimly
over minor characters or is posited in mere speculative possibility.

The Scarlet Letter, then, like the majority of the best tales,
suggests that Hawthorne's vision of death was a good deal
stronger and more constant than his vision of life.* This is
indeed, as Hawthorne calls it, a dark tale, and its mesh of
good and evil is not equally strong in all its parts. Hawthorne
was right in not wanting to be judged as a man solely by it,
though I think he must have known, as we do, that it is his
greatest book. For in it there is perfect charity, and a real,
though defective, faith, but almost no hope. Unlike most of

---

* W. Stacey Johnson has marshaled considerable evidence for the con-
trary view in his "Sin and Salvation in Hawthorne," *The Hibbert Journal*,
October 1951. My comment on the argument of a part of this excellent
article is that, while it is true that Hawthorne believed in the possibility of
redemption, he did not "believe in it" in the same way, with the same kind
of conviction, that he believed in sin and death.

us today, Hawthorne was close enough to historic Christianity to know its main dogmas, even those he did not fully share. He preferred not to seem to be denying so central a part of the Christian Gospel as that men can be saved from their sins.

CHAPTER SIX

THE HOUSE OF THE SEVEN GABLES

The House of the Seven Gables was written far more deliberately than *The Scarlet Letter*. If Hawthorne's first novel was "wrung from the heart," his second was the product in much greater degree of conscious, even of self-conscious, artistry. He was right, as he so often was in his judgment of his work: it was indeed more representative of the whole man. It was more comprehensive, more like the man his family knew.

But if Hawthorne was not wrong in thinking that this work represented him better, neither is the modern reader wrong in his preference for the earlier novel. For Hawthorne recognized aspects of himself that he did not like, traits and tendencies that were hard to live with, insights and feelings that left him ill at ease. The traits he liked, on the other hand, were those his age also admired. It is little wonder, then, that whereas *The Scarlet Letter* shocked his contemporaries, and to some degree Hawthorne himself, *The House of the Seven Gables* pleased everybody. But to say that for the modern reader it is not wholly convincing is almost certainly to understate the case.

Yet for all its archaisms, there are reasons for calling it inferior in interest only to *The Scarlet Letter* and *Moby Dick* among American novels before the work of James. The variety of the ways in which it has been interpreted by perceptive critics is one clue to its richness. It can be read as a parable on the nature and effects of Original Sin. It can be read as a more complete working out of the theme of "Lady Eleanor's Mantle," that pride and death are inseparable companions: they sit together in the darkening room that is at once the heart of the old house and the tomb of the judge's ambitions. It can be read as the most impressive artistic statement of Hawthorne's democratic beliefs: the aristocratic Pyncheons discover that death and suffering are no respecters of persons and that they must give up their pretensions to superiority and mingle with "the common life" and the plebeian Maules. It can be read as a statement of the archetypal theme of withdrawal and return, which Hawthorne interpreted as isolation and redemptive reunion. It can even be read as Henry James seems to have read it, as a piece of charmingly poetic realism, a sort of forerunner of the "local color" tales of old New England that were so popular after the Civil War, a delicate evocation of a way of life that James remembered having known as a boy.

It can be read in all these ways, and others too, but they are all partial readings. Hawthorne himself provided hints for a no less partial reading. In his preface he tells us that the subject of his romance is wrong and retribution, sin and suffering, carried on through generations. He seems only partially serious as he tells us that the "moral" he has provided for his romance is that "the wrong-doing of one generation lives into the successive ones, and divesting itself of every temporary advantage, becomes a pure and uncontrollable mischief." In a somewhat more serious tone he adds that he wishes the work might convince mankind "of the folly of tumbling down an avalanche of ill-gotten gold, or real estate, on the heads of an unfortunate posterity, thereby to maim and crush them, until the accumulated mass shall be scattered abroad in its original atoms." The romance provides, then, in Hawthorne's view of the matter, texts for sermons on the sins of pride and avarice and on the fact of mutability, illustrating meanwhile the ways of Providence.

But Hawthorne knows, as he also says in his preface, that "when romances do really teach anything, or produce any effective operation, it is usually through a far more subtle process than the ostensible one." He knows that what he wants to say cannot after all be said in the preface, that the real meaning of his work cannot be expressed in a generalization. For all its moralizing then, this preface, in which Hawthorne comments more freely on his intentions in the work than was customary with him, tells us to read the romance attentively if we would know the meaning.

2

The opening sentences, familiar though they are, are worth quoting:

Half way down a by-street of one of our New England towns, stands a rusty wooden house, with seven acutely peaked gables, facing towards various points of the compass, and a huge, clustered chimney in the midst. The Street is Pyncheon-street; the house is the old Pyncheon-house; and an elm-tree, of wide circumference, rooted before the door, is familiar to every town-born child by the title of the Pyncheon-elm.

In view of what we have discovered of Hawthorne's habit of emphasizing in his descriptions only those details that are most significant, we shall do well to note certain images here. Hawthorne opens his story of the house that, as we later discover, was built by pride and possessed by death on the very day of the housewarming with a description that stresses the darkness and angularity of the structure and the "wide circumference" of the great tree that is said later to "overshadow" it. A careful reading of the story will disclose no significant feature of structure or texture, image or concept, that is not associated in some way with the suggestions contained in the house and the elm.

The outward appearance of the house, Hawthorne tells us in the sentences immediately following those I have quoted, had always reminded him of a human face. The interior, especially the great chimney in the center, he repeatedly presents in terms of heart imagery. The elm introduced in the second sentence is described more fully later in the first chapter and again in chapter nineteen, where we are once more reminded that it has the shape of a "sphere." It is the source, we learn, of whatever beauty the house possesses, and it makes the house "a part of nature." At the end the few leaves left it by an autumn gale "whisper unintelligible prophecies" as the last of the Pyncheons leave the house forever.

The associations clustered around the house and the elm, and particularly the straight lines and angles of the one and the curves, circles, and cycles of the other, are not equally present everywhere or scattered at random throughout. In the first ten chapters angular images predominate, from their introduction in the title and the first sentence through the portrayal of Hepzibah to their last new embodiment in the Pyncheon fowls in the tenth chapter. Meanwhile, however, images of curve and circle, though subordinate, are also present, especially in the several reminders of the shape of the elm, in the introduction of Phoebe, and in the treatment of Clifford's portrait. In the last eleven chapters the action is dominated by the presence of Phoebe and Clifford, both clearly associated with images of curve and circle. When in the last chapter Pyncheon and Maule are united and depart from the house, the theme which has been rendered visible by straight lines and angles is overcome by that embodied in curves, circles, and cycles.

This contrast between two strongly contrasted patterns

of imagery, one of which diminishes in frequency and emphasis while the other increases in both, seems to me to lead us to the heart of the novel. The house is both setting and symbol: it is the antagonist in a drama of good and evil. But the elm is taller even than the house, and overshadows it: appropriately enough, it has the last word. Hepzibah, in whose gaunt angularity and frown we see again the features of the house, is in the spotlight in the opening chapters, only to be supplanted by Clifford after his return from prison. As the climax approaches and the two victims of the past make an abortive attempt at flight, it is he who takes command. At the end he too retires into the background while Phoebe and Holgrave lead the way to the new life. The soft lines of Clifford's oval face, the rounded grace of Phoebe, the seasonal-cyclical prophecies of the elm — these replace the rigid angles of the house and Hepzibah and Pyncheon fowls as the revolution of the hands on the face of his watch mock the dead judge's ambitious plans and delusions of permanence.

3

The whole structure of the romance is designed to keep these images and their symbolic extensions always before us. A closer look than we have yet taken at the structure of the work, and particularly at the plot and the characters, will show the extent to which Hawthorne subdued his materials to the demands of his pattern.

The recounting of family history in the first chapter is in essence a summary statement of the cycles of mutability. Prosperity, we learn, has given way to poverty before, so that Hepzibah has only to *reopen* the shop once before resorted to by an impoverished ancestor. The cycles of nature embodied in the yearly "death" and "rebirth" of the elm are apparent, to the long view, on the human level also: original injustice has been reënacted as original retribution will be reënacted. The same things have happened over and over again as generation has followed generation, so that in this glance at the past in which time is foreshortened until death seems almost immediately to follow birth we see what Hawthorne says he wants us to see, "how much of old material goes to make up the freshest novelty of human life." We see the past alive in the present. The wheel of fortune revolves before us and circles not apparent to the mind that lacks memory take shape. But the Pyncheons do not see them, for their vision is taken up with the more palpable reality of their great house and the social position of which it is a symbol.

The Pyncheon withdrawal from the mass; their willed isolation within the mansion "withdrawn," as Hawthorne says, "from the line of the street, but in pride, not in modesty"; their attempt to build a house and a fortune that would always endure — all this is negated by Hepzibah's forced opening of the cent shop. This act, so crucial and central in the rising action of the novel, and presented with emphatic circle imagery, may be seen as connected with the concept of the cycle in three ways. First, it is a simple repetition of an action that occurred in the past. Second, it means that for this branch of the family the wheel of fortune has turned full circle, from poverty to riches to poverty again, as it will later turn in another way for the branch represented by the judge. And third, though Hepzibah's pride is yet undiminished, her contacts with her first customer mark the beginning of that return after withdrawal which is one of the basic themes of the novel.

The coming of Phoebe, a Pyncheon reduced to plebeian status and so renewed in vitality and grace that now she seems to shed a circle of light around her, is another movement in the same direction, and one that is even more clearly a part of a cyclical process. Her presence, bringing new life and color and happiness to a house that had long known only isolation and darkness and death, subtly modifies Hepzibah's point of view as it partially destroys her isolation after her long solitude; and for Clifford, after his still more complete alienation, it becomes the very principle of life. Clifford's attachment to Phoebe, so cruel in its implications for Hepzibah, is the first willed, and so efficacious, step in the Pyncheon regeneration.

Chapter eleven, "The Arched Window," is perhaps the most explicit key to thematic structure. Hawthorne's chapter titles are seldom without significance, and sometimes, as here and in "May and November" and "The Flower of Eden," the modern reader will surely feel that they point too insistently to the deeper import of the chapters they introduce. For from beneath the only segment of a circle to be seen in the angular house, Clifford looks out at the "stream of humanity" in the street, and from this window he makes, in his attempt to jump out, what is in effect his first violent effort at reunion. Still later, seeing from it the throngs of churchgoers, he persuades Hepzibah to start with him for church, not from any sense of piety, but from a compulsion to participate in a common activity. Clifford's extreme suffering and ruin have prepared him for escape from the house of the Pyncheons.

But escape is not possible, in Clifford's way, by merely willing it. Even after the death of the judge, the flight precipitated by Clifford fails. The two old people return, unable to escape their past until after the engagement of Holgrave and Phoebe. This union of Pyncheon and Maule makes possible their reattachment to "the magnetic chain of humanity."

4

The texture of the novel is such as constantly to reinforce the themes thus embodied in the larger aspects of structure. After the opening sentences the continued description of the house centers on the contrast of its evidences of former grandeur with its present darkness and decay. But flowers grow from the rotten shingles of a roof kept moist by the overshadowing elm, visible emblems of that cycle whereby life requires death for its nourishment. Again, there is a suggestion that the overhanging second story, rendering the rooms below doubly gloomy by casting them in its shade, represents a predominance of head over heart, an imbalance later reversed in Clifford, whose sympathy, we are told, was unchecked by judgment. And the references to vegetable and seasonal cycles first introduced by the mention of the elm are continued in the descriptions of the garden, in the continuous light and shade imagery, particularly in the opening of chapter five, with its reminder of the diurnal revolution, in the description of the sun dial on the roof, and in the elaborate attention given to the judge's watch. "The shadow creeps and creeps, and is always looking over the shoulder of the sunshine."

Maule's well, introduced early and later made to supply the title of a chapter dealing with the relations of Phoebe and Holgrave, symbolically unites the two contrasting image patterns of house and elm. For though its waters are continuously renewed, still they carry the taint first noticed at the time of the building of the house. In the waters of this spring past and present are somehow one. As Hawthorne said of another spring in "Egotism," "How strange is the life of a fountain! — born at every moment, yet of an age coeval with the rocks, and far surpassing the venerable antiquity of a forest."

Frequent circle imagery, particularly after the arrival of Phoebe, continues, defines, and expands some of these implications. When, for instance, Hepzibah received payment from her first customer in the cent shop, the coin itself is a reminder of the cycle she is now taking her first step to complete:

The little *circlet* of the schoolboy's copper coin — dim and lustreless though it was, with the small services which it had been doing, here and there about the world — had proved a talisman, fragrant with good, and deserving to be set in gold and worn next her heart. It was as potent, and perhaps endowed with the same kind of efficacy, as a galvanic *ring*.

Out of context, the words I have italicized in this passage may seem so casual and "natural" as to be hardly worth noting, but when we recall the way Hawthorne worked in *The Scarlet Letter*, and then consider that the theme of this romance asks us to consider whether history should be conceived in cylical, linear, or some other terms, we see that they serve as textural enrichments of a motive that is embodied everywhere, on all levels, from the most abstract to the most sensuous. They are a part of a running stream of circle images of all degrees of literalness and emphasis. Phoebe, for instance, is said to move in a "circle," where the drained image means literally a group of acquaintances. And we have pure images when we are told that she wears her hair in "ringlets" and that she seems to Clifford, whose intuitions seem unfailing though his reason is weak, to shed light around her "like the circle of reflected brilliancy around the glass vase of flowers that was standing in the sunshine."

The stream of circle imagery is conceptualized by Clifford when he talks to the strangers on the train. Having attempted to jump from an "arched" window in order to "plunge into the surging stream of human sympathies," and having attained his present illusory identification with mankind by passing through the "arched" entrance to a railway station, he now speculates on the nature of time and history in a passage that comes closer than any other to presenting explicitly the chief themes of the novel. The railroad, he suspects, will "bring us round again to the nomadic state." "You are aware, my dear sir, — you must have observed it, in your own experience, — that all human progress is in a circle; or, to use a more accurate and beautiful figure, in an ascending spiral curve."

One aspect of the implications of the circle imagery is strongly reinforced by the imagery of light and darkness that Hawthorne scatters so profusely through his story. The "black" old house that "never lets in the sunshine" admits a very brilliant ray indeed when Phoebe enters. One of the stumbling blocks in the novel for the modern reader is in fact the way in which Hawthorne has made Phoebe, "the bright young girl . . . whose fresh and maidenly figure was both sunshine and flowers" and whose name in Greek meant *shining* — the way he has made her seem more like a ray of sunshine than like a person.

But if he fails here in his color and light imagery, he is sometimes successful, particularly, and symptomatically, in handling the darker shades. When he feels the darkness of time and death in the "Governor Pyncheon" chapter, when he places before us again and again the cold and the darkness of the house, when he describes the "gloom of sky and earth" during the great storm in which Clifford and Hepzibah fled, when he visualizes death as a descent into the black depths of water in the opening of "The Departure" — here and elsewhere he succeeds in imparting the life of the imagination to a chain of color images that sometimes seems forced and merely ingenious. But on the whole I think we shall have to decide that the light and color imagery is handled too emphatically and that its chief effect — aligning with positive values those things and persons associated with circles, and with negative values their angular opposite numbers — would have been clear anyway.

More sparingly and subtly used to reinforce the circle and angle images are the running allusions to Eden. They begin in connection with the color and flower symbolism of chapter five, on the morning of Phoebe's first day in the house. Outside her window the girl discovers a bush covered with "a rare and beautiful species of white rose." She discovers also that "a large portion of them . . . had a blight or mildew at their hearts; but, viewed at a fair distance, the whole rose-bush looked as if it had been brought from Eden that very summer, together with the mould in which it grew." The references continue in chapter seven with a description of the sunshine which Phoebe has let into the house — "as fresh as that which peeped into Eve's bower, while she and Adam sat at breakfast there." And these two apparently casual references are revived and reinforced in chapter ten when the Pyncheon garden becomes the Christian Garden and Clifford a new Adam: "It was the Eden of a thunder-smitten Adam, who had fled for refuge thither out of the same dreary and perilous wilderness into which the original Adam was expelled." Finally, this line of reference is explicitly united with the stream of flower imagery in the chapter called "The Flower of Eden." Then Phoebe and Holgrave "transfigured the earth, and made it Eden again."

These connections with the Eden myth take us of course to the heart of the story. For Adam's sin, like that of the Pyncheons, was pride; the penalty, alienation from God and man and the corruption of man and nature — the introduction, as it has been interpreted, of death; and the cure, love. And the Christian myth of the origin and cure of evil embodies the concept of a cycle as surely as the ancient figure of the wheel of fortune and the pagan vegetation myths do. For the story told is one of union, alienation, and reunion, withdrawal and return. The Eden allusions then help to expand Pyncheon history into man's history.

Even the rhythm and syntax of the style contribute to the symbolic pattern Hawthorne is creating. Again and again at crucial points the sentences move to a rhythm more regularly undulatory than is common in prose: they rise and fall and return upon themselves with a controlled movement in contrast with the first and consistent with the second, the finally triumphant, motive. Frequently the longer sentences start with modifiers, move slowly to the main clause, and end with modifiers: "At the moment of execution — with the halter about his neck, and while Colonel Pyncheon sat on horseback, grimly gazing at the scene — Maule had addressed him from the scaffold, and uttered a prophecy, of which history, as well as fireside tradition, has preserved the very words." Or through balance, repetition, and antithesis they achieve a circular effect with main clauses: "Beauty would be his life; his aspirations would all tend toward it; and, allowing his frame and physical organs to be in consonance, his own developments would likewise be beautiful." Frequently, as in the foregoing sentence, the last word, after the accretions of insight and qualification achieved by the development, repeats or alludes to the first: "He had no right to be a martyr; and, beholding him so fit to be happy, and so feeble for all other purposes, a generous, strong, and noble spirit would, methinks, have been ready to sacrifice what little enjoyment it might have planned for itself, — it would have flung down the hopes, so paltry in its regard, — if thereby the wintry blasts of our rude sphere might come tempered to such a man." Or the effect is achieved more subtly by rhythm alone: "But no sooner was she a little relieved than her conscience smote her for gazing curiously at him, now that he was so changed; and, turning hastily away, Hepzibah let down the curtain over the sunny window, and left Clifford to slumber there."

This is the antithesis of Emerson's staccato sententious style, his pulpit exhortation — which was, of course, as suited to his purpose of arousing the youth of the land to nobler lives as was Hawthorne's to his purpose. It is the style of a man whose insights are too qualified to be succinctly summarized. What Hawthorne wrote of Donatello's progress in *The Marble Faun* could be said of the style of the *Seven Gables*: it travels "in a circle, as all things heavenly and earthly do." The very sound and structure of the predominantly loose and heavily modified sentences express the returns and contradictions, the ambiguities and cycles of a reality which he saw as containing at its very core an "entanglement of something mean and trivial with whatever is noblest in joy or sorrow."

Now it is true of course that Hawthorne's style is basically the same in all his work, and that the rhythm in it might always be called in some sense "cyclical." Which is to say that the style of the *Seven Gables* is not wholly organic to the structure of the novel. But that it should be "wholly organic" is of course impossible, unless we were to assume that a novelist could create a completely distinct style for each of his works and that the works themselves were not each a partial expression of persistent attitudes and ideas and a persistent sensibility. Hawthorne's style is obviously Hawthorne's style, everywhere; and on the other hand, many of his works embody the theme of withdrawal and return. But such qualifications do not invalidate the conclusion that here the style is functional to a degree not usual in novels, even in Hawthorne's novels.

Finally, several other devices characteristic of Hawthorne's technique are here put to use to enrich the theme. The "ambiguity device," for instance, allowing multiple interpretations of a single incident, is an expression of Hawthorne's way of viewing things from all possible vantage points, circling round them to discover all the implications. Hawthorne tells us in his preface that his work is not a novel but a romance because it takes liberties with actuality in order to "connect a by-gone time with the very present that is flitting away from us," to show, that is, the cyclical reality which, as Clifford says, we do not normally perceive. To do this in an ordinary realistic novel Hawthorne thinks is impossible; so, as he tells us in his preface, he will base his work on legend and superstition, take the superstition seriously without believing in it, and examine it to see what human truth it may contain.

Tradition, legend, and superstition, then, are at the heart of the tale, but the tale itself is not superstitious. It is ambiguous, with an ambiguity as deeply intertwined with its meaning as the ambiguity of *Moby Dick*. The "village gossips . . . hinted" that the house of the Pyncheons was built over an unquiet grave. "Some people thought" that the digging of the foundation disturbed the waters of the spring, as Rappaccini's pride had brought death into the garden. There was a "tradition, only worth alluding to," that a voice spoke out at Colonel Pyncheon's death saying, "God hath given him blood to drink." "There were many rumors" about the cause of the death, rumors no doubt unfounded in "fact" but very possibly grounded in the moral law.

Now it is commonly pointed out that this characteristic device of Hawthorne's represents a late and serious use of a Gothic tradition for moral and psychological purposes. "Modern psychology, it may be, will endeavor to reduce these alleged necromancies within a system, instead of rejecting them as altogether fabulous," Hawthorne tells us in his first chapter. Less commonly remarked is the fact that the method itself is basically mytho-poetic, the end here being the creation of epiphanies of cyclical reality. So Joyce in our time linked myth with actuality, Ulysses and a Dublin Jew, to create epiphanies of a reality he conceived in terms of Vico's cyclical theory of history. Hawthorne's naturalization of the supernatural, his serious, but not superstitious, examination of those profoundly revealing expressions of the human mind and soul by which man in his ignorance of the true and final "facts" creates an interpretation of the raw data of experience, his candid, rational, and sympathetic analysis of the irrational — these connect him with the present century's discovery of the fundamental importance of myth. And the premise of the method was a sense, and the

purpose a demonstration, of the cycles in which we are involved but which we do not see.

This is also one of the effects of another characteristic of
Hawthorne's writing as we find it here: his habit of slowing
down the action until we can study its minutest aspect, analyze it from all sides, and realize, among other things, its
connections with the past and its foreshadowing of the
future. Between the time when Hepzibah leaves Judge
Pyncheon to summon Clifford and the time when she returns, only a few minutes elapse but it takes a full chapter
to present them. In "The Pyncheon Garden" no overtly significant actions occur: the characters meet and talk a little,
Phoebe reads to Clifford, the summer afternoons seem, as
James remarked, drowsy and motionless, with time suspended and reality concentrated here and now; yet what
finally emerges is a keener sense of the revolutions in which
we are all involved.

In short, the images of angle and circle implied in the
description of the house and the elm which opens the romance are, like the images in the opening chapter of *The
Scarlet Letter*, the first suggestions of a pattern that may
profitably be thought of as the figure that Hawthorne worked
into the carpet. Though an alternative reading could be
made which would give the central place to images of light
and dark — for they are very numerous and prominent — yet
it seems clear that Hawthorne himself has given us the clue
we need to decide this question by beginning and ending
his work with the house and the elm and by making his
theme explicit in Clifford's speech. It requires no forcing to
see that all the motives, on whatever level of abstraction or
concreteness, are connected with this basic pattern of circle
and angle. The secular movement of light and dark, the
rhythm of flower and blight, the allusions to prelapsarian
innocence and post-Adamic sin, the themes of isolation and
reunion and permanence and change, even the contrasts of

head and heart and pride and humility, all are linked in some way with the basic image pattern. Phoebe, for instance, is associated throughout with roundness, light, flowers, innocence, the heart, humility, and a balance between permanence and change. Clifford finds in her the principle of life, Holgrave the correction of his ingenious speculations. Her arrival is the coming of grace after sin and suffering. In her marriage with Holgrave we see both the end of the male Pyncheon line and of the name, and the promise of renewal. She carries the redemptive theme of the romance. Though the burden is too heavy for her to bear, she is certainly supported by every device Hawthorne knew how to use.

5

It is paradoxically true of *The House of the Seven Gables* that it is at once more realistic and more consistently allegorical than *The Scarlet Letter*. It has a richer evocation of atmosphere, a more palpable recreation of a definite time and place and way of life than Hawthorne's masterpiece. But it is also more directly and completely controlled by a conscious conceptual framework, a framework involving the most abstract levels of thought. If the work is to be recovered for mature readers in our time, it can only I think be through an appreciation of its symbolic structure. This may not be possible, but we shall not know whether it is possible or not until we see how far Hawthorne succeeded in conveying "more of various modes of truth" than he could grasp "by a direct effort."

The first of the themes to demand comment is the one that Hawthorne emphasizes in the preface and continues to underscore throughout, the relation of past and present. Superficially, the relation seems to be one of contrast. Past evil makes present suffering, past wealth leads to present poverty, the house once magnificent is now decayed. When the inadequacy of this insight becomes clear, we find another, which turns out to be its very antithesis, emerging from the pattern: there is nothing new under the sun, past and present are essentially identical, as seen in the deaths of colonel and judge. But this too turns out to be only a partial insight, needing correction. The correction, we discover, has been foreshadowed from the very beginning by the symbolism of the elm, which experiences yearly death and rebirth, and by the symbolism of Maule's well, which combines permanence and change.

But when we relate these conceptions to the image patterns we discover what seems to be an essential ambiguity. The angles of the house are associated only with death and the *illusion* of permanence and linear progress, but the circles of the elm are associated both with sterile repetition and redemptive renewal, with the death of the judge and with Phoebe's coming. We must somehow distinguish between the movement of the hands around the face of the dead judge's watch and the circles of light shed by Phoebe.

The "light" shed by the judge's sultry smile is deceptive. Despite his appearance he is really a creature of darkness. If he had his way he would continue and compound the original injustice. He is therefore unable to escape the compulsive cycles of nature. The circles in which he is involved are his only reality; his dreams of achievement, his plans for his day and for the continued building of his fortune, are as illusory as the dreams of permanent magnificence his ancestor embodied in the house. The circles associated with Phoebe, on the other hand, are not compulsive but liberating. Her light is as real as the sunshine and as healing as love. Hers are not the circles of nature but the cycles of grace. She is natural, but as the flowers are natural: like the lilies of the field, she is not worried about achieving security or ambitious to achieve distinction. She is emblematic, Hawthorne might have said, of the redemptive power of love, by which alone man may break out of the cycles of futile repetition and participate by choice in a cycle of a different kind.

But if Phoebe illumines and transforms nature by the power of love, we are still left with a difficulty when we return from the level of abstraction to the level of the imagery. How can the circles of nature and grace be so different and yet look so much the same? If we conceive of the circles of history in terms of the ancient figure of the wheel of fate, then the death of the judge and much else in the history of the family would make it appear that the wheel is merely going around. But the union of Pyncheon and Maule suggests that the wheel is moving somewhere as it revolves. To see whether its progress is real or merely apparent, we should I suppose have to get somehow off the rim of the wheel itself. And this stepping "out of" or "above" history to achieve a vantage point from which we may perceive the progress as well as the revolutions of the wheel is just what Hawthorne invites us to do in his conclusion, with its reliance on the hope of heaven for Alice Pyncheon. If faith can afford a vantage point outside the wheel, we shall be able to see how the two kinds of circles are related.

It is Clifford, with his ruined mind and his intuitive certainties, who provides the chief clue. Talking wildly to his neighbors on the train, he asserts that both permanence and the kind of progress that is conceived in linear terms are always delusions; the circle, he thinks, supplies us a better analogy. When we are engrossed in life, he says, we "fancy ourselves going straight forward" toward something quite new and entirely of our own design; but when we look back over history we come to suspect that what we have fancied to be new will really "bring us round again" to the old. The truth, he thinks, is best expressed in a different figure, neither straight line nor revolving wheel on a stationary axis, but "an ascending spiral curve" in which the present "repeats" the past, but the past "etherealized, refined, and perfected to its ideal." Thus the intuition of Clifford discerned what the simple faith of Uncle Venner discerned in the last chapter, that as the wheel revolves it moves upward.

I suspect that the modern reader will find it easier to accept Clifford's figure of the spiral curve than his words about the etherealization of the past. Hawthorne too had his difficulties with Clifford's solution, as his aesthetic failures in the work suggest and as one sentence in the last chapter implies. "It is a truth," he says, "(and it would be a very sad one, but for the higher hopes which it suggests) that no great mistake, whether acted or endured, in our mortal sphere, is ever really set right." Is there, then, or is there not, a possibility of redemption from sin and suffering? Apparently only if our "higher hopes" are justified. If we may trust "wise Uncle Venner," they are: for the novel ends with the Pyncheon elm whispering to him "unintelligible prophecies" as he "fancies" the spirit of Alice Pyncheon moving "heavenward from the HOUSE OF THE SEVEN GABLES!"

So Hawthorne ends his romance with the very words with which he began in his title. He was fond of this device, but here it was peculiarly fitting. This is the last of the circles he drew for us, and perhaps the one that pleased him most. Only the "from" before the title words indicates any movement. Without it the wheel would merely have revolved. With it, the wheel has moved somewhere as it revolved. So that we are back now where we started, with the house and the elm standing before us in deeper contrast than we were prepared to understand at first; but all who merited it, even Alice Pyncheon, have escaped. Withdrawal in pride has given way to return in love; head and heart have come together to temper each other in the marriage of Holgrave and Phoebe; redemption has come out of suffering. Hawthorne's closing words clearly express the meaning he intended us to get.

The achieved meaning is something else again. Hawthorne

wanted to correct the impression he feared he had left in *The Scarlet Letter*, that there is no real escape from the past, no redemption from sin. This was to be his "happy" novel, his assertion of faith in the possibility of freedom and a fresh start, his statement of his belief that goodness is as real as evil and genuine choice as real as necessity. To achieve these "affirmations" Hawthorne translates certain central Christian dogmas into psychological, or human, terms. He shows us self-centeredness, as pride, the "original" sin, bringing about destructive isolation, then love making possible a redemptive reunion. But in order to make this translation, to achieve this *naturalization* of Christian belief, Hawthorne had to rely on the agency of an unstained heart to effect the redemption, though he had gone on record as not believing that any heart was unstained, and the best of his stories had all supported his stated conviction. We shall see how this problem of the exception to the sinful nature of man emerges again in *The Marble Faun*. Here it is sufficient to say that it is no wonder that the redemptive theme in the novel is unconvincing; for it rests finally on the possibility of a Phoebe, a ray of light untouched by darkness, a flower immune forever to the possibility of blight. Phoebe was the product of an act of faith, of faith not in Christian doctrine but in "the religion of the heart."

6

The House of the Seven Gables represents the beginning of that decline in the quality of Hawthorne's writing which did not end until it had reached the almost complete failure of creativity of the unfinished romances. If the novel still has sufficient charm and interest to make it worth the time of readers interested in serious fiction, as I think it has, then surely its virtue must be found in what remains after we have made some rather large deductions.

After we have made all possible allowances for changes in taste, I think we shall still have to eliminate Phoebe and Holgrave from the list of really created characters in the work. Holgrave is interestingly drawn, but he never comes alive. In their analysis of the nature of the new American, Hawthorne and Emerson for once agreed: a comparison of Holgrave with Emerson's various statements of the new American characteristics would show that Hawthorne could have lifted his young pragmatist entire out of Emerson's pages. But Holgrave also anticipates James's estimate of the American in Christopher Newman and elsewhere. Holgrave is an interesting creation, the product of a shrewd analysis; he is right from a thematic and symbolic viewpoint; but his actions and motives in this story do not ring true. He is considerably more of an allegorical character than even Chillingworth in *The Scarlet Letter*.

Phoebe I have already dealt with at more length than she deserves, except on an allegorical level. The portrayal here is both sentimental and frivolous, with a frivolity characteristic of the "playful" side of Hawthorne's fancy at its weakest. She is of course only one of a long line of spotless maidens in Hawthorne's work: she is first cousin to Eve of "The New Adam and Eve"; to the unnamed maidens with the hearts of dazzling white who fortunately appear only on the periphery of *The Scarlet Letter*; to Priscilla in *The Blithedale Romance*, that most shadowy of Hawthorne heroines; to Hilda in *The Marble Faun*. She is Hawthorne's tribute to his wife, his gesture of *rapprochement* toward the optimistic humanism of his time, his Pelagian heresy. That she is quite unbelievable all will agree, though there will be different explanations given as to why she is so unconvincing. My own suggestion is that Hawthorne could not draw the type "realistically" because "in his heart" he did not really believe in her; and he did not believe in her because the type does not exist in nature. Hawthorne might have been better ad-

vised, as it turned out, to have made her still more frankly
allegorical than she is — and to have named her Grace!

Beside this failure in Phoebe, the other failures are almost
negligible. Often Hawthorne ceases to "translate" felt reality
and falls back on ingeniously contrived fancies. The decay
in the old house is fine — until the rats frisk about too play-
fully and conveniently. Alice's posies on the roof are good —
until they are insisted upon once too often. The death of the
judge is splendid in a baroque way — until the chapter goes
on too long and the pretense that the judge has not really
died ceases to have point.

Of a different order are the failures in the handling of the
marriage, the new house, and the fortune. The marriage,
though thematically demanded, is perfectly unconvincing
for two reasons, either of which would be sufficient alone:
neither of the partners to it is a real character; and we have
had no preparation for it, since there is little evidence before
the betrothal is announced of any growing love between the
two. The new house, larger and finer than the one being left,
seems a convenient adjunct to the happy ending only if one
is careful not to think about it. Since the old house has not
only symbolized but in some sense actually abetted the
"withdrawal in pride" which ended in isolation and death,
one wonders how long it will take for the new great house
to assume a similar role. Like the old one, it is built on a
foundation of iniquity by "ill-gotten gain" — for the judge's
fortune is as tainted as the colonel's. It is even "withdrawn"
like the old house, the suburbs being the present equivalent
of what had once been Pyncheon Street's rural privacy. How
many generations will it take in such an abode for the new
Pyncheons bearing a new name to start repeating the tragic
cycle? As for the fortune, the less said the better. Fortui-
tously acquired by a law sacred to the sentimental novel
since the days of Fielding, it is intended to solve problems
but only succeeds in multiplying them. This "avalanche of

ill-gotten gold," to use a phrase which Hawthorne used in his preface but carefully refrained from applying to the judge's fortune at the end of the novel, will surely "maim and crush" someone again, as it has in the past. But if we are to continue to take the ending as "happy," we had better not look too deeply into this matter.

One of the most acute of Hawthorne's critics remarked to me in conversation several years ago that *The House of the Seven Gables* is a finer novel than most people have realized, and that it needs to be reëvaluated and given its proper place among the great novels in English. Against this opinion we may set the immediate reaction of most modern readers: that the novel is "dated" to the point of being archaic, that its machinery creaks in the joints, that Hepzibah is the only really created character in it, and that the ending is forced to the point of absurdity.

If we can manage to read the work with the care which it requires and the sympathy it deserves, I think we shall come finally to decide that a just evaluation must lie somewhere between these two extremes. Clearly, there are excellent things in the romance, and there are great weaknesses. But what may interest a student of Hawthorne more than an attempt to arrive at a nice balance is the implication of these merits and defects for an understanding of the whole body of Hawthorne's work. If, as I believe, Hawthorne is a writer whose importance for us is living and even increasing, then *The House of the Seven Gables* gains a considerable part of its significance for us from its role as one act in the drama of sin and salvation that Hawthorne worked on in installments labeled "tales" and "romances" between 1825 and 1864.

CHAPTER SEVEN

THE BLITHEDALE ROMANCE

We do not often read *The Blithedale Romance* nowadays. If we do read it, or, more likely, plan to read it, it is usually because we are interested in its portrayal of life at Brook Farm, that abortive experiment in communal living in which Hawthorne rather inexplicably joined for a while. Read this way, it is very disappointing. Where we had hoped for a gallery of portraits and a re-creation of historic details, we find instead the most Gothic of Hawthorne's romances, with only one historical character we are likely to recognize and even that one greatly disguised. For Zenobia is not Margaret Fuller, as Hawthorne was careful to point out in his preface; she is a literary creation in some respects suggestive of Margaret Fuller. And if the work proves disappointing as history, it is equally, or at least so we are apt to feel at first reading, disappointing as a romance: for its Gothicism is too evident and its machinery too contrived.

But there is another way to read *The Blithedale Romance*, a way which, while it will not make it seem a great historical novel, will make it seem an acute analysis of the meaning of history; and while it will not completely salvage it as a romance, will make it appear a very interesting work of art. I mean reading it with the closest attention to texture, as

though it were not a novel but a poem. To read it this way
is to read it the way Hawthorne wrote it. It is also to read
it in the only way likely to give us a fresh insight into its
meaning and value for us.

2

We may fairly begin with the title. *Blithe dale* may be
read as Happy Valley, and the body of the novel suggests
that we not only may but should read it this way. The title
contains, then, an echo of one of Hawthorne's favorite authors, for Johnson's *Rasselas* tells how the Prince of Abyssinia, reared in a secluded happy valley where there was no
sin or suffering of any kind, journeyed through the outer
world in search of a man both happy (for he had not been
contented in the happy valley) and wise, only to have to
return at last, disillusioned, to his refuge from the world.
Hawthorne's book uses a similar journey plot, but inverted.
Coverdale the narrator goes from the real world of Boston to
the happy valley of Blithedale and then, disillusioned, returns to Boston. Johnson set up a mythical Happy Valley in
order to test the nature of the real world against it; Hawthorne started from the real world of Boston in order to
test the reality of Blithedale. Johnson ended on the theme
developed in his poem "The Vanity of Human Wishes";
Hawthorne ended on a theme that may be partially suggested by such phrases as "the failure of reform" and the
folly of expecting utopias if the heart of man remains unchanged, the same theme, essentially, as that developed in
"Earth's Holocaust."

That sketch had ended, we remember, after the reformers
had attempted to do away with all the world's "trumpery"
and injustice and superstition, with the warning that unless
we could find some way to purify the heart of man, all reforms would prove in the end to have been in vain, for it is

from the heart that evil springs. There is no happy valley to be found or created merely by altering man's outward habits of living or getting a living. The title *Blithedale* then is ironic: the happy valley turns out to be a fool's paradise.

So much emerges from a literal reading of the two parts of the word. But the second part is also a covert heart image. We have seen Hawthorne use a valley (or dale) to suggest a heart before.* This reading points not to the conclusion Coverdale came finally to share with the Prince of Abyssinia but to a fallacy he came to see as lying behind the failure at Blithedale. The reform rested finally on the assumption of the natural goodness of man's heart: if man is good "at heart," then by changing those social arrangements that corrupt him we can create utopia. All hope for man rests in political and economic, or, more broadly, social manipulation; communists and pragmatists, who equally follow Rousseau in this respect, are right: man's heart is "blithe" in the sense of happy, fortunate, just as we should desire it to be. Whether read in this way, then, as an ironic reference to the error at the root of the matter, or as an allusion to *Rasselas*, the title is revealing. Ignoring the tendency to evil in man's "foul cavern," from which the old evils or their duplicates would issue all over again even if we should succeed in eliminating their superficial manifestations, the experiment was doomed to failure from the start.

Coverdale, whose voice and personality are central in the work, has a name as suggestive as that of the community. The first part suggests what is perhaps his most striking characteristic, his tendency to cover up, to be secretive, to hide and withdraw. He is constantly keeping out of sight; he peers and peeks and eavesdrops. What he is finally covering, we come to suspect, is the secrets of the heart, as he

---

* For a thorough treatment of the subject of heart imagery, see John Shroeder, " 'That Inward Sphere': Hawthorne's Heart Imagery and Symbolism," *PMLA*, March 1950.

conceals his love for Priscilla until the end of the story and as the last part of his name suggests. The concealment motive suggested by his name is connected, as we shall see, with a good many other disguise images that run though the novel.

Hollingsworth's name suggests both "holy" and "worthy." But here too, as in the title, there is irony. For despite his devotion to what is, abstractly considered, a good cause, the reform of criminals, he is an egotist who is blind to all that is most holy and worthy of our devotion. He loves mankind in the abstract but not actual men. His flaw comes finally to reveal itself to Coverdale as spiritual pride, which blinds him to the real complexity and mixed nature of man and the world. His name, though it points to a real nobility in his character, is finally ironic.

Zenobia bears the name of a queen both splendid and tragic, and she herself is regal in appearance and manner and comes to a tragic end. She is described in terms of her natural vitality and her luxuriant womanhood, and her name carries the significance of "one having life from Zeus." But here too there is a touch of irony, for the flower that she always wears in her hair, and that Coverdale finds emblematic of her nature, is at first a hothouse bloom, an exotic, and later a piece of jewelry wrought in imitation of a flower. She too, though less obviously than the others, is somehow false.

These are the clearly symbolic names in the work, though there may be vaguer, or more debatable, suggestions in some of the others, especially in Westervelt. But they are enough to make it clear that there is more going on here than meets the eye of the researcher looking for Hawthorne's memories of Brook Farm.

3

The texture of *The Blithedale Romance* is remarkably rich and interesting, even for Hawthorne. Two main streams of imagery clarify, reinforce, and expand the themes suggested by the name symbolism. In the early chapters fire imagery is dominant. Hawthorne insists on it so much, in fact, that at the beginning of chapter four he apologizes for "harping on it." But the imagery of masks, veils, and disguises, though subordinate to the fire imagery in most of the opening chapters, is introduced earlier. It is doubly present in the first sentence of the first chapter, explicitly in the reference to the Veiled Lady and implicitly in the reference to Moodie; and thereafter it dominates the chapter. It is apparent, as we have seen, in the name of the narrator. And it finally overshadows the fire imagery. Both it and the fire imagery are enriched by being associated with other image patterns, but the two of them are so much more frequent and emphatic than the others that they establish the pattern within which all the images have their place.

Readers often find Hawthorne's first chapter puzzling and unsatisfactory. He devotes it to introducing, first, the Veiled Lady, who except for Coverdale is the first character to appear, and second, old Moodie, whose name supplies the chapter with its title. Toward the end of the chapter we hear of Zenobia. One of the peculiarities of the chapter for the modern reader is that it is devoted to introducing three people of whom only one, Zenobia, is apparently a character of any consequence in the novel. I say "apparently" because we eventually discover that the Veiled Lady is really Priscilla and old Moodie is the father of both Priscilla and Zenobia. But by the time we discover this we are likely to have ceased to care, for the "mysterious" aspects of Hawthorne's plot are certainly not likely to hold our attention long today. Is this chapter then, we wonder, simply a rather extreme example of the trouble Hawthorne often had with the mechanics of his stories?

I think we may assume that Hawthorne felt he was gaining a valuable addition to suspense by this device of introducing characters whose identity remains hidden. But the chapter served Hawthorne in another way, and for us this is surely the more important. It introduces and places in the foreground of our attention veil and fire images. And it is typical of Hawthorne that the images which will be the chief carriers of the theme grow out of the plot, which thus functions symbolically even though it remains clumsily contrived and Gothic on the literal level.

The introduction of a mysterious Veiled Lady in the first chapter of a work that is to be full of disguises is obviously appropriate, but the thematic function of the chapter does not end there. Old Moodie, too, wears his own kind of veil. "He was a very shy personage, this Mr. Moodie." He wears a patch over one eye, and he never, as Coverdale immediately notices, reveals more of himself than is absolutely necessary. When he visits Blithedale and eats lunch in the field with Hollingsworth and Coverdale, he eats "with" them but not in sight of them, for he manages to sit so that a screen of leaves hides everything about him but his shoes. When he follows the two to the farmhouse he walks behind Hollingsworth so that Hollingsworth "could not very conveniently look him in the face." Coverdale notes that he gave the impression of "hiding himself behind the patch on his left eye." At the funeral of Zenobia he keeps his face "mostly concealed in a white handkerchief." He is as much a veiled character as the Veiled Lady and more obviously so than Coverdale.

The only other character introduced in the first chapter is Zenobia, and from what we learn of her later we first get the impression that she is unlike Coverdale, Moodie, and the Veiled Lady in being quite lacking in a veil. (Coverdale pictures her once lacking not only a veil but any other sort of drapery or covering.) She does not share Moodie's tendency to hide behind bushes or Coverdale's to peer out of thickets or into windows; she seems in fact to Coverdale to

be rather immodestly open in her manner, disturbing him
with her frank acknowledgment of her womanliness. Yet
there is one secret she will not reveal, the secret of her
very identity. So it is that Coverdale remarks to Moodie in
the first chapter that "Zenobia . . . is merely her public
name; a sort of mask in which she comes before the world
. . . a contrivance, in short, like the white drapery of the
Veiled Lady, only a little more transparent." Every character
in the first chapter, then, wears his mask. When finally we
discover that Priscilla is the Veiled Lady and the half-sister
of Zenobia, we realize that these two who are so unlike in
almost every respect are connected in a significant way: one
wears a veil by choice, the other by necessity. It is not difficult, knowing Hawthorne, to guess which will serve as
heroine.

But we are not quite through with this first chapter yet.
When Coverdale replenishes his fire we have the unobtru-
sive beginning of a chain of fire imagery that does not cease
until the end of the romance. Thus the opening chapter does
in fact accomplish a good deal: it introduces all but Hollingsworth among the principal characters and it first states the
leading images. The distance between this and the opening
chapters of *The Scarlet Letter* and *The House of the Seven
Gables* is after all not so great as it at first seems.

After this Hawthorne never lets us forget for long the
theme signalized by the veil imagery. We are reminded of
it, according to a hasty count, on some thirty-five of the
subsequent pages. But to say that we are "reminded" is not
to convey adequately what is really going on. For the veil
is not a static or allegorical symbol, and the first chapter
merely introduces, it does not define, it. Twenty-two of the
twenty-nine chapters develop the theme explicitly, and all
of them, of course, do so implicitly.

Coverdale, for instance, journeys to Blithedale in a snow-
storm that veils the "conventionalism" of the world against

which Blithedale is a protest. Zenobia wears her unnatural flowers, which Coverdale decides are a "subtile expression" of her character. Westervelt hides his true character behind a false laugh and false teeth: his laughter, "brief, metallic," reveals that his "remarkably brilliant" teeth are "a sham." Coverdale feels "as if the whole man were a moral and physical humbug; his wonderful beauty of face, for aught I knew, might be removable like a mask." Even the pair of spectacles Westervelt later puts on are masking devices: they "so altered the character of his face" that Coverdale "hardly knew him again." The reformers spend an evening at charades and Zenobia remarks that the identity of the actors is too apparent through their improvised disguises. Later the whole company, with the exception of Coverdale, put on masks and play at being Arcadians. Coverdale does not need a mask. He remains hidden as usual even without one, peering at the others through the leaves and later retreating, when he is discovered, to his "bower," from which he observes Priscilla, Zenobia, and Hollingsworth without disclosing his own presence. Everyone at Blithedale has a mask, veil, or disguise on at some time in the story.

4

The fire imagery is only slightly less prominent than that of veils, masks, and disguises. Chapter one closes with Coverdale building up his fire. Chapter two opens with his admission that he is not likely ever again to know so cheery a blaze as that which he remembers from his first day at Blithedale. The remainder of the chapter develops the implications of this initial imagery. The fire that first day warmed the heart as well as the body. The cheer it provided in contrast to the cold outside strengthened Coverdale and his companions in their hope that here they might begin "the life of Paradise anew." After several reminders of the pres-

ence of the fires in chapter three, chapter four turns again
to extended treatment of the subject. The great old kitchen
fireplace, with its "cavernous" opening, is now described.
The fire that burns in it is very cheery, but it is not such as
any real farmer would build: it is too large to be perfectly
natural even in such a fireplace, and, as Silas Foster sardoni-
cally points out, it is built of brushwood, which burns very
brightly but will not last.

Silas Foster's doubt about the permanence of the fires at
Blithedale is paralleled by Priscilla's inability to be warmed
by them. She finds "the sense of vast, undefined space, pressing from the outside against the black panes of our un-
curtained windows . . . fearful . . . The house probably
seemed to her adrift on the great ocean of the night." And
so it was later to seem to Coverdale. Very soon after arriving,
indeed, he was forced to go shivering to his "fireless chamber" with a cold in the head.

While Coverdale is still confined to his sickbed, Hollingsworth builds a fire to warm the room, and it is very welcome
to the sufferer from cold. Yet "there never was any blaze of
a fireside that warmed and cheered me, in the down-sink-
ings and shiverings of my spirit, so effectually as did the
light out of those eyes, which lay so deep and dark under
his shaggy brows." When it becomes clear to Coverdale later
that his friend has given way to "the terrible egotism which
he mistook for an angel of God," the light that warms disappears. Coverdale is left thereafter with more cause than
ever to deplore the coldness of his own heart. His "cold
tendency," which has gone far as he thinks toward "un-
humanizing" him, leads him to want fires everywhere, even
when he does not need them: "Summer as it still was, I
ordered a coal-fire in the rusty grate, and was glad to find
myself growing a little too warm with an artificial tempera-
ture." The cold from which Coverdale suffered was more internal than external. Like that of Gervayse Hastings in "The

Christmas Banquet," it was the cold that proceeds from a frozen heart.

At least eight other image patterns are related, some obviously and some obscurely, to the veil and fire clusters. It has already become clear how coldness comes in as the counterpart of the fires and warmth, and how these two lead naturally, as always in Hawthorne, to heart imagery. These four, veil and fire, coldness and the heart, take on added meaning in their relationships with the iron imagery associated with Hollingsworth, the flower imagery and the frequent allusions to the theater and acting associated with Zenobia, the images of laughter that make an interesting connection between Westervelt and Coverdale, and the images of dreaming that are associated with Coverdale alone. And all these running metaphors are tied in with the frequent allusions to Eden, Arcadia, and Paradise. Some, like the iron imagery that helps to characterize Hollingsworth, grow naturally out of the main image patterns, extending and reinforcing them; others, like the flower imagery associated with Zenobia, serve to qualify or counter the suggestions of the dominant images. Though each of these might profitably be given separate treatment, I shall comment on only two of them, the heart and cold clusters, which may be treated together.

The cold is at first external. We see it in a set of pure images which at first reading have no obvious metaphorical force: Coverdale and his friends begin their enterprise in a snowstorm, and as they gather around their fires the cold seems to press in from without. Then, following a brief spring and summer which some of the less perceptive of the utopians seem to expect to last forever, Coverdale returns to the farm in the fall. Once again the weather is cold, but by now the metaphorical implications are clearer, so that the images are like those I called "mixed" in *The Scarlet Letter*: Coverdale finds the "ice-temper" of the air invigorating because he is experiencing a momentary resurgence of faith. When his heart is warm, he can defy, or even enjoy, the outer cold. And what is implicit here, the uniting of the streams of heart, fire, and cold imagery, is also made explicit. Zenobia is talking to Priscilla about the latter's probable future as Hollingsworth's wife:

"Poor child! Methinks you have but a melancholy lot before you, sitting alone in that wide, cheerless heart, where, for aught you know, — and as I, alas, believe, — the fire which you have kindled may soon go out. Ah, the thought makes me shiver for you! What will you do, Priscilla, when you find no spark among the ashes?"

We were prepared for "that wide, cheerless heart" by the descriptions of the kitchen hearth, with its "old-fashioned breadth, depth, and spaciousness," much earlier. We see now that the hearth has been a symbolic heart all along. And the brushwood fires prepared us for the ardor which Priscilla has awakened in Hollingsworth and which Zenobia believes is bound to be short-lived. We can now see that the groundwork for all this was laid as early as the first chapter and elaborated in the meditation of Coverdale which opens chapter two:

There can hardly remain for me (who am getting to be a frosty bachelor, with another white hair, every week or so, in my mustache), there can hardly flicker up again so cheery a blaze upon the hearth, as that which I remember . . . at Blithedale. It was a wood-fire, in the parlor of an old farm-house, on an April afternoon, but with the fitful gusts of a wintry snow-storm roaring in the chimney. Vividly does that fireside re-create itself, as I rake away the ashes from the embers in my memory, and blow them up with a sigh, for lack of more inspiring breath. Vividly, for an instant, but, anon, with the dimmest gleam, and with just as little fervency for my heart as for my finger-ends! The staunch oaken logs were long ago burnt out. Their genial glow must be represented, if at all, by the merest phosphoric glimmer, like that which exudes, rather than shines, from damp fragments of decayed trees, deluding the benighted wanderer through a forest. Around such chill mockery of a fire some few of us might sit on the withered leaves, spreading out each a palm towards the imaginary warmth, and talk over our exploded scheme for beginning the life of Paradise anew.

5

When the novel opens Coverdale is returning to his apartment after having spent an evening watching "the wonderful exhibition of the Veiled Lady." Though he suspects that mesmerism and its attendant clairvoyance and telepathy are rather "the revival of an old humbug" than "the birth of a new science," yet he has asked the Veiled Lady to predict the success or failure of the Blithedale enterprise. In view of his skepticism about the new "science," he is not surprised when the answer he receives is "of the true Sibylline stamp, — nonsensical in its first aspect, yet, on closer study, unfolding a variety of interpretations, one of which has certainly accorded with the event." The answer, in short, is a kind of riddle, with its "truth" hidden behind a veil of ambiguities. Like the identity of the Veiled Lady herself, the meaning of her reply will become clear only as time uncovers it. The most obvious thing a veil does is to cover, hide, or disguise.

Yet this raises an interesting question. Why, if this is so, is veil imagery introduced at the beginning, then pushed into the background to make way for the fire imagery that predominates in the next four chapters, then later brought back into the foreground again? Why, in other words, as the meaning of the answer to Coverdale's question becomes clearer, as the veil of obscurity is lifted from the prophetic words, does the veil imagery increase? There would seem to be movements in opposite directions going on here: the identity of the characters is being gradually unveiled, as is the answer to the initial question about the success of the enterprise; but Coverdale, after the first flush of his enthusi-

asm has worn off, covers his tracks more completely than
ever, Zenobia takes to wearing artificial flowers in place of
her hothouse bloom, Westervelt comes into the picture with
his profusion of masks, and at last all the utopians together
put on disguises.

One thing such a statement of the problem seems to me
to make clear is that the veil imagery does not function in
terms of an allegorical sort of symbolism. Like the laughter
in "My Kinsman" and the colors in *The Scarlet Letter,* it
functions symbolically in terms of context. The veil which
is at first merely a piece of gauze hiding the features of the
mesmeric subject quickly expands to metaphor as it gets
associated with the obscurity of her answer to Coverdale's
question, then becomes a metaphor for the mystery surrounding the identity of Moodie and Zenobia — all this in
the first chapter. As the tale progresses it takes on the character of a snowstorm, a hothouse flower, a set of false teeth,
a pair of spectacles, a window curtain, a "leafy retreat," the
black water of a river at night hiding a body, and even
Coverdale's habits and personality. It becomes finally, perhaps, whatever hides from us the frustration, the futility,
which lie hidden, suspected but not clearly seen, in the
future.

As the years darkened around Coverdale he saw, one sup-
poses, the meaning of the veil changing from that which
hides a truth one wants to know to that which hides a reality
one fears to know. Thus it was, perhaps, that though he
knew, when he wrote, the folly of the kind of utopianism
he had taken part in at Blithedale, yet he could not wholly
regret having been involved in it; for it had been a generous
folly, resting upon a belief in the possibility of progress.
And his words and his tone suggest that it came to seem to
him, in some of his moods at least, that without the veil that
mercifully conceals reality we could undertake no generous
or noble action whatever. If the reality of Blithedale had

been clear to him at the beginning, he never would have been warmed, even momentarily, by the blazing fires in those early weeks of the adventure.

If this is the final meaning of the veil, then the content of the fire symbol must be modified accordingly. The brushwood fire, even the fire of great logs, long since reduced to ashes, suggests in such a context not so much true comradeship and "holy sympathy" and faith as a mere illusion of these things. The outer cold, the blackness Priscilla saw pressing in upon the little group, must have been more real, then, than the flames all along. The comradeship, the sympathy, and the faith were indeed made possible only by the presence of the veil. If this is what Coverdale comes finally to suspect, as his tone seems often to imply, then here certainly is the ultimate failure of hope. If this is what he suspects, then it is little wonder that many have found this the coldest, the most completely negative of all of Hawthorne's novels.

But if Coverdale suspects this at times, he does not *believe* it — quite. For the veil is also, always, that which isolates man from man and the desired truth from our perception of it. It destroys the connections in "the magnetic chain of humanity." As Mr. Hooper, in an earlier story, had been cut off from his congregation by his black veil, so the partners in the Blithedale attempt at practical brotherhood are isolated from one another by their veils. And if the veils cannot be removed, if it is not possible to bring out into the light that which is hidden, to "be true" as Dimmesdale finally was true, then no experiment in brotherhood can ever succeed. Again, in so far as the veil hides the ultimate truth from us, it puts us all in the unhappy position of Aylmer in "The Birthmark," whose scientific idealism led to such awful results; for we recall that he "failed to look beyond the shadowy scope of time, and living once for all in eternity, to find the perfect future in the present." Aylmer failed to look,

Coverdale suspects we may be unable to look beyond the veil: whatever the cause, the result may be the same.

When we pursue this interpretation of the veil imagery we approach Hawthorne's consciously intended meaning. Priscilla is obviously his redemptive character, whose love will save Hollingsworth if anything can. She is, despite the veil thrust upon her in her role as the Veiled Lady, the only major character who does not either wear a veil by choice or manifest spiritual and intellectual pride. She is the only character motivated consistently by love. (Zenobia is "in love" with Hollingsworth, but her love is a manifestation of *eros* rather than *agape*; and Hollingsworth protests that he loves humanity, but he doesn't care very much for actual men.) Priscilla is a paler Phoebe, a more helpless Hilda of *The Marble Faun.* Her love is redemptive so far as the others will let it be.

But they will not let it be if they can prevent it. They admit her to their circle at first somewhat reluctantly and, as Coverdale notes, do very little to make her feel at home with them. The remarkable thing about this community founded on the theory of the brotherhood of man is the almost complete absence in it of any actual brotherhood. The leading characters, Zenobia, Hollingsworth, and Coverdale, are scarcely concerned at all about the fate of the community; each uses it for his own purposes. And they care less and less for each other as time goes on. So that in addition to being set, as Coverdale says, in a "relation of hostility" to the world outside in their effort to compete with it commercially, they come finally to be hostile to each other. Removal of their veils, being true, would have been no doubt the first prerequisite to lasting success of the experiment; a change of heart would have been the second. Certainly the chief intended meaning of the work is that we cannot create "Paradise anew" while maintaining our separateness, our disguises, and the fundamental self-centeredness or pride of which they are a manifestation. Hawthorne is saying again what he had said in "Earth's Holocaust," that all reform is superficial so long as the heart remains unchanged.

That this is indeed the intended meaning of the work may be shown by an examination of the fire and veil imagery in such a way as to make clear the comparative weight Hawthorne has given to each of them in the various parts of the novel. The pattern that emerges looks like this:

Chapters	Images
I	VEIL — fire
II–V	FIRE — veil
VI–IX	fire — veil
X–XXIX	fire — VEIL

I have set chapter one apart from the others because it simply introduces what is to follow. And it is clear now that in addition to its other, already noted, introductory functions, it foreshadows the dominance of the veil imagery in the last chapters. It supplies in fact a veiled answer to the question Coverdale asks of the Veiled Lady.

Now this is an admirably balanced and functional structure. It suggests the cyclical pattern of *The House of the Seven Gables,* which starts with the HOUSE and the elm and ends with the ELM and the house. If this sort of thing ever happens by accident — which one may reasonably doubt — it does not happen by accident in Hawthorne's work: he knew what he was about, as we have ample evidence by this time to believe. What he was about in this instance was creating a work of art that would say again more fully and clearly what he had often said before. The largest pattern that emerges from the imagery here says that the reformers could not succeed in reorganizing society because they could not, or would not, put off their veils and emerge from their separateness. It says that the fires of faith, hope, and love burned brightly at first at Blithedale but were soon extinguished by the selfishness of men and women who could not afford to be "true."

The implication of this is of course that a redeemed society can only come when there are enough redeemed individuals. And the ending *means* to suggest the possibility of this: Priscilla may be able to "humanize" Hollingsworth. But this possibility is surely too slight to encourage us to pin our hopes on it. And there is another reason why the record of Blithedale's failure is so very much more impressive than the suggestion that another kind of effort might succeed: as we have noted, there seems to be some question in Coverdale's mind about what the veil finally is and does. Aylmer would have been wiser to look beyond, but that was because what he would have learned by doing so would have been the message of the Gospel: it would have chastened his hopes of man's achieving perfection by his own efforts, but it would not have overwhelmed him with any revelation of the final futility of all effort. But what if there is nothing but darkness and cold "beyond"? Then clearly the veil is a saving ignorance, making possible a precious illusion, permitting us for a little while to be warmed by the ephemeral fire. Whether the veil is this as well as that behind which individuals hide themselves from others, Coverdale does not seem able to make up his mind.

His ambivalence, and the resultant suggestion of uncertainty about the meaning of the veil as symbol on the most abstract levels, almost make it possible to read the novel in two different ways. Either the experiment failed because men could not sufficiently put away their veils and be true and loving; or it would never have been started had there not been a veil draped over the facts of life and death, making faith and hope momentarily possible. Of these two readings there can be no question about which one Hawthorne meant us to make. Even if there were no evidence at all available from his other works and his life, or if we decided to rule all that other evidence out, the structure and texture of this work should be decisive — unless we wish to assume that Hawthorne did not know what he was about and that the design he wrought is not meaningful. For if we were to decide that the primary meaning of the veil is that of a saving ignorance making possible a valuable illusion, then the largest pattern made by the images in the work would be at odds with the work's meaning. For in this reading we should expect that as the veiling effect increases, the fires, being dependent on the veil for their being, would burn brighter. But this is precisely the opposite of what happens: the veils become more prominent, and the fires go out. Form and content do not come apart in this way in Hawthorne. The veil cannot be intended, as the structure of the work itself shows, primarily to be that which makes hope possible.

Yet the doubt creeps back and will not be argued away. The ambiguity remains and will not be dissolved in paraphrase. It is not that there is any conflict here between intended and achieved meanings in the usual senses of those terms, for what we have decided is the primary intended meaning is "achieved"; it is thoroughly and consistently and even elaborately embodied in structure. It is not that structure and theme are at odds but that structure and theme together are to some extent at odds with feeling, with tone. Coverdale, for instance, says he has been in love with Priscilla all along; and, considering Priscilla's role and his, we find this appropriate on the thematic level. But we have trouble believing him. Again, he does not say he has no hope left of any kind for man, but his tone speaks more eloquently than his words, and the disillusion he means to apply only to the kind of effort that was made at Blithedale we find difficult to restrict to that effort.

This is not the ambiguity of the "double mood." It is Hawthorne's own special brand of ambiguity, the ambiguity of head and heart. What Coverdale believes he cannot trust

himself always to feel; and what he feels he does not believe.
Hawthorne the conscious artist makes the fires die as the veils
come to the fore. At the same time Hawthorne as Leonard
Doane and Gervayse Hastings and Goodman Brown, Hawthorne of the haunted mind, was aware, or felt without being aware that he felt it, that the fires might have been
impossible without the veils.

6

Even those who may find the work less ambivalent than
these speculations suggest can hardly deny that it is very
cold. Hawthorne wrote only one novel and very few stories
with happy endings that are even partially convincing, but
surely this is more negative and hopeless than most of the
works. As Coverdale writes he seems to be chiefly aware of
the death that is involved in time, with the "years that are
darkening around" him. He says he does not want to regret
his part in the Blithedale enterprise, but his tone suggests
a great weariness. "Whatever else I may repent of, therefore, let it be reckoned neither among my sins nor follies
that I once had faith and force enough to form generous
hopes of the world's destiny."

We are invited to assume that Coverdale means only that
the generous hopes were misdirected at Blithedale, that this
kind of effort at redemption is a mistake. But this is not
always what he seems to mean, despite his recognition that
Priscilla points the way to a more fruitful effort:

> Therefore, if we built splendid castles . . . and pictured beautiful
> scenes, among the fervid coals of the hearth around which we were
> clustering, and if all went to rack with the crumbling embers and
> have never since arisen out of the ashes, let us take to ourselves no
> shame. In my own behalf, I rejoice that I could once think better of
> the world's improvability than it deserved.

Does Coverdale's doubt about the "world's improvability"

go beyond Fourierist reform to include any coöperative effort, or even any individual effort? There are times when he makes it seem so. There is a sense in which it may be said that what finally emerges from the novel most vividly is death. It is not surprising that the most powerful scene is the midnight search in the river for the body of Zenobia, in which Hawthorne drew upon an experience he had had while living in the Old Manse. There were a good many kinds of experience that Hawthorne could not use successfully in his writing, but this he could use. The stream that hid the body, that veiled it from the searchers, Coverdale called, fittingly in his character as minor poet, the "Black River of Death." When the water's veil was finally lifted it revealed something so grotesque and fearful that Coverdale was moved, for once, to a profound emotion. "Ah, that rigidity! It is impossible to bear the terror of it."

In creating Coverdale, Hawthorne isolated and projected a part of himself that he disliked. Coverdale is of course not Hawthorne. He is a minor transcendentalist poet, a slightly comic figure even in his own eyes. His tastes in reading are very nearly the opposite of Hawthorne's, and there is irony in the whole portrait. Yet the irony is partially self-directed, for he is that part of Hawthorne that Hawthorne had earlier projected in his cold, proud, faithless men. Since he is both narrator and analyst — "Greek chorus," he calls it — of the story, his character gives the work the tone of icy coldness it has. Whatever he may say of his own reactions, the reader is never warmed for a moment by the roaring fires at Blithedale.

And this is no doubt one of the reasons for the lack of popularity of the book, in Hawthorne's day and in our own. Others perhaps are the too sharp break between the chapters dealing with Blithedale itself and those relating Coverdale's stay in town; the too evident influence of the Gothic romance, with its machinery of mysterious persons, "marvels" like mesmerism, and very villainous villains; and the surprising revelation at the end that Coverdale is in love with Priscilla — for we had thought that he could not love anyone but himself.

But surely the chief difficulty in the way of a greater enjoyment of the novel is created by Coverdale. He is, as we are tempted to say today, a very Jamesian character, highly conscious, and self-conscious, a reflector rather than an actor, given to irony, which he as frequently directs at himself as at others. He is a preliminary sketch for some of James's later characters. But whereas James manages to make us feel sympathy for his characters, Hawthorne makes us feel little or none for Coverdale. Perhaps the basic reason is that Hawthorne disliked the Coverdale in himself too much, so that he was not in sympathy with his own central creation.

But today there is no good reason for emphasizing the failure. The flaws are perfectly evident: given contemporary taste in fiction, we are not likely to miss them. What we have tended to miss is the remarkable textural richness and beauty of the work. Missing this, we have missed too a great deal of the meaning. The book deserves to be read more carefully than we have generally read it.

CHAPTER EIGHT

THE MARBLE FAUN

Anyone content to judge novels principally by the number and importance of the ideas in them, without much regard for aesthetic matters, might be tempted to conclude that *The Marble Faun* is Hawthorne's most significant romance. For in it Hawthorne made an attempt to treat directly the largest conceptions of the nature of life, and particularly of the effects of evil, that had formed a substructure of assumption and attitude in his earlier works. In *The Marble Faun* Hawthorne was trying to think out the problems raised by his artistic career.

A very great deal of what he had written in more than a third of a century had been a preparation for this romance. Most of his stories, the best of them surely, had been concerned with the facets of a single great theme. Now he approached that theme, which we may call the nature and significance of evil, from a different angle, with a different interest. Now it was to be examined philosophically and theologically. What had been assumed while the experiences of sinful hearts were scrutinized was now to be looked at directly, on a higher level of abstraction. Having written for more than thirty years chiefly of the problem of evil, Hawthorne tried in his last completed romance to carry his thinking through to the end. If *The Marble Faun* is not actually as meaningful as its position in relation to the earlier works would suggest, we must look elsewhere than in the nature of its theme for the reason.

Again, if the work must finally be judged a failure, despite some great merits — and it has been so judged by most of its readers — then it is not because it is structurally ill conceived. Aristotle's word *mythos* seems wholly justified as a descriptive term for this plot. Count Donatello, an innocent, childlike young man, almost animal-like in his "naturalness" and lack of conscience, visits ancient, corrupt, and beautiful Rome and falls in love with Miriam, a woman with some secret guilt in her past. Through her he comes to know sin, committing a murder because of love for her. Though his experience with good and evil develops him into an adult and responsible human being, he is nevertheless punished for his sin. Others suffer too, as his sin has repercussions on his friends. Hilda, pure in heart, watches in horror, tries at first to avoid becoming involved, but finally grows more charitable and becomes engaged in human life more fully than she has been before. Kenyon, watching the business with speculative interest, finds himself wondering whether sin can be so dreadful a thing after all if it has the consequence of making man human, even if it does so at the cost of his innocence and happiness. Warned by Hilda of the dangers implicit in such ideas, he puts them behind him and proposes to Hilda: head and heart come together at last, the one to give up its irresponsible ideas, the other to give up its virgin innocence, both to leave the mystery unsolved.

Now I have the impression that a summary of the plot suggests that this romance might well be Hawthorne's best. Not that there is any formula for classifying plots as good or bad and that this is a good one according to the formula, but that for Hawthorne one would think this perfect: perfect because suited to his sensibility and related to those central concerns on which we have seen him do his greatest work, perfect also because logically symmetrical and complete, unified in scene and action and implied theme, perfect because capable of extension without loss of symmetry or coherence. Here are all of the old themes in a new and, as it were, definitive, arrangement: sin that is kept hidden in the heart, the effect of the guilty conscience on the individual and on others, the impact of the past on the present, the relations of head and heart, and the path to redemption through the union of the two — all brought together in a structure dominated by the Eden myth.

And there are some new themes here too, as we shall discover, though they are not apparent from the summary I have attempted. They too should, one would think, enlarge the area of meaning of the work: for here we find the theme that James was later to do so much with, the problem of European culture and American morality, of the contrasting and complementary virtues and defects of the innocent and the civilized; and the related antinomy of progress and primitivism; and the — still related — contrast of knowledge and faith as ways to redemption. All these questions are raised in *The Marble Faun* in addition to Hawthorne's usual themes. It is, in fact, the work which most clearly brings him into relation with the leading ideas of his century. Thematically it demands comparison with the work of Melville, James, Dostoevski, and others who raised the century's special concerns to dimensions of universal significance.

2

To identify the overarching theme more exactly, we may turn, since Hawthorne made his allegory explicit, to two speeches near the end. Miriam, one of the best of Hawthorne's dark ladies, attractive yet obscurely sinful, worthy of our respect and calculated to arouse our pity, yet dangerous, as ambiguous a character as Zenobia, first dares to make explicit what has already been suspected by the perceptive reader. "I delight to brood on the verge of this great mystery," she tells Kenyon:

"The story of the fall of man! Is it not repeated in our romance of Monte Beni? And may we follow the analogy yet farther? Was that very sin — into which Adam precipitated himself and all his race — was it the destined means by which, over a long pathway of toil and sorrow, we are to attain a higher, brighter, and more profound happiness, than our lost birthright gave?"

Kenyon replies that he cannot follow her so far: this is too dangerous a speculation. But a little later we find him pursuing the same train of thought, using indeed almost the identical words. This time it is Hilda who is shocked by the "dangers" in this line of reasoning. "Did Adam fall," Kenyon asks, "that we might ultimately rise to a far loftier paradise than his?" " 'Oh, hush!' cried Hilda, shrinking from him with an expression of horror."

The theme then is the fall of man into evil. And the particular question that is asked, and that determines the point of reference from which the analogy with the Christian myth of the Fall is framed, is whether or not man's fall should be considered fortunate. When Miriam asks the question there is a strong implication that she thinks the answer should be "yes." But Miriam is an unregenerate character, however much the modern reader may sympathize with her. When Kenyon asks the same question he almost immediately rejects the answer which his words have implied, prompted in part apparently by a desire not to offend Hilda, with whom he is in love, and in part by agreement with Hilda's analysis. So the two characters with whom Hawthorne expected the reader to be most in sympathy decisively reject the notion of the Fortunate Fall. And the plot, too, symbolically rejects it: for Miriam, who first proposed the theory, ends in tragic exile; Donatello, who seemingly exemplified it,

ends in prison; Kenyon, who for a time speculatively entertained it, ends by denying it and marrying Hilda; and Hilda,
Miriam's antitype and the strongest critic of the theory,
"saves" Kenyon by guiding him "home," where such speculations will presumably not recur.

If the explanation of Donatello's career as a fortunate fall
into sin is rejected, so likewise is the only other interpretation explicitly presented in the work. This too is offered by
Kenyon and rejected by Hilda. It is the very opposite of the
paradoxical fall upward to a higher bliss: it is a simple
one-directional fall downward from the golden age into
civilization. "Faun or not," says Kenyon,

he had a genial nature, which, had the rest of mankind been in accordance with it, would have made earth a paradise to our poor friend.
It seems the moral of his story, that human beings of Donatello's
character, compounded especially for happiness, have no longer any
business on earth, or elsewhere. Life has grown so sadly serious, that
such men must change their natures, or else perish, like the ante-
diluvian creatures, that required, as the condition of their existence, a
more summer-like atmosphere than ours.

From this point of view, which Kenyon seems not to have
held very seriously, and which Hilda rejects decisively as
too pessimistic, man has declined into civilization. Since no
one in the work shares Thoreau's optimism about the possibility of a return to nature and innocence, man must adapt
himself to sadly changed conditions and practice resigna-
tion. This is a pessimistic version of Rousseauistic primitivism, identifyng the happy with the simple, the desirable
with the uncomplicated. Donatello had been happy in nature
on his estate in the mountains, but in Rome the world was
too much with and for him. Most modern readers will rejoice, I imagine, that this interpretation, so far removed from
Hawthorne's usual and central ideas, is rejected even more
summarily than that of the fortunate fall.

Thematically, then, on the explicit level and on the most

obvious of the implicit levels, *The Marble Faun* is "good Hawthorne." But when we look a little more deeply beneath the surface we come upon some things that a reading of the earlier works has not prepared us for. Though most critics have found that the romance "reads better" than *Blithedale*, what we find when we examine it closely is not, I fear, intentional ambiguity so much as unintentional confusion and failure of embodiment. There is a sense in which, despite the less damaging intrusion here of the Gothic elements that so greatly weakened *Blithedale*, it represents a stage in confusion beyond that work, a further step toward the paralysis of the unfinished romances.

3

In his conclusion to *The Marble Faun*, added to the second edition in response to letters from those whose curiosity was left unsatisfied by the original ending, Hawthorne protested that many were misreading his tale. He attempted once again to explain his aims as a writer, writing in a somewhat defensive tone that may in part be a reflection of his awareness of the rising vogue of the new realism. Speaking of himself in the third person he wrote:

He designed the story and the characters to bear, of course, a certain relation to human nature and human life, but still to be so artfully and airily removed from our mundane sphere, that some laws and proprieties of their own should be implicitly and insensibly acknowledged.

The idea of the modern Faun, for example, loses all the poetry and beauty which the Author fancied in it, and becomes nothing better than a grotesque absurdity, if we bring it into the actual light of day. He had hoped to mystify this anomalous creature between the Real and the Fantastic, in such a manner that the reader's sympathies might be excited to a certain pleasurable degree, without impelling him to ask how Cuvier would have classified poor Donatello, or to insist upon being told, in so many words, whether he had furry ears or no.

Hawthorne was not, as he here felt the need to insist once more, a realist. He had called his work a "romance," and he now reminded his readers of that fact, hoping thus to make clear the irrelevance of their questions. Now in so far as his remarks were an attempt to correct the taste and judgment of the literal-minded who had missed the symbolic aspect of his story, we tend to feel today that he was quite within his rights. But if he hoped by this apology to be excused from the necessity of embodying his conceptions in tangible form — that is, from being a novelist, as the word is used today — he was mistaken. For though the emphasis in fiction falls, from period to period and tradition to tradition, in different places, yet there seem to be some permanent laws too, and one of the most important of them is that the writer of fiction, however abstract his conceptual framework may be, must embody it, give it substance. Our age is perhaps too impatient with allegory to do the form justice, but there is a core of truth in what we hold as a prejudice: pure allegory is not what we mean by fiction.

The Marble Faun comes closer to being pure allegory than any of Hawthorne's other romances, and this despite the "realism" of the elaborately wrought Roman background and the fine chapters on the Italian countryside around Donatello's home. The reason that this is so is surely not that the Eden myth exercised a controlling influence on the story; this could have been an advantage, as it was in "Rappaccini's Daughter." The reason is rather to be found in Hawthorne's double failure of embodiment. He fails, on the one hand, to give even the necessary minimum of specification to some of his characters and events; and, on the other, to suit to his purpose all the specification he did give. *The Marble Faun* is sometimes bare where it should be rich, and sometimes misleading in the texture which is supplied. And these twin weaknesses are most evident in the characters, that is, precisely at the center of the work.

We may grant Hawthorne a degree of success with Donatello. He was, as he said, faced with a special problem in the
creation of a character existing in the borderland "between
the Real and the Fantastic," and though most of us will
probably wish that he had not let the Faun of Praxiteles
influence him quite so obviously as it did, still there is a
firmer illusion of reality surrounding Donatello than Hawthorne succeeded in creating for some of his less "anomalous"
characters.

Kenyon and Hilda, for instance, are "real people" in a
sense in which Donatello is not, but they are apt to seem
not more but less real to the reader. Kenyon is at times a
mouthpiece for one side of Hawthorne, at times the *type* of
reason, but at no time an interesting or wholly believable
human being. He is not so much a created fictional character
as a name and a convenience. And Hilda is even less satisfactory, for while Kenyon is shadowy, without much reality,
he is believable in so far as there is anything there in which
to believe or disbelieve.

But Hilda is wrong both ways. Chiefly she appears to be
a lifeless convention lifted bodily from nineteenth-century
romances and the steel engravings of the Christmas gift
books: the "pure" maiden, Cooper's "genteel female," Mark
Twain's conception of Olivia and Hawthorne's of Sophia.
She appears, in short, to be a stereotyped "culture-symbol,"
the embodiment of nineteenth-century feminism, sentimen-
talism, and the "religion of the heart." She is "pure," "spiritual," the guardian of moral values and the inspiration of
sinful men, exercising her power by appealing to man's
"higher self." Now that the culture has changed and this
stereotype has lost its irrational appeal, she is completely
unbelievable. I shall delay comment on the other way in
which she is wrong for the story until later. For the moment
it is sufficient to note that the two chief carriers of the positive theme, Kenyon and Hilda, "hero" and "heroine" by their

place in the work, are remarkably pale characters. If the novel survives despite this, it must be because of some other extraordinary merits.

But Hawthorne's failure to give much fictional reality to two of his three chief characters is complemented by a very different failure. To the extent that he succeeds in creating the illusion of reality in his characterization he does so largely at the expense of, or in a way that weakens, his explicit theme.

Miriam has seemed to almost all readers the most interesting and memorable character. With the possible exception of "poor Donatello," she is the only really created character in the book and is, I suspect, the only character strongly appealing to the modern reader. She comes of course of a long line of dark, attractive, strong, sexually mature and appealing, yet "guilty" women in Hawthorne's works. She is, as has been remarked, sister to Hester and Zenobia. But note what effect Hawthorne's success with her has on the achieved content, as contrasted with the explicit meaning. Miriam is sinful. She has been involved in some dark crime in the past, and now she wills the murder which precipitates the fall of Donatello. No hope of redemption or escape is suggested for her. It is she who proposes the anti-theme, the Fortunate Fall, which hero and heroine and the whole structure of the plot finally reject. Her presence makes possible the conflict, out of which emerge the chastened Hilda and the wiser Kenyon. Yet because she is by far the strongest character, she runs away with the book, imposes her will on it, and actually determines the achieved content to a far greater degree than the supposedly more sympathetic characters.

Because of Miriam, then, those who believe that the "meaning" of the work is expressed in the idea of the Fortunate Fall are partially justified. But the "meaning" they are getting is not the one Hawthorne intended — to judge his intention, for the moment, solely by the novel he produced.

Reading the work simply in terms of an identification with Miriam and her ideas is rather like reading *Moby Dick* in terms of a sympathetic identification with Ahab alone: the temptation to do so is great, the strength of Miriam and Ahab almost compel us to do so, but we should resist the temptation if we want to understand either novel in its wholeness. The only way Hawthorne could have prevented his success in creating Miriam from confusing the meaning of his novel would have been to have created in Kenyon and Hilda characters who were more than a match for her.

Instead he created in Hilda a character not simply pale and unreal but calculated, so far as she becomes real at all, to strengthen the reader's preference for Miriam. As Hilda becomes ridiculous in her much insisted upon Virgin Purity, the theme of which she is the chief defender becomes ridiculous with her. As she becomes offensive to pragmatist and Christian alike in her priggishness and lack of charity, the theme takes on something of her unattractiveness. If she can be judged in moral terms at all, she must be considered guilty of a pharisaical form of spiritual pride, a far more deadly vice than any specific sinful act such as that Miriam is supposed to have been implicated in.

Richard Fogle, to whose generally excellent analyses of Hawthorne's work we all are indebted, has recently argued that Hilda is intended as a superhuman being, somewhere between men and angels, and is thus another "anomalous" creature in the work, like Donatello.* I think there is every reason to doubt that Hawthorne intended her to be taken this way. But if we were to grant the point for the sake of exploring the idea, then two remarks would immediately be in order.

First, if she is a "pure spirit," exempt from sin, her arguments can have no relevance for Kenyon or Miriam, or for

---

* *Hawthorne's Fiction: The Light and the Dark* (Norman: University of Oklahoma Press, 1952), pp. 162–183.

us: we are not pure spirits, and any redemption that may come to us must come in a way possible for human beings. That of course is the point of the doctrine of the Incarnation; it is also a part of the meaning of the doctrine of the Third Person of the Trinity, the Holy Ghost, which works in and through human beings in their human condition in nature. It seems unlikely that Hawthorne was so confused in his understanding of Christianity that he was unaware of the significance of God's taking on human flesh. The reasoning behind St. Paul's "No man has seen God" was surely not unknown to Hawthorne. And just as a God who remained completely transcendant could not speak to us, so a superhuman Hilda could have no real relevance for the plot. The effect of Donatello's sin on her would be completely foreseeable: it would necessarily be nonexistent, so that there would be no conflict and no development at the center of the novel. And her coming down from her tower at the end to marry Kenyon would be both meaningless and ridiculous.

Second, if we see her as superhuman by intention, then we have not only the absurdity of Kenyon's taking a Spirit to wife but the further anomaly that Hilda as a representative Spirit would, at least in the first four-fifths of the novel, make the supernatural world look very unattractive and even immoral, inferior indeed in grace to the human world. Now I am sure that Hawthorne faltered in creating Hilda, but he did not falter that badly. Hilda the Virgin, safe from the sinful world in her high tower, busy feeding her doves and tending the flame of faith, may seem to the modern reader to have been immaculately conceived, but Hawthorne knew too much about the Christian tradition to attribute to Heaven uncharitableness and self-righteousness. Yet surely the modern reader is right in detecting these traits in Hilda. She prefers not to associate with Miriam for fear she may be stained by her sin; she will not help her for the same reason. Throughout most of the story she rejects the world because it is sin-

ful while she is perfectly pure. If we disregard the change
Hawthorne tried, not very successfully to be sure, to show
in her at the end, what we have in her is not a *type* of what
Hawthorne understood as the essence of Christian faith but
a feminine version of the man of adamant, the Puritan bigot
and pharisee.

But if, both from what we have seen of the blonde maidens
who foreshadow Hilda and from an inspection of this novel
in its entirety, we must accept Hilda as human by intention,
we shall still find her the weakest character in a novel that
could have been convincing only if she had been strong.
There is no need to point out in detail what is wrong with
her; any perceptive reader will detect it immediately. But I
should like to emphasize one problem she raises. If, as Hawthorne reiterates so insistently, she is absolutely spotless,
then she must be exempt from the human condition as Hawthorne had always pictured that condition in the successful
characters of all his best work and as he had characterized
it in his only direct statements on the subject. If she is perfectly without stain, then from a purely logical point of view
she is justified in "disclaiming" her "brotherhood" with the
sinful. For we recall that Hawthorne had argued in earlier
years that the reason why we must not disclaim our brotherhood even with the guiltiest is that all have sinned, if only
in wishes that have never come to fruition. In Hilda, Hawthorne is forgetting his Pauline theology and opening an
intercourse with his age by toying with a notion peculiar to
"the religion of the heart."

Even the earlier blonde maidens have not fully prepared
us for Hilda. Priscilla is subject at least to the ills of the flesh,
if not to the corruption of the will, and her spotlessness is
not emphasized. Phoebe plays a redemptive role similar to
the one that Hilda is supposed to play, but fortunately we
know of her chiefly that she is fresh, healthy, cheerful, and
plebeian. She may be a ray of sunshine but she is never a pure

spirit; even what we must presume to have been her virginity
is not insisted upon. In short, these and other blondes are
Hawthorne's weakest characters, but never before this was
the type wholly absurd. Their existence in the earlier works
should suggest to us that Hilda is intended to be human;
but her absolute purity should have suggested to Hawthorne
her violation of what he had once believed, and still believed
with a part of his mind, to be a general law of humanity,
and hence her impossibility as a central character. A character exempt from sin can have at best only an allegorical
relevance in a novel on the meaning of sin.

4

The chief interest of *The Marble Faun* for the modern
reader probably derives from its intricate tissue of symbolism, a large part of it explicit. Like the letter in *The Scarlet
Letter*, the statue of the faun, though most prominent, is
least interesting. Though it is theoretically justifiable as a
basic structuring symbol, Hawthorne seems to modern taste
to make too much of it, to insist too much upon its symbolic
import. Yet his procedure is not wholly wasteful, for the
mythical half-human, half-animal creature who is intelligent
but has no soul suggests the major thematic concerns of the
romance.

The next most prominent symbol is of course the (possibly) furry ears of Donatello. Here most of us will feel,
as Hawthorne himself seems to have felt, there is even less
success. The symbol is too obvious; we do not need the ears
to see that Donatello is a modern faun. And there is even a
sense in which the ears are an obstacle rather than an unnecessary aid to this perception: for by making him literally
a faun, they not only effectively block the work of the imagination but render him unreal, since fauns, as we cannot cease
to know even in the novel, were mythic, not historic, crea-

tures. Of course we never discover whether he actually had furry ears or not. But if this is an example of Hawthorne's ambiguity device, surely it is one of the weakest.

When we move beyond the Faun of Praxiteles and the ears of Donatello, we find much that is interesting and valuable. Once again in the old way — and, except for the three chapters of the fragmentary *Dolliver Romance*, for the last time in his career — Hawthorne makes his setting work for him. Rome is civilization, an old, deep, decayed civilization — a civilization resting on the ruins of a civilization. It is both culture and corruption, paradoxically both superior and inferior to "nature." It is "the world" that the romanticists sometimes found too much with them and that St. Paul urged Christians not to be conformed to, and it is learning, beauty, and art. The Roman background enriches the theme.

More deftly handled, because less prolix, is the opposed symbol of nature. The chapters on Donatello's native country and on his relation to it in the past are I think among the best that Hawthorne ever wrote. Everything contributes to the effect of innocence and vitality. Foreshadowing the priest's cold clean country in *A Farewell to Arms* and the landscape of the fishing trip in *The Sun Also Rises*, Donatello's Appenine country suggests all the truth there is in primitivism without committing the novel to primitivism's errors. If Donatello, like Rima in *Green Mansions*, could communicate with the animals, the limitations of his simple existence are likewise apparent, even to him. And it is interesting to note that Hawthorne finally brings the primitivism of these episodes into line with Christian doctrine by having Donatello's innocent relation with nature destroyed by his sin.

The images of light and dark that Hawthorne has used here as elsewhere consistently and effectively are connected with the nature and civilization symbols. The ruins of an earlier civilization in Rome are buried in darkness both lit-

eral and figurative, the catacombs where the past is encountered are dark, Hilda tends a flame, the several towers in
the story are said to reach up into the light, and Kenyon
at the top of Donatello's tower is impressed by the shifting
patterns produced by the patches of sunlight and shadow
on the landscape below him. When Hawthorne carries the
imagery of light and dark, along with the implications it has
picked up, into his characterization, making redemptive
Hilda a blonde and sinful Miriam a brunette, we are apt to
feel more amused than impressed. But on the whole the use
of light and darkness in the romance is effective.

The other symbolic effects are highly uneven, ranging
from the clear but thinly allegorical to the suggestive and
the confused. Kenyon, for example, as a "head" symbol in
Hawthorne's usual contrast of head and heart, is clear
enough but, because of his inadequate development as a
character, quite lacking in power. Only once it seems to me
does he come alive as a person and at the same time function as a symbol of the reasoning mind, and that is when
he climbs Donatello's tower and looks off across a wide ex-
panse of mountain scenery. His enlarged physical perspec-
tive is easily translatable into an enriched understanding
of the mottled sun and shade of life. For the rest, we have
chiefly his own word for it that he is a "thinker" whose
thoughts have wandered "wild and free."

Hilda's and Donatello's towers are successful or not de-
pending on how closely we examine them. Superficially,
it would seem appropriate that the two originally innocent
characters should inhabit towers, thus living high above
the corruption of society. Hilda with her lamp and doves
and Donatello with his mountains and wild creatures are,
or once were, equally close to heaven, whether because of
faith or innocent naturalness. But when we ponder on this
curious equivalence of optimistic primitivism and Christian
orthodoxy, we enter a realm of confusion that is not les-

sened by the recollection that Miriam too lives in a tower.
What *she* is doing in one is difficult to decide. Presumably
her tower, the first one mentioned in the story, is not supposed to have the connotations acquired by the tower
image in the next chapter, "The Virgin's Shrine," which is
about Hilda's tower. But when we hold the whole story in
mind at once, the effect of the three towers is confusing.
We can measure the distance Hawthorne has traveled in
his few European years by his handling of these towers:
whatever defects we may find in the symbolism of the
Seven Gables and *Blithedale*, there is nothing like this.

The heart imagery is also uneven. The walk through the
catacombs is certainly one of the best scenes in the book,
and one of the reasons for its excellence is that here, for
once, the heart imagery is clear, powerful, and richly suggestive without being overemphasized. The catacombs are
perfectly adapted to symbolizing Hawthorne's normal conception of the heart: they are dark, underground, full of
secret passages and mysterious labyrinths. In them Miriam's
shadow, her link with the dreadful secret of her past, appears and is recognized by her, but not by the others. In
the darkness of the catacombs that which paradoxically is
hidden by the light of day becomes clear. Of all the heart
images in Hawthorne's work, this is one of the best.

But the others in the romance are not so good. Miriam's
shadowy room is a heart, the darkly sinful or stained heart.
Emphasizing what would be clear anyway, Hawthorne tells
us that it seems not to belong to the "actual world" but
rather to be a "type of a poet's haunted imagination." And
Hilda's room in her tower is her heart, pure, light, and
lofty. The sharpness of the distinction between the two
rooms, appropriate enough if the contrast between Hilda
and Miriam is to be very much emphasized, suggests why
Hilda cannot enter Miriam's room and is reluctant to allow
Miriam to enter hers: to do the first would be to enter the

sinful heart, to do the second would be to let sin enter the spotless heart, in either case risking contamination. If hearts can be thus neatly divided into sinful and sinless, no doubt these antiseptic precautions are reasonable enough.

There are other examples of confusion in the heart imagery, and some of them are even less excusable, though perhaps in another sense less disturbing to the reader. For if we read this work without remembering anything from the earlier works, the implications of the heart imagery in Hilda's and Miriam's rooms are clear, if not very intelligent; but the implications of the heart imagery connected with Donatello's tower, though they are less heavily underscored by Hawthorne, are confused from any point of view.

During his innocent youth, Donatello had enjoyed his old room at the top of his tower, close to heaven. But by the time of Kenyon's visit, Donatello's heart is no longer pure, so he is reluctant to enter the room: he feels he has no right there any more. So far, so good — or bad, since this reinforces the dichotomy of good hearts and evil hearts already set up. But what are we to make of Kenyon's climb up the tower and his experience on the battlements? Are we to suppose that he is in some way appropriating to himself the former innocence of the Monte Benis, climbing back toward heaven by returning to nature in some fashion? If so, we must suppose it possible for reason to undo itself, for Kenyon is a head symbol, and it was by the awakening of reason and conscience that Donatello fell from virtue. Are we to suppose that the "regenerative power" of nature is so great that it can work even on a purely rational man like Kenyon? Hawthorne had not been in the habit of presenting nature as regenerative. He could never, we would have said, have written a story like "The Luck of Roaring Camp," in which nature, in the form favored by nineteenth-century melodramas, a baby, works a miraculous regeneration of a whole community of corrupt miners, changing them almost over-

night from villains to heroes. (The question of how they
got to be villains, since they live far from civilization and
since the nature they are so close to is supposed to be regenerative, must not be raised.) The whole body of Hawthorne's
work and the whole weight of his opinions expressed outside
his fiction from 1825 to 1850 had run counter to the sentimental primitivism so common in his age. Was he at the
end of his career at last "catching up" with a notion he had
rejected thirty years before?

Again, what are we to make of some other aspects of the
tower? When Kenyon finally persuades Donatello to guide
him up to the top, the following conversation ensues:

> "Come, then," said the Count, adding, with a sigh, "it has a weary
> staircase, and dismal chambers, and it is very lonesome at the summit!"
> "Like a man's life, when he has climbed to eminence," remarked
> the sculptor; "or, let us rather say, with its difficult steps, and the
> dark prison-cells you speak of, your tower resembles the spiritual
> experience of many a sinful soul, which, nevertheless, may struggle
> upward into the pure air and light of Heaven at last!"

How seriously are we to take Kenyon's analogies? A tower
with prison cells at its base and with long flights of steps
which must be laboriously climbed is not the sort of tower
in which Donatello in his innocent days, before he had experienced sin, should have had his room at the top. He may,
let us grant for the moment, have been perfectly innocent
in his youth, close to nature and so close to heaven; but he
cannot be conceived on any set of assumptions as having
achieved this position. If we take Kenyon's similes seriously,
then this tower is surely not symbolic of the situation of the
Monte Benis, who had never undergone "the spiritual experience of many a sinful soul." In his better work, Hawthorne had not been in the habit of throwing in figures of
speech which could not be taken seriously. Even if we decide
that Kenyon's fancies should be passed over lightly, the
tower will still not do. We do not need to take Kenyon's

word for its design, and its design is all wrong for the context. We can hardly say that Donatello's living at the top, above the dark prison cells, means only that in his innocence he has been above the corruption of the world; for he would have had to climb up and down daily, passing through or beside the prison cells. And once down from his lofty perch he could never have returned, for, as Hawthorne has insisted, he was not fitted for laborious spiritual struggle. Of if he had attempted to return, the prison cells and the staircase would have given him an introduction to evil which should have prepared him for his acquaintance with Miriam. If it is supposed that it is quibbling to take the symbols in this way and consider them in such detail, I can only say that in the earlier works it is usually possible to do just this, and that, it seems to me, is one of the reasons why the earlier works are better.

5

In plot too, as well as in characters and explicit symbolism, Hawthorne faltered. And he faltered at precisely that point where, if we remember "Alice Doane's Appeal," we should expect him to falter, in dealing with the question of the responsibility for the sin that precipitates Donatello's fall.

Yvor Winters has written with penetration on Hawthorne's relation to his Puritan background, emphasizing what he sees as a contradiction equally present in the Puritans and in Hawthorne, between the denial of the reality of choice in predestinarian theory and the magnification of that same power of choice in practical Puritan moralism. Thus the Puritan preachers told their congregations that good works were wholly inefficacious,* that whether they were elect or

* Or even, when performed by any but the elect, sinful. See for example Article 13 of the Anglican Thirty-nine Articles, in which good works performed outside Grace are said to partake of "the nature of sin." This and certain other articles were intended to keep the Puritan party within the English church.

damned had been determined at the beginning of the world, and that they could not of their own will repent and be saved. Yet simultaneously they urged them to repentance, condemned them for their wickedness, and created a way of life that has become synonymous with legalistic moralism. Franklin's early tract, "The Doctrine of Liberty and Necessity, Pleasure and Pain," which he came later to regret as indiscreet, had exposed some of the implications in this system, and Mr. Winters' extension of Franklin's analysis seems to me essentially sound.

But as we have already seen, Hawthorne was not, in his usual point of view, so close to Puritan thought as Mr. Winters would make out. "Rappaccini's Daughter," for instance, is closer to Catholic (not necessarily just Roman Catholic) doctrine than to Puritan Calvinism. Though Hawthorne often wavered between his feeling of fate and his tentative belief in freedom, he wrote not a single story which must be interpreted as clearly predestinarian in its point of view. ("Alice Doane's Appeal" is a piece of uncriticized self-revelation, not a story in the usual sense.) If there is lack of clarity in many of the works on this matter, it may be a positive advantage: it avoids the doctrinaire solution and simply presents the paradox, which is after all one that no philosopher or theologian in any age has ever resolved without suppressing some of the facts.

But the allegory of *The Marble Faun* is concerned, as we have seen, with the largest, the most abstract generalizations about the meaning of the experience of sin. When such questions are addressed directly, it is not sufficient to rest on the sensed paradox, the psychological antinomy. And Hawthorne has not done so. He resolves the conflict as he had in "Alice Doane's Appeal" at the beginning of his career, with a denial of freedom. But there is another element here that reminds us more of the Puritans than of "Alice Doane's Appeal": for while he implies a denial of freedom he empha-

sizes at the same time the significance of moral acts. Donatello "sins" with little, if any, conscious intention, and Hilda
is good without ever having been tempted by evil. The world
is neatly divided, as the Puritans divided it, into the elect
and the damned, and the division was an act of God before
man existed, bearing no relation to man's life. It is not surprising that despite its concentration on the problem of the
meaning of evil, *The Marble Faun* has considerably less
moral significance than any of Hawthorne's finished romances.

The point I am making here involves the distinction sometimes made between sin and guilt. Though the terminology
will seem archaic to some, the distinction is real, as the distinction between murder and manslaughter or between manslaughter and justifiable homicide is real. The imputation of
moral guilt involves intention, which cannot be determined
behavioristically, and it assumes some degree of freedom
of choice, which can never be proved logically or empiri-
cally but which must be assumed if the moral dimension of
experience is not to be declared nonsense. When theologians
use the word "sin" to mean what Hawthorne usually called
guilt, they define it as "evil will," not as evil action.*

Now this is another way of saying that the problem of sin
may be only abstract and theological, while the problem of
guilt is always moral. In his earlier work Hawthorne had
been concerned with guilt, and only indirectly and by impli-

* For example, Claude Beaufort Moss, in his semi-official statement of
Anglican orthodoxy, *The Christian Faith: An Introduction to Dogmatic
Theology* (*SPCK*, 1943, p. 137), writes: "Nothing is evil, or can be evil,
but a personal will disobeying God. The will is not material: no material
thing can be evil." Compare, for representative medieval and modern, and
Catholic and Protestant expressions of the same point of view, St. Thomas
Aquinas and Reinhold Niebuhr. Augustinian-Calvinistic emphasis on the
body as the source of evil will did not exclude, though it sometimes mini-
mized or obscured, the significance of *choice* of evil on man's part. Even
the American Puritans with their crude and somewhat distorted version of
Calvinism asserted this with one breath while denying it with another.

cation with the problem of sin. Was Reuben Bourne guilty
in "Roger Malvin's Burial," and if so, of what? Who was
more guilty, Dimmesdale or Chillingworth? These are relevant questions to ask about "Roger Malvin's Burial" and *The
Scarlet Letter*. If no questions like them can be framed for
The Marble Faun, or if, when they are asked, they seem not
entirely relevant, then it should be clear that this is not a
moral romance in the sense in which that phrase can be
applied to most of the tales and to the other three romances.
Hawthorne is here moving away from what had been the
center of his writng. We may call *The Marble Faun* a philosophical allegory with a good deal more appropriateness
than we can apply the term to *The Scarlet Letter*.

An examination of the way Hawthorne has treated Donatello and Hilda and managed the crucial "original sin" will
tend to support these general considerations. I have said that
it is not clear that Donatello *chose* evil. That this is so becomes apparent if we remember two things: first, the great
emphasis Hawthorne has laid on the modern faun's innocence. He is so childlike that the other characters treat him
as an amiable boy, almost as a household pet. They recognize, that is, that they cannot attribute to him even that
limited responsibility for his actions that the common sense
of mankind attributes to sane adults under normal circumstances. He is a throwback, symbolically, to the mythical
childhood of the race. We do not hold children, the insane,
or animals responsible legally or morally for a very good
reason: we do not suppose that they know enough, or are
free enough, to choose. And to the extent that we decide
that foreknowledge and freedom are not attributable to
them, we refrain from attributing guilt. As a "child," Donatello must be judged "not guilty" of the murder of Miriam's
shadow.

And Hawthorne manages the event in such a way as to
emphasize this very point. Childlike Donatello loved Miriam

as a child may love a parent, with unreserved devotion, complete trust, blindly. When he saw her in apparent danger from her persecutor, he acted instinctively, as a child or a faithful dog would act. And what he did was done at least with Miriam's implicit consent, perhaps even at her command.

Though the evidence on this point is not wholly decisive, yet it is impressive. When, in "The Faun's Transformation," Donatello tells Miriam "I did what your eyes bade me do, when I asked them with mine, as I held the wretch over the precipice," Hawthorne tells us that the words "struck Miriam like a bullet." She could only reply by repeating, "And my eyes bade you do it." Falling back here on his ambiguity device, Hawthorne still has not avoided the implication that the guilt is not Donatello's but Miriam's, or at any rate not so much Donatello's as Miriam's. But if the romance concerns the fall of man, this would mean that Adam's "original sin" did not involve any *guilt*; or, to translate the Eden myth into other terms, that sin is foreordained, so that individuals are not responsible for it. This is a view which it is possible, theologically, to explore and even to hold; doctrines of the Fortunate Fall, with which it is connected, have suggested themselves in several periods to many besides Milton. But it would seem not to be a view well adapted to serving as a basis of the type of moral romance Hawthorne had done his greatest work in.

Again, if it is doubtful whether Donatello can be blamed for his actions, it is clear that Hilda cannot be praised for hers. Both characters are morally neutral; they do not exist in the moral dimension. Since a significant, perhaps the central, aspect of the humanity of human beings is the fact that they are moral beings, capable of incurring guilt, a character of perfect innocence like Hilda, absolutely immune to stain, cannot seem real to us. Hilda becomes somewhat real only in the last part of the work, after she has been touched, de-

spite her efforts, by mankind's fate. Up to this point, as she
has had no temptation, she has had neither reality nor virtue.

The predestinarian tendencies of *The Marble Faun,* I
think we must decide, make it impossible to find any value
in it as an exploration of the nature of moral action. There
is left the possibility that it has value as an allegory on that
most difficult of questions, the origin and meaning of evil.

6

Hilda, we recall, rejected Kenyon's theory of man's decline
from Arcadia as too pessimistic. Hawthorne calls her at this
point, "hopeful and happy-natured," thus attributing to her
traits which he himself conspicuously lacked; so that here
as elsewhere we see that through Hilda Hawthorne is indulg-
ing in self-criticism. When Kenyon, "remembering what
Hilda had recently suggested," proposed his alternative
theory, offering Hilda her choice between the two, she rejected the alternative even more forcibly than the original.
"Do not you perceive," she asked, after expressing her
"horror" so strongly as to wound "the poor, speculative
sculptor to the soul,"

"what a mockery your creed makes, not only of all religious sentiments, but of moral law? and how it annuls and obliterates whatever
precepts of Heaven are written deepest within us? You have shocked
me beyond words!"

"Forgive me, Hilda!" exclaimed the sculptor, startled by her agita-
tion; "I never did believe it! But the mind wanders wild and wide;
and, so lonely as I live and work, I have neither polestar above, nor
light of Cottage-windows here below, to bring me home . . . Oh,
Hilda, guide me home!"

The dangers Hilda perceived in the notion of the Fortunate Fall were real enough from Hawthorne's point of view.
Though the idea has a long history, going back indeed to the
later patristic period and finding expression in the Roman

Missal in a hymn for Easter Evening ("O felix culpa"), though it may also be found in such later writers as Du Bartas and Milton, yet it does have some curious consequences. Seemingly harmless enough as an expression of a desire to magnify God's greatness by showing how He in His omnipotence and mercy turns evil into final good, it nevertheless greatly sharpens the existing paradox of God's foreknowledge and omnipotence and man's responsibility.

The resulting antinomy has led some minds into what used to be called Antinomianism, which suggests that sin is only apparent. The elect either cannot sin at all, or if they sin, can incur no personal guilt. (Sin is either nonexistent and so impossible, or only an appearance and really good as well as necessary.) Adam's sin, so the argument runs, was the necessary means to man's final salvation, for if he had not sinned, Christ would not have needed to come and we would not know our present hope of glory. Just so, the reasoning was sometimes continued, each one of the elect repeats Adam's history, "sinning" for the greater glory of God and his own salvation. However one takes it, then, it is at least clear that sin is only good in disguise. In the rather secularized version of the idea presented in *The Marble Faun*, it is a necessary part of our education, a stepping stone to higher things. It is of course an apparently logical deduction from this that man should welcome and perhaps positively seek sin in order to coöperate with Providence.

There is every reason to believe that such a line of reasoning seemed to Hawthorne, as it did to Hilda, to make a "mockery" of religious doctrine and moral law. It does quite literally "obliterate" conscience. Though it has often occurred to believers, it has never been accepted as official doctrine by any branch of the Church, and for obvious reasons. It is easy to see how it occurred to thoughtful minds contemplating Genesis and Pauline theology and desiring to express their sense of the glory of God, but it is clear that it either has no moral meaning at all or the wrong meaning, if taken literally and extended. Hilda's rejection of it is a sign of her orthodoxy. It suggests that, however far from his earlier faith speculation had carried Hawthorne during his last years, he had not yet lost his instinct for the central meaning of Christianity.

But Hawthorne had to reject the notion for another reason too, though he may not have been conscious of it. The implications of the idea were all wrong for the work of his lifetime. The earliest affinities of the idea are with the Gnostic heresies: Adam's eating the fruit of the tree was really a good thing, because knowledge is always good. Its later affinities are with modern naturalism: sin is only error, or sickness, or the result of being "underpriviliged," or a lack of knowledge, to be cured by more knowledge. Both the Gnostic and the naturalistic implications make sin unimportant because only apparent or symptomatic, or because it is easily cured by education or social change. But if sin and guilt are unimportant, then the great bulk of Hawthorne's writing must really be, as one modern naturalist has said, concerned with a "trivial" subject.

If the idea of the Fortunate Fall, with all its implications, were accepted, then Hawthorne had misapplied his whole creative energy. If there is really no moral problem and guilt cannot be incurred, then there is literally no sense to most of what he had written. Chillingworth and Ethan Brand and Rappaccini should have been applauded and encouraged, and neither Hester nor the Puritans sinned at all, so that *The Scarlet Letter* is really concerned with an illusion, or, at very best, makes a mountain out of a molehill.

The *achieved* content of *The Marble Faun*, then, contains a meaning that was very ominous for any future career as a novelist that Hawthorne may have hoped for. In so far as the idea of the Fortunate Fall has implications that correspond with some of the currents of nineteenth-century naturalistic thought, we may say that he had at last nearly "caught up" with the advanced thought of his age. The result was that he had to choose now between giving up writing and becoming an entirely different sort of writer. When he got back to Concord he tried to avoid the dilemma by doing neither, by going on writing in the old way. But the inner meaning was gone. The result was the mechanical repetition of devices that had ceased to be functional, of symbols that no longer symbolized anything, of plots ever more intricate to hide the fact that they were meaningless. The result was the late romances.

Meanwhile he could rely on Hilda to protect him from the dangers of modern antinomianism — or he hoped he could. But Hilda was a weak reed. What he had said effectively in *The Marble Faun* he had said through Miriam and, to a lesser degree, through Kenyon. The passage in the book which, apart from the scene in the catacombs, sounds most like the old Hawthorne of the great tales and romances is the discussion of Guido's Archangel. Significantly, the words that express the point of view that we have come to know as Hawthorne's most permanent and central opinion are given to Miriam. The sculptor, she says, has made the archangel conquer evil too easily: his feathers should have got ruffled in the struggle.

One of the troubles with the idea of the Fortunate Fall is that it too disposes of evil too easily. It is symptomatic of the confusion in the novel that Miriam, who first puts forth the doctrine, is also the one who in the comment on the archangel speaks for the part of Hawthorne's mind that still had a strong intuitive grasp of the unarguable reality of evil and guilt. But the intuition was useless without its rationale, and the rationale it had once had, now seemed only doubtfully available. There is a deep personal pathos in the cry that Hawthorne assigns to Kenyon, "Oh, Hilda, guide me home!"

For we must suppose that Kenyon, whose mind has wandered "wild and wide" in free speculation, will scarcely be content for long in the narrow confines of Hilda's thoughtless orthodoxy. Hawthorne's letters and other personal records show that Kenyon was expressing a feeling very familiar to his creator when he said that "the years . . . have a kind of emptiness, when we spend too many of them on a foreign shore." But Hawthorne did not find in Concord that "home" for which the longing had become acute. He found the emptiness there too — and in Washington, Boston, Philadelphia, and Plymouth, New Hampshire. That emptiness is preserved for us in the late unfinished romances.

CHAPTER NINE

THE LATE ROMANCES

In the last five years of his life Hawthorne tried to write one more romance to bring his career to a fitting close. He had lived long with a premonition of early death, and now, with an increasing sense of urgency, he wanted both to make money to provide for his family after he was gone, and to say some things that he felt he had never yet succeeded in getting said.

He failed in both these aims. He failed miserably, desperately, shockingly. Against a growing certainty of failure he forced himself to write on and on, to discard what he had done and start afresh, writing in torment and desperation of spirit, concealing from his family how much he was writing that they might not realize how completely he was failing. In five years he accumulated some twenty-two "studies" for four romances which he left unfinished at his death: twenty-two studies, four fragmentary romances, one of which exists in two different versions — and except for the three chapters of The Dolliver Romance and a few scenes in Septimius Felton, nothing with the power and authority of the earlier work, almost nothing indeed that was not positively bad, and that he did not, with his still acute self-criticism, recognize as bad. His own comments in the margins of his

manuscripts tell the story: "Here I come to a standstill! . . .
I have not the least notion how to get on. I never was in
such a predicament before. . . There must be a germ in
this — I don't know. . . How? Why? What sense?"

All the evidence of the failure is now open for inspection.*
Only the causes of it still are hidden. We can *see* the chaos,
follow the fumbling and the false starts, watch the old tricks
being used without effect, without meaning. We can watch
Hawthorne parodying himself, recognizing the parody, stop-
ping, discarding what he had done, starting again, only to
fall into the same traps. We can watch him returning to the
apprenticeship of *Fanshawe* all over again, as though he had
never written the great tales and *The Scarlet Letter*. We can
watch him struggling against ill health and inner desolation,
forcing himself by sheer acts of will to go on when he had
no hope. The drama that we may watch in Hawthorne's last
period is as strangely and movingly tragic as anything in the
life of any writer; tragic, not merely pathetic, for Hawthorne
as actor in his own drama had been a great writer and now
he could write nothing, or almost nothing, of any worth.

What had happened to his talent?

2

In all the complicated, seemingly chaotic confusion of
Hawthorne's last five years of writing only one element of
clarity is apparent. The twenty-two studies and four fragmentary romances treat just two themes. Hawthorne's English experiences had suggested to him the subject of the
American claimant to an English estate. He first tried to
treat the subject in *The Ancestral Footstep*, which he was
planning as early as 1855 and which he actually began in
1858; then he tried all over again in *Dr. Grimshawe's Secret*,

* See E. H. Davidson, *Hawthorne's Last Phase* (New Haven: Yale University Press, 1949).

which he worked on in 1860 and 1861. When this subject failed him, his own situation, which brought again into the foreground a lifelong interest, suggested to him the subject of the elixir of life, the subject both of *Septimius Felton*, which he worked on from 1861 to 1863, and of *The Dolliver Romance*, with which he was occupied in the last months before his death in March 1864. Though he tried, especially in *The Ancestral Footstep* and *Dr. Grimshawe's Secret*, to work in material from his English Notebooks on the differences between English and American cultures, as he had used his Italian Notebooks in *The Marble Faun*, and though he had some hope of capitalizing on the timely subject of civil war in *Septimius Felton* — for the Revolution he felt was also a civil war — yet the claimant and the elixir are the organizing centers of all his last efforts at fiction. And they were at once inevitable and impossible: inevitable because all his career had pointed to them, impossible because now that he tried to treat them directly in major works he no longer had any means of dealing with them.

Superficially, the subject of the first two of Hawthorne's unfinished romances was new to him and seems to suggest that he was trying once again to treat "present actuality," to use directly the English experiences just behind him. But a second look is enough to suggest that this lost English inheritance situation is more than a result of the English years and more than a stock device of the popular romance: it is the old Eden-Arcadia theme in a new, timely guise. For both the American claimant and man exiled from Eden or Arcadia share the memory of a lost birthright, the memory, conscious or buried, of a nobler condition. In both themes, man is sadly fallen from his former condition, whether to his final good or ill not being quite clear.* Hawthorne had been haunted

* See, in *Hawthorne's Last Phase*, the various endings Hawthorne contemplated for the American heir in *The Ancestral Footstep* and *Dr. Grimshawe's Secret*; compare the theme of *The Marble Faun*.

all his life by a memory of a lost innocence. That memory lies behind and beneath the Gothic claptrap of *The Ancestral Footstep* and *Dr. Grimshawe's Secret.*

In his youth Hawthorne had thought a good deal about the fallen and shrunken estate of his family, exaggerating in his fancies no doubt their former affluence and social position as he contemplated his own poverty and obscurity and the necessity of accepting help from his uncles. At the beginning of his writing career he had given compulsive expression to some of the deeper layers of these fantasies of a lost estate in "Alice Doane's Appeal." In the great tales written between 1830 and 1850 he had returned to the theme often, peripherally and indirectly, as in "My Kinsman, Major Molineux" and "Roger Malvin's Burial," through symbolic reference and allusion in "Rappaccini's Daughter," or directly, as in "The New Adam and Eve." Of the four novels, only *The Scarlet Letter* does not have the theme in a prominent position. Eden imagery is a controlling factor in the *Seven Gables* and *Blithedale*, and the fall of man is the explicit theme of *The Marble Faun*. The return of an American heir to claim his ancestral estate is, in short, only a variation on a theme that had often appeared in Hawthorne's works because it expressed an interest that lay close to the center of his deeper mind.

And now, as he approached the end of his life, with what seems to have been full consciousness of the fact, the idea came to the surface and refused to be dismissed, even when it was clear that he was not succeeding in doing anything with it. He had gone to England with a recurrent sense of "returning home": "My ancestor left England in 1630. I return in 1853." He had tried to look up the records of the family but he had found out little that he had not already known. Long ago he had identified himself in his imagination with an English relative when he had written stories of Jervase Helwyse and Gervayse Hastings, for there had been a Gervase Elwes, a baronet, in the family; the thread connecting the Jervase Helwyse of "Lady Eleanor's Mantle" and the Gervayse Hastings of "The Christmas Banquet" with Hawthorne's genealogical interests in England is unbroken.* Now he entitled his book about his English experiences *Our Old Home*, and he was quite sure in the end that the Wayside in Concord was not and never would be the home he sought. Once, after visiting the English village of Eastham, he had written in his journal, "Eastham is the finest old English village I have seen, with many antique houses, and with altogether a rural and picturesque aspect, unlike anything in America, and yet possessing a familiar look, as if it were something I had dreamed about." Now he tried to write romances about Americans returning to claim estates they had never seen but knew instinctively. Hawthorne anticipated in some degree the symbolic careers of James and Eliot.

The other theme too, the elixir of life, or earthly immortality, was also inevitable, and not only because Hawthorne knew he was dying. Septimius Felton's search for power and happiness in an unending future is but the reverse of the search for the lost birthright. Eden and Immortality are two sides of the same preoccupation. There is a sense in which we may say that Hawthorne's failure with *The Ancestral Footstep* and *Dr. Grimshawe's Secret* required that he reverse the coin and search the future for what could not be found in the past.

Hawthorne had always written of life with one eye on death. Fanshawe, his earliest clearly recognizable projection of himself in fiction, had been doomed to die young. "Alice Doane's Appeal" and "The Hollow of the Three Hills," probably his earliest surviving tales, have death at their center. And from these youthful pieces down to *The Marble Faun*, death, in one of its several disguises if not directly, occupies

* See the *English Notebooks* for 1854.

the center of the scene. Just as Hawthorne's negative or evil characters are more vividly created than his good ones — Judge Pyncheon more so than Phoebe, Zenobia than Priscilla, Miriam than Hilda — so it might also be said that in nearly all of his works death tends to be *felt*, life only surmised, hoped for, or postulated. Judge Pyncheon's death is vivid and powerful; Phoebe's life and love pale, relatively unconvincing. The death of Zenobia in *Blithedale* is the strongest scene in the book.

And now that his own death appeared to Hawthorne very close, the theme of the elixir of life which he had long ago treated in "Dr. Heidegger's Experiment" appealed to him with a new urgency. Over and over he wrote on pieces of paper the number 64, which he had long since connected with "some destiny." "God himself," he had written in his English Notebooks in 1855, "cannot compensate us for being born for any period short of eternity." Now he made Septimius Felton reply to his friend's question as to whether their countrymen were "worthy" to live: " 'It is hardly worth answering or considering,' said Septimius, looking at him thoughtfully. 'We live so little while, that (always setting aside the effect on a future existence) it is little matter whether we live or no.' "

Mark Van Doren has commented very justly on Hawthorne's self-portraiture in the figure of Dr. Dolliver. But it should be added that an aspect — and, on the whole, a very important aspect — of Hawthorne is portrayed likewise in Septimius Felton, that morbid scholar-recluse who is first cousin to Fanshawe but who is not willing, like Fanshawe, to accept his doom. When Hawthorne deplored his well-loved Dr. Johnson's "morbid" dread of death, he was speaking from the top of his mind and protesting too much. His own frequent protestations of faith in immortality cannot be taken wholly at face value: he was more like Dr. Johnson than he cared to admit even to himself. As, in an increasing "intensity of desolation," he made himself write on and on, the subject of the elixir of life forced itself on him as naturally as the subject of the American heir had, until he had found beyond all possibility of doubt that he could do nothing with it. It seemed that he could do nothing with this, either.

3

Many reasons have been suggested for Hawthorne's final failure, some of them based on bad logic, others obviously superficial, all of them finally inadequate. Among those that are worthy of comment, the one that seems, at first thought, most cogent is failing health. But there are several reasons why this is not sufficient to account for what happened. In the first place, Hawthorne's health did not begin to fail until about 1861 or even later, while his artistic failure is obvious in all the work he did on *The Ancestral Footstep*, begun in 1858, and in *Dr. Grimshawe's Secret*, 1860–61, and is foreshadowed, as we have seen, in *Blithedale* and *The Marble Faun*. This consideration alone would be conclusive, but we may add to it a second: the kind of failure we find in the late romances is not such as simple physical illness could easily account for. It is, rather, a failure at the center, a failure at the very point where Hawthorne's creative greatness had lain, a failure of meaning and values. Something deeper than physical pain or lack of energy would be needed, one suspects, to produce this kind of failure.

The same line of reasoning is sufficient to show that it was not the Civil War that made Hawthorne unable to write as he once had. The war may have been for him, as Mark Van Doren has said, "pure disaster," though I suspect that this is overstating its effect. But the war did not break out until after he had stopped working on the two most completely bad of the last romances, *The Ancestral Footstep* and *Dr. Grimshawe's Secret*. And while it was in progress, at the very end of his life, he wrote the only thing in this whole period that has any sustained value, the fragments of *The Dolliver Romance*. The war, then, will surely not do as the reason for his failure.

Slightly more plausible perhaps on the face of it is financial worry. It is true that Hawthorne had not succeeded, for various reasons, including both bad luck and bad judgment, in building up sufficient savings from his consular income to make his family secure. But he had known, earlier in his life, that security is not possible in the world; and during a period of real financial distress he had written some of the greatest tales and sketches and *The Scarlet Letter*.

An explanation of about the same degree of plausibility is offered by the "twilight of romance" theory: that by the end of Hawthorne's career the rise of the realistic mode in fiction had rendered his type of writing obsolete, and that his realization of this confused and frustrated him. It is true that Hawthorne began his career rather late in the Romantic movement and that by the final years of his life the new realistic fashion was already under way in Europe and faintly stirring in America. It is likewise true that Hawthorne admired the work of the English Victorian novelists and sometimes regretted that he could not write like Trollope. But it is also, and more significantly, true that this was not a new development at the very end of his career. If his genius had been nourished on Scott, it had been nourished just as obviously on Bunyan, who can hardly be called a "romantic." Hawthorne's favorite writers at all periods in his life were "old time" authors, not, with the exception of Scott, men of his own century — Dante, Cervantes, Spenser, Shakespeare, Bunyan, Milton, Johnson. If he was "old fashioned" at the end of his career, he was not very much less so in the middle of it, when he was doing his best things. The "twilight of romance" had in fact already set in before even *The Scarlet Letter* was written, so it can scarcely be used to explain the total failure of almost everything written after *The Marble Faun*. It is, no doubt, one of the reasons for Hawthorne's increasing uncertainty in his last ten years, but it must not be used to explain too much.

There are, I think, two approaches to this problem which offer more reward. I mean the psychological and the theological or philosophic. The two are interrelated, but for convenience I shall treat them separately. In making the psychological approach I must beg to be excused from attempting any definite analysis. Psychology is a highly specialized study, and I am not a psychologist. But a few facts are clear, and one or two inferences from them seem inevitable.

Some psychological factor as yet unidentified by any of Hawthorne's biographers, presumably the Oedipus situation that Freud considered universal at some stage in male development, was apparently at work during all of Hawthorne's adult life to produce his lifelong restlessness, unease, and sense of guilt and estrangement. This is not to say that there were no objective bases for these feelings: simple moral realism and self-knowledge should be sufficient to produce a sense of sin, and only the insensitive are likely to be wholly contented. But no reader of Hawthorne's letters and journals can escape, it seems to me, the feeling that the cause of the discontent and dissatisfaction that amounted to spiritual malaise lay far deeper than the causes constantly suggested by Hawthorne himself and by his family — causes like the size and shape of the houses in which they lived, the neighbors, the climate, the need to work at uncongenial tasks.

Much of the time after 1850 Hawthorne found all tasks uncongenial, even writing. He frequently protested that he could not write in the winter because of the cold. In England his consular duties were extremely light, almost nominal, yet he got no creative work done. Even in the comparatively onerous position in the Salem Custom House he worked at earning a living only a part of each day, yet could do nothing on his writing during the rest.

There was, to be sure, a period when Hawthorne seems to have been relatively at peace: the first two or three years after his marriage. But though his was an ideally "happy marriage," the fact that Hawthorne was not happy during twenty or so of the twenty-two years it lasted seems to me undeniable. His restlessness, his dis-ease shines out through the very attempts of his wife and son to deny it. In the last ten years of his life the dissatisfaction in his letters amounts at times to petulance and at times to hopelessness. A very deep-seated ambivalence of feeling becomes apparent. Everything is Janus-faced, nothing is clear, nothing gives any real satisfaction. As he had hated Salem, yet been unable to turn from it and all that it stood for in his mind, so later in England he both longed for and dreaded his return to America, longing and dreading not mildly, superficially, with the surface of his mind as moods and circumstances changed, as might be natural, but deeply, agonizingly. He longed also for a real home, and one of the most moving passages in the English Notebooks recounts his longing:

The house is respectably, though not very elegantly, furnished. It was a dismal, rainy day yesterday, and we had a coal-fire in the sitting-room, beside which I sat last evening as twilight came on, and thought, rather sadly, how many times we have changed our home since we were married. In the first place, our three years at the Old Manse; then a brief residence at Salem, then at Boston, then two or three years at Salem again; then at Lenox, then at West Newton, and then again at Concord, where we imagined that we were fixed for life, but spent only four years, and afterwards another year or two in Italy, during all which time we shall have no real home. For, as I sat in this English house, with the chill, rainy English twilight brooding over the lawn, and a coal-fire to keep me comfortable on the first evening of September, and the picture of a stranger — the dead husband of Mrs. Campbell — gazing down at me from above the mantel-piece, — I felt that I never should be quite at home here. Nevertheless, the fire was very comfortable to look at, and the shape of the fireplace — an arch, with a deep cavity — was an improvement on the square, shallow opening of an American coal-grate.

Yet the reason he was never able to establish a permanent home was inward, not outward. When circumstances, including the result of a former decision, forced him to live longer in the Wayside than he had ever lived in any house since his marriage, he protested vehemently that the place was a "prison" from which he would never escape. A good deal of the time he hated everything about it, as he had hated Salem and Rome and even, at the end of his stay there, the Old Manse.

The evidences of this dis-ease of his became more pronounced in the last decade, especially in the last five years — and several years before there were any visible symptoms either of his sudden "aging" — if that is really what it was — or of his final unidentified physical illness. The temper and tone of his English and Italian letters and journals provide the hint of the failure in the writings to come that is not provided by conditions of physical health, or money matters, or politics, including war. The secret that cannot be communicated, that estranges one even from those one loves and that takes the *life* out of everything, had provided the substance of many great tales and the principal theme of his greatest romance. When it ceased to be projected into stories it did not cease to exist. There seems to me to have been a strong resurgence of guilt feelings and of hopelessness in Hawthorne's life in the final decade, and particularly in the last American years. The mystery of the late cramped handwriting, so suddenly changed, the greatly increased manifest isolation, even in the midst of a loving family, the altered tone of the letters, all suggest that the memory of lost innocence and the sense of death have become almost obsessive.

If this is so, it means among other things that Hawthorne

and Melville were more alike in their experiences than they knew or we have realized. It is interesting, and perhaps instructive, to set up a parallel between Melville's *Typee* and Hawthorne's "Alice Doane's Appeal"; and between *Pierre*, with its evidences of breakdown of control, and *Blithedale*, with its much less evident signs of trouble to come; and between *Billy Budd* and *The Dolliver Romance*, each of which suggests a new control and peace coming just before the end. Such a parallel is useful only in so far as it suggests similarities in the psychological histories of the two great writers. It could be highly misleading if misapplied. What it suggests is the possibility that Hawthorne's personality was not so much unlike Melville's as his greater self-control and the different circumstances of his life would seem to indicate. And if that is so, then a psychological explanation of the failure of the last romances is as appropriate as is Professor Henry A. Murray's psychological analysis of the failure of Melville's *Pierre*.

We may attempt, then, to find the reason for the failure of the late romances by studying Hawthorne's life, or we may look at his work, and especially at the fragments themselves, and see what we find there. The essence of what we find may be expressed in two ways, but the two come finally to the same thing. We find a loss of meaning, or a failure of belief. The two come to the same thing because once a highly conscious mind like Hawthorne's has lost its moorings in its most generalized beliefs, then particular events and objects lose their discrete meanings; and because, conversely, if particulars are not numinous with meanings, then generalized meanings cannot be formed from them, to complete and organize them.

The most striking difference between Hawthorne's work before the late romances and the first three of the late romances themselves is that the best of the early work is either directly or indirectly moral, while the late romances are not. Even when the early tales are explicitly historical, like "The Maypole of Merrymount" and "The Gray Champion," with a very few exceptions, the most obvious of which is "Alice Doane's Appeal," they have moral overtones, are informed with moral meaning, are written from within a coherent moral tradition, which the tale assumes and which may be deduced from the tale. The novels likewise, and most obviously, are "moral romances." But *The Ancestral Footstep, Dr. Grimshawe's Secret,* and *Septimius Felton* are not, except sporadically and peripherally, moral at all; and the fragments of *The Dolliver Romance* are too incomplete for us to tell what that would have become, though what was written is in the old vein.

The late romances are not moral, they are Gothic, as *Fanshawe* and "Alice Doane's Appeal" are Gothic. They are personal, as those early works were. They are conventional, as those were. They are at the same time far more conventional and far more personal than *The Scarlet Letter* or *The House of the Seven Gables,* personal in their lack of distance from Hawthorne's private anguish, conventional in plot and incident and device. They are at once "expressionistic" and stereotyped; which is only to say that they fail completely as art. But they are not significant in moral terms. Their failure of meaning — again except in *Dolliver* — is everywhere so apparent that I shall give only two examples. In both *The Ancestral Footstep* and *Dr. Grimshawe's Secret* Hawthorne tried to use the "bloody footprint" legend he had picked up and recorded in his Notebooks in England. His past works are full of such Gothic "wonders" — men with glowing eyes, scarlet letters on the chest or in the sky, branches of trees that die when a handkerchief is tied around them, beautiful flowers that are deadly poison. But now he could see no meaning in his wonders, and that made all the difference. The bloody footprint as used in the late romances has no moral overtones whatever; it remains what it was when Hawthorne found it, a meaningless marvel. It was never transmuted by his imagination.

Again, Hawthorne tried to use in all of the late romances except *Dolliver* his memory of — or notes on — the giant spiders he had seen in the British Museum, but again he could do nothing with them. Though they are presented as though they were symbolic, a close reading of the passages in which they occur makes it perfectly clear that they symbolize nothing whatever. Dr. Grimshawe, who worked in his study beneath an enormous and repulsive spider, is not an evil man (in so far as he is sufficiently created so that we can judge him at all) but merely crotchety and old and addicted to the bottle. The spider adds "atmosphere" but no meaning, and the "atmosphere" is finally useless. When we think of what Hawthorne had done with a cat and the hens in *The House of the Seven Gables,* or with a snake in "Egotism," or with a dog in "Ethan Brand," we see both the measure and the nature of his failure here. "What meaning?" Hawthorne asked himself repeatedly in his marginal notes on his manuscripts.

What meaning indeed! Hawthorne had not had to ask himself such a question when he was writing his great works. His grasp of an object and of its meaning had been simultaneous, and both "object" and "meaning" — to imply a separation that did not exist for him — had preceded the embodiment in a tissue of character and incident that made the tale out of a "moral idea." This had been Hawthorne's way of working, the only way he could work. Now he was searching out "marvels" and wondering desperately what meaning he could arbitrarily assign to them.

That this failure of his "particulars" to have meaning was in part a result of the loss or weakening of Hawthorne's most general — philosophic and religious — beliefs seems to me clear, though it cannot, of course, be "proved" conclusively enough to convince anyone who prefers to believe that the psychological factors alone are sufficient to account for the failure. One can only recall and weigh the significance of such matters as the implications of the imagery in *Blithedale* and of the general theme of *The Marble Faun* and the assigning of the function of guarding traditional values in that novel to Hilda (Sophia). Or one may assess the significance of the fact that Septimius Felton, the last of the long line of secretive scholar-recluses created by Hawthorne as partial self-portraits, is made a materialistic naturalist who has "too profound a sense of the marvelous contrivance and adaptation of this material world to require or believe in anything spiritual."

Or we may note the tone of Hawthorne's repeated assertions of belief in immortality, a tone which seems to me to run from the matter-of-fact, the tone in which one utters a conventional truism, in the early letters and journals, to that of a labored attempt to believe in the last years. Or one may note the words he used to describe Melville's discussion of problems of faith and immortality in 1856: "deserts . . . dismal . . . monotonous." A man who believes in immortality, as Hawthorne always said he did, does not find speculation on it "dismal." We do not, I think, need to choose between psychological and philosophic or religious explanations. The two are always interwoven and to some degree inseparable. All that I would protest against would be a completely mechanistic explanation that would leave conceptual matters, matters of belief, completely out of account.

Hawthorne's religion had always, it is true, been more emotional than logical; it had been instinctive, conventional, undebatable. He had never gone to church and what theology he knew he got mostly by reading history — the works of the American Puritans — or indirectly from the great Christian writers whose works he loved — Dante, Spenser, Bunyan. But as long as his religion had been merely assumed and not questioned — at least in any essentials — it was serviceable: it provided him with a frame of value and meaning. It is true, again, that Hawthorne's interest had never been directly in morality in the abstract, but in *morality as experienced* — that is, in the human heart. It is not true in my opinion to say, as one Hawthorne scholar has, that Hawthorne was not deeply concerned with "the eternal verities," or that he dealt with morals as "mere conventions," or that his thought turned usually on "fundamentally trivial" moral problems.

Hawthorne was interested in moral experience. That is why his works have to be distinguished from what we usually think of as purely "didactic" fiction, even though they begin and end in moral meanings. But experience can only have moral significance in terms of some set of moral values — explicit or implicit, inherited or created, consciously held or unconsciously assumed — some moral system. The Christian tradition had supplied this for Hawthorne for thirty years of writing. But it is my impression that toward the end of his life he began to question the basis of this system, and that when he did so the whole system crumbled and slid into meaninglessness. In 1857 he had recorded in his English Notebooks (in a passage that Mrs. Hawthorne revised, to protect her husband's reputation for piety) that the fog obscured the statues of the saints on St. Paul's so that they looked down "dimly from their standpoint on high, faintest, as spiritual consolations are apt to be, when the world was darkest." I think it was his experience of this failure of "spiritual consolations" that lay behind an image that he worked into *Septimius Felton* and that is one of the half dozen or so happy strokes in that novel:

In short, it was such a moment as I suppose all men feel (at least, I can answer for one), when the real scene and picture of life swims, jars, shakes, seems about to be broken up and dispersed, like the picture in a smooth pond, when we disturb its tranquil mirror by throwing in a stone; and though the scene soon settles itself, and looks as real as before, a haunting doubt keeps close at hand, as long as we live, asking, "Is it stable? Am I sure of it? Am I certainly not dreaming? See; it trembles again, ready to dissolve."

I can only suppose that the sort of experience suggested by this image prompted the curious phrase — curious for Hawthorne — in *The Dolliver Romance*: "the old man, a hater of empiricism (in which, however, is contained all hope for mankind)." Hawthorne is speaking out directly as author here, not characterizing anyone by assigning a belief to him; and when we think of the meaning of "The Birthmark" and of much else that Hawthorne had written, the sense of the oddity of this statement grows. It seems unlikely that assigning a meaning of "trial and error" to Hawthorne's use of the word *empiricism* here removes all the oddity. Historic Christianity has never rested primarily and ultimately on empiricism, in any of that word's possible meanings.

4

Dr. Grimshawe's Secret contains several touches that remind us of the earlier writings without suggesting parody. One of them is the explicit heart image in chapter eleven. It is worth quoting at some length:

There is — or there was, now many years ago, and a few years also it was still extant — a chamber, which when I think of, it seems to me like entering a deep recess of my consciousness, a deep cave of my nature; so much have I thought of it and its inmate, through a considerable period of my life. After I had seen it long in fancy, then I saw it in reality, with my waking eyes; and questioned with myself whether I was really awake.

Not that it was a picturesque or stately chamber; not in the least. It was dim, dim as a melancholy mood; so dim, to come to particulars that, till you were accustomed to that twilight medium, the print of a book looked all blurred; a pin was an indistinguishable object; the face of your familiar friend, or your dearest beloved one, would be unrecognizable across it, and the figures, so warm and radiant with life and heart, would seem like the faint gray shadows of our thoughts, brooding in age over youthful images of joy and love. Nevertheless, the chamber, though so difficult to see across, was small. You detected that it was within very narrow boundaries, though you could not precisely see them; only you felt yourself shut in, compressed, impeded, in the deep centre of something; and you longed for a breath of fresh air. Some articles of furniture there seemed to be; but in this dim medium, to which we are unaccustomed, it is not well to try to make out what they were, or anything else — now at least — about the chamber. Only one thing; small as the light was, it was rather wonderful how there came to be any; for no windows were apparent; no communication with the outward day . . . Let us forth into the broad, genial daylight, for there is magic, there is a devilish, subtile influence, in this chamber; which, I have reason to believe, makes it dangerous to remain here. There is a spell on the threshold. Heaven keep us safe from it! *

This passage, with its suggestion of the increasing loneliness of the man who envisaged his own heart as "dangerous" and without communication with "the outward day," and the Colcord–Jesus relationship that is quite skillfully set up (but not developed) are, I think, the only things worth remembering in this novel on which Hawthorne worked harder and longer than he had on *The Scarlet Letter*.

Septimius Felton has, as Mark Van Doren has said, a number of good things in it. The killing of the young Englishman, the burial, some of Septimius' thoughts — these things and perhaps one or two others are memorable enough to deserve to be preserved, out of context, in a small anthology that could be made of the worthwhile passages in Hawthorne's last writings. But the significant thing about these passages is that they do not draw upon Hawthorne's recent experience at all but upon experience as old as the earliest of the tales. The material from the English Notebooks that he had

---

* From the Julian Hawthorne edition (Boston: Houghton Mifflin, 1890), p. 130. A scholarly edition of the romance, E. H. Davidson's *Hawthorne's Doctor Grimshawe's Secret* (Harvard University Press, 1954), was not yet published when this work went to press.

tried so hard to work into *The Ancestral Footstep* and *Dr. Grimshawe's Secret* and the parallel between the Civil and the Revolutionary wars that he hoped to develop here were totally unsuccessful.

What there is of *The Dolliver Romance* is good. Again, as on *Septimius Felton* and on the period of the late romances in general, Mark Van Doren is the most penetrating critic:

> By some miracle the pieces of it [Hawthorne] did produce came near to being the brightest and best of all his work. The surviving fragments of this fourth fragment . . . have an astonishing force, a reassuring grace . . . *The Dolliver Romance* is an intricate, a delicate, a cunning comment upon its author's developing senility. Dr. Dolliver, who lives beside a graveyard with his great-granddaughter Pansie and her kitten, is neither Mr. Kirkup of Florence nor Dr. Grimshawe of the black bottle and the bloated spiders; he is Hawthorne grown old, and the good wife Bessie who died so long ago is perhaps Sophia, and Pansie is certainly the Una of 1849 . . . Hawthorne is now free of his notebooks and his plans . . . The striking thing is Hawthorne's amusement. The self-portrait is not in the least line sentimental.*

All this, and more that Mr. Van Doren says with his usual felicity, is very just. But the comment that Hawthorne is now free of his English Notebooks, though valuable, is insufficient as an explanation of why he is writing so very much better than he had for a long time. We shall never, I suppose, have a sufficient explanation of this remarkable resurgence of power in the last months of Hawthorne's life, when his physical powers were failing daily. But we may note that in addition to the self-portraiture in old Dr. Dolliver there is another element in the fragments, and that is by no means a product of Hawthorne's contemporary experience, but rather a group of symbols lifted bodily from his earliest writings. The child running toward the open grave, the flower, the coiled serpent, the glowing eyes, the sparkling elixirs, the villainous Colonel Dabney — these are all familiar ingredients handled

* *Nathaniel Hawthorne* (New York: Sloane, 1949), pp. 260–261.

in the old way. There is, in fact, except for the portrayal of senility, nothing new in *The Dolliver Romance*. The amazing thing is that what had once been Hawthorne's by right of creation has been recovered.

And not by any "technical device," not because Hawthorne suddenly remembered what he had forgotten how to do. In the final months of his life, after he had lost all hope that his symptoms were temporary, it may be that he gained a fresh hold on, or a new vision of, those values that had been his, despite his doubts and his questions, earlier in his life. A personality is not only a product of anterior and exterior forces. There is a very real and important sense in which it is self-created by the values it espouses. For a long time Hawthorne's hold on the only values he could really accept had been weakening, and his work had been weakening with it. Now at the end the old values seem to have reasserted themselves.

At any rate, some sort of "elixir of life" worked for Hawthorne's writing at the end: it returned to the manner and matter of his youth. From internal evidence alone we would have no way of knowing that *The Dolliver Romance* was not written a quarter of a century before it was. Here is a mystery unlike that of the failure of the other late writings: it does not seem to give promise of any definitive solution.

CHAPTER TEN

CONCLUSION

At the height of his career Hawthorne described himself as a man who had spent his creative life "burrowing, to his utmost ability, into the depths of our common nature, for the purposes of psychological romance, — and who pursues his researches in that dusky region, as he needs must, as well by the tact of sympathy as by the light of observation." For "the purposes of psychological romance": no such purpose in literature had been conceived, before Hawthorne conceived it; and no form of fiction appropriate to such a purpose existed, before he created it. In the deepest sense of the word Hawthorne was a creative writer.

He and Poe began creating an American fiction at the same time, under many of the same influences, and with results in many ways comparable. It seems to most critics today that Hawthorne had the richer imagination; yet whatever may be our judgment of the comparative merits of the two, it is clear that before them there was nothing in American fiction that either writer could take very seriously. Turning to European fiction, and especially to the Gothic tale, each of them in his own way, but particularly Hawthorne, took what served his needs and transformed it, to create a form, a language, and a meaning that had never before existed.

What Hawthorne had to do when he started writing was more than just what any writer always has to do, to adapt a tradition to his individual sensibility and his talent and to his time. Hawthorne lived in an age of revolution both social and intellectual, which was also a time when fiction was beginning to take over functions previously fulfilled by other forms of literature or not fulfilled at all. No existing form of fiction very closely approached being suitable for his purposes. Perhaps traditional allegory, whether in prose or in verse, was more help to him that anything else. But the one thing most obviously demanded by allegory, a clear, fixed, publicly accepted scheme of values, was not available to Hawthorne. He was no philosopher; more relevantly, not a Christian in the sense that Bunyan and Spenser were, with their literal acceptance of the Bible as history. He was a man of the nineteenth century who had read and valued Voltaire when young, Christian in sympathy and conservative in temperament to be sure, with a kind of intuitive grasp of the essentials of Christian faith, a man who retained a tragic sense in an age of romantic primitivism and the religion of progress, but a man of the nineteenth century still. Allegory as it had been known and practiced was impossible to him in any but a limited and occasional and peripheral sense.

As for the Gothic novel and tale, these were at once more obviously available and finally less suitable. The amount of Hawthorne's indebtedness to the form has been explored in a learned volume.* But no one reading *The Castle of Otranto* or *The Monk* without preconceptions would be likely to see any but superficial resemblances between these or similar Gothic romances and Hawthorne's work. The matter can be

---

* Jane Lundblad, *Nathaniel Hawthorne and the Tradition of the Gothic Romance* (Upsala, Sweden, 1946).

stated very briefly: Hawthorne drew extensively upon this popular form, as Shakespeare used the revenge tragedy and James used the comedy of manners, but the form itself, as he found it existing, was not to his purpose. Taking from it certain elements and turning them to new purposes, he transformed what he used. Only an examination which artificially isolates form from meaning will fail to note the difference between the Gothic elements in Hawthorne's fiction and the same elements in the popular Gothic novel. The house of seven gables is first a decaying New England mansion and then the kind of edifice that pride always builds and finally an image of the human heart; its resemblance to a long line of castles in the Gothic novels is interesting but not of primary significance to one who is concerned with the meaning and value of this work. Hawthorne's use of the formulas of the Gothic romance is of much the same order as Robert Penn Warren's use, in *World Enough and Time*, of the currently popular form of the historical novel.

What we now think of as the main stream of the English novel from DeFoe and Fielding through Jane Austen to Scott and Dickens was realistic in intention, taking the cue for its form from the histories, journals, letters, and memoirs of "real life," or from the stage, and very largely divorced from the mytho-poetic sources of modern fiction. That this tradition of the "novel," with its aim at realism and social criticism, as opposed to the "romance" was unsuited to Hawthorne's sensibility and purposes is too clear to need extended comment, and that despite Hawthorne's occasional wish that he might write like Trollope. At least in the formative first twenty-five years of his writing career, Hawthorne had little desire to "picture" society; and at no time in his career did he have either the desire or — in his own opinion — the ability to "instruct," in the sense of urging appropriate courses of action as Dickens instructed, taking his reader by the elbow and pointing out abuses that needed correction.

Despite its tendency toward allegory, Hawthorne's work is not didactic in the usual sense of that word, but contemplative, aimed at the imagination and the understanding rather than at action. His own temperament was such that even in private life he could not readily bring himself to give advice, not even when his position seemed to make it appropriate that he do so. The reason he gives in *Our Old Home* for not "meddling" in the affairs of others while he was a consul at Liverpool suggests an attitude that would seem to militate against the writing of didactic fiction. "For a man, with a natural tendency to meddle with other people's business," he noted in his description of his consular experiences,

> there could not possibly be a more congenial sphere than the Liverpool Consulate. For myself, I have never been in the habit of feeling that I could sufficiently comprehend any particular conjunction of circumstances with human character, to justify me in thrusting in my awkward agency among the intricate and unintelligible machinery of Providence. I have always hated to give advice, especially when there is a prospect of its being taken. It is only one-eyed people who love to advise, or have any spontaneous promptitude of action. When a man opens both his eyes, he generally sees about as many reasons for acting in any one way as in any other, and quite as many for acting in neither . . .

And his work had as little in common with the realistic aim of the contemporary novel as with the didactic. Both in theory and in practice, his work looks back to epic and romance and myth and forward to such writers as James, Conrad, Kafka, Faulkner. The gulf between it and the work of Fielding, Richardson, Smollett, Dickens, or even Scott, whose romances Hawthorne liked to read aloud to his family, is very great. One reason for this is surely that any "burrowing" that had been done in the main stream of the English novel up to Hawthorne's time had been quite incidental to other purposes.

When Hawthorne defined his purpose as a writer of "romances," his first care was to distinguish the romance from the novel.

> When a writer calls his work a Romance, it need hardly be observed that he wishes to claim a certain latitude, both as to its fashion and material, which he would not have felt himself entitled to assume had he professed to be writing a Novel. The latter form of composition is presumed to aim at a very minute fidelity, not merely to the possible, but to the probable and ordinary course of man's experience. The former — while, as a work of art, it must rigidly subject itself to laws, and while it sins unpardonably so far as it may swerve aside from the truth of the human heart — has fairly a right to present that truth under circumstances, to a great extent, of the writer's own choosing or creation. If he think fit, also, he may so manage his atmospherical medium as to bring out or mellow the lights and deepen and enrich the shadows of the picture.*

We get the feeling when we reread Hawthorne's prefaces that he was groping toward a conception of fiction that was more novel than he realized. Others before him, from Fielding on, had wondered where to place fiction among the several kinds of literature, but Hawthorne's emphasis on it as an art form, his insistence that it be tested by laws appropriate to its mode of existence rather than its accuracy as document, clearly foreshadows James's thinking on the same problems. And his choice of painting as an analogy points in the same direction. But most important of all is his life-long insistence that the kind of truth he wanted to portray was the "truth of the human heart," and that the best way to portray this is by the strategy of indirection. The truth so conceived is of a different order from the truth conveyed by ordinary didactic fiction, by philosophy (unless, with Whitehead, we conceive of philosophy as a kind of poetry), or by the univocal symbolism of the exact sciences. It is a truth that not only cannot be expressed except in the images of the imagination but, as Hawthorne himself thought, cannot be "grasped" except in such images. The most striking way in

---

* From the Preface to *The House of the Seven Gables*.

which Hawthorne's work is seminal for modern fiction is the
suggestion it contains that he was working toward a conception of technique as discovery.*

2

But if Hawthorne conceived of his work as being more
like poetry than like history or journalism, the question of
how this general conception could be translated into actual
works of fiction had still to be faced. For nearly forty years
of active writing he experimented with various forms in an
effort to find the one best suited to the composition of that
natural history of the soul that he wished to write.

Fanshawe was his experiment with the fictional formulas
popular in the 1820's. Almost immediately recognizing the
error of this, he turned to two forms that might be considered two versions of the opposite extreme: from the contrived plot, the exaggerated suspense, and the melodrama of
the sentimental Gothic tale to a retelling of "true" tales from
local history and to semifictional sketches. He felt at ease in
both forms, but in the sketch in particular he felt that he
could exercise his peculiar talent. Developing it out of the
periodical essay of the preceding century as handled by
writers of the romantic period who had given it a more personal cast, he valued the form because it allowed him to
glimpse truth out of the corner of his eye and to give fancy
full sway. And surely he was not wholly wrong. The essay
has almost disappeared today as a literary form and we find
find it difficult to appreciate the sketches, or to avoid com-

* I have in mind here especially Mark Schorer's "Technique as Discov-
ery," in W. V. O'Connor, ed., *The Forms of Modern Fiction* (Minneapolis:
The University of Minnesota Press, 1948). See also Susanne K. Langer,
Philosophy in a New Key (Pelican Books); Allen Tate, "Literature as
Knowledge," *On the Limits of Poetry* (New York: Swallow-Morrow, 1948);
W. K. Wimsatt, "The Structure of the Concrete Universal," *PMLA*, March
1947; Eliseo Vivas, "Literature and Knowledge," *Sewanee Review*, Autumn
1952.

paring them with the best of the tales, invariably to the disadvantage of the sketches. But he did some of his best work in them, and we need to read again not simply the several best but such little-known ones as "Main-Street," "The Devil in Manuscript," and "Old News."

But the sketch was not entirely suited to his purposes. Between it and the tale he contrived a sort of intermediate form having some of the characteristics of the older allegory and some of the features of the personal essay. "The Haunted Mind" is more nearly an essay than an allegory, "The Procession of Life" more nearly an allegory than an essay. The advantage of this intermediate form over the sketch lay in the greater opportunity it offered for objectification of feeling and thought in symbolic form. The disadvantage — from our point of view at least, since it is not clear that Hawthorne's consciousness of his purposes brought him to this point in analysis — the disadvantage lay in the inadequate autonomy of the symbols so created. The figures in "The Christmas Banquet" do not move by themselves in accordance with their own necessities but only as their very present creator moves them. "The Celestial Railroad" is saved from the subjectivity and inadequate, because wholly allegorical, meaning of "The Procession of Life" only by Hawthorne's reliance on the structure of incident and value supplied him by Bunyan.

No sharp separation can be made between the allegorical "processions," the sketches with some narrative ingredients, and the "tales proper," as we think of the short story today. Is "Wakefield" a sketch or a story? Is "Earth's Holocaust" an essay, an allegory, or a tale? The unity of all of Hawthorne's work must not be forgotten while we categorize the diversity. Yet the impossibility of making neat distinctions should not obscure such important differences as those between, say, "Fancy's Showbox" and "Ethan Brand," or "The Christmas Banquet" and "Major Molineux." Between "The Man of Adamant," which Hawthorne called an apologue and we might be more likely to call an extended parable, and "The Wives of the Dead," which would appear to have no conceptual theme beyond what may be called a feeling for the "strangeness" of life, the opacity of experience, there are significant differences; but both grow out of history, both take the form of legends, and both are concerned only with the significance of history, not with history as fact. "The Gentle Boy" is comparatively "realistic" in its exploration of the theme of religious fanaticism through the Puritan persecution of the Quakers; "Young Goodman Brown" is comparatively allegorical in its treatment of the nature and consequences of the Puritan belief in the total depravity of man. The two stories are very different in their effect, and one of them, the more allegorical one, seems to most readers of Hawthorne today very much the greater of the two. (The other was a favorite of Hawthorne's contemporaries.) Yet it would be misleading to set up sharply contrasting categories, label them "realism" and "allegory," and assign the stories to them. What holds these two stories and the others together is the tendency of all of them, even of those that are more nearly sketches than tales, to move toward the mytho-poetic.

Some of Hawthorne's writing for children provides an interesting commentary on his assumptions and his procedure in the rest of his work. Grandfather's chair, for instance, in the book to which it supplies a name, is not an emblem or type of anything, in Hawthorne's usual sense of these words. If it is a symbol, it is not such a symbol as can be translated in abstract terms. Rather it is intended to be for Hawthorne's young readers what we might describe today in Eliot's phrase, an objective correlative: a formula for a particular set of emotions. Explaining his general purpose as that of retelling episodes from the American past in such a way as to create "picturesque sketches of the times," Hawthorne tells why he gives the chair so prominent a place in the book:

There is certainly no method by which the shadowy outlines of departed men and women can be made to assume the hues of life more effectually than by connecting their images with the substantial and homely reality of a fireside chair. It causes us to feel at once that these characters of history had a private and familiar existence, and were not wholly contained within that cold array of outward action which we are compelled to receive as the adequate representation of their lives. If this impression can be given, much is accomplished . . . The human heart may best be read in the fireside chair.

Though this has its "dated" air, sounding perhaps to a generation suspicious of the simpler emotions a little rustic and naïve, there are some interesting assumptions behind it. The human heart cannot be read directly, nor can what Hawthorne wanted to say about history be said directly. For what Hawthorne wanted to say there was not a more "literal" language, indeed for precisely what he wanted to say, no language at all until he created it. And creating it involved finding the adequate symbols, whether emblems or types or objective correlatives or, in the larger sense of structure, significant form. Hawthorne realized that fiction is an art form long before James began to write in the Hawthorne tradition. He realized it when other writers thought of fiction as document or as the vehicle for something extraneous to itself or as a harmless form of entertainment. His experimentation with the various forms and combinations of parable, allegory, legend, sketch, tale, and romance were demanded by his attempt to accomplish a task not very different, despite the more abstractly intellectual character of his art, from that William Faulkner set before himself in the opening of his story of the man called Monk:

I will have to try to tell about Monk. I mean, actually try — a deliberate attempt to bridge the inconsistencies in his brief and sordid and unoriginal history, to make something out of it, not only with the nebulous tools of supposition and inference and invention, but to employ these nebulous tools upon the nebulous and inexplicable material which he left behind him. Because it is only in literature

that the paradoxical and even mutually negativing anecdotes in the
history of a human heart can be juxtaposed and annealed by art into
verisimilitude and credibility.

3

Judgment of Hawthorne's achievement as an artist is
certain to reflect our judgment of the validity of allegory as
a form of literature. If allegory is, as many assume, an "inferior" form, then we may well ask whether it is possible
to assign Hawthorne a major place in fiction. Since labeling
him an allegorist and so dismissing him without discussing
the reasons is the most significant form that negative criticism of his work takes, I should like to add a few final notes
to what has already emerged as we have examined the separate works.

To the question of whether or not what Hawthorne wrote
should be called allegory, only a carefully qualified answer
seems possible. Some of the works are allegories in a rather
loose sense, and a great deal of the work shows a tendency
toward allegory, that is, toward giving priority to a highly
intellectualized, abstract framework of meaning rather than
to the discrete and sensuous. If this is damning, then Hawthorne is damned.

Most of the negative criticisms that may be made from
this point of view were made long ago by Hawthorne himself. When he spoke, in the preface to "Rappaccini's Daughter," of his "inveterate love of allegory" the words were
meant to be taken as disparagement; when he added that he
generally contented himself with "a very slight embroidery
of outward manners," the implication was strong that this
was what made his work seem "shadowy" and "unsubstantial." He anticipated James's condescension toward the tales
when he decided on another occasion that they resembled
"flowers that blossomed in too retired a shade." After 1850

he regularly disparaged the tales, professing once not to know what he had ever meant by those "blasted allegories." Such comments, however, are hardly sufficient to conclude the discussion; indeed, they perhaps tell us more about Hawthorne's personality and changing opinions than about the tales they are meant to categorize. If the broadest accurate generalization that can be made about Hawthorne's works in this connection is that many of them tend rather markedly toward the allegorical mode, then we are left to look once more at the assumption that allegory is an inferior mode.

I think we shall all agree that allegory is a peripheral form of imaginative literature. Pure allegory would be by definition only philosophy in disguise; in this strict sense even Dante, Spenser, and Bunyan did not write allegory. Like "pure realism," which presumably would be "facts" without any governing scheme of interpretation, it is probably an impossibility. Where shall we find an allegory worthy of any consideration which has no lifelikeness of character and event? Surely the difference between allegory and realism — for these seem to be the forms that should be contrasted — is one of degree: the degree to which a pattern of meaning dominates, or the "givenness" of the material dominates, the complete structure and texture.

If this is so, then we shall have to say that the kinds of distinction that must be made between the more and the less allegorical tales and romances of Hawthorne are not of secondary but of primary importance, since all fiction is more or less allegorical. And it would seem pertinent to go on to add that the best of Hawthorne's work is not so very different from, say, the work of James as it has been customary to imply by classifying the one as an allegorist and the other as a realist. It could even be argued plausibly that "Roger Malvin's Burial" is less allegorical than "The Real Thing." In terms of achieved content, rather than in terms of Hawthorne's explicit statement of his "moral," is "Ethan Brand"

more or less allegorical than "The Jolly Corner"? Surely "The
Wives of the Dead" is less allegorical than "The Beast in
the Jungle." (It is also of course less valuable.) Hawthorne
and James do not work in the same way, but the differences
between their stories are probably more obscured than clarified by the allegory-realism contrast.

If both symbolism and illusion of reality are typical of
fiction at its best, it does not follow that a work of fiction
to be good must have both qualities in equal degrees. In the
best of Hawthorne's more allegorical tales a certain defi-
ciency in illusion of reality is compensated for by a depth
and completeness of symbolization rare in fiction. Though
they lack the textural density that springs from the illusion
of perfect lifelikeness, they have a complexity of their own,
not simply intellectual but emotional and imaginative, to
balance their remarkable coherence. Defective perhaps as
fiction, as we have come to define fiction in the last century,
they are rewarding as poetry. But to say even this is to
assume a sharpness of distinction between the two forms that
Hawthorne did not recognize either in theory or in practice.

One final consideration on this matter of Hawthorne as
allegorist. It seems to me impossible to arrive at completely
separate judgments of the "reality" that fiction has and the
"meaning" that it has. We cannot wholly separate the "fact"
from the *Gestalt* of which it is a part and from which it gets
not only its meaning but a part at least of its reality. So it
is that to the extent that Hawthorne's values seem to us mistaken, his characters and events are likely to seem to us unreal too; and we shall say then with stronger emphasis that
he is too allegorical, meaning that he has let general beliefs
(which we do no accept) guide him in the creation of characters and situations (which we cannot accept either, because they bear the stamp of the concepts which "discovered" and shaped them).

4

The statement in "The Haunted Mind" about the tomb or dungeon contained "in the depths of every mind" was no casual or passing idea, explored once and then dropped, but a ruling conception in Hawthorne's life, perceptible through-out his work at all stages. The image of the heart as a place of darkness and death or imprisonment is of course a hall-mark of his style, and here and there throughout the works are statements that approach explicitness. In "The Birth-mark" it is the sleeping rather than the waking dream that is referred to, and the idea has literary antecedents as well as a very personal relevance for Hawthorne, but the relation to the constant heart images is clear enough: "Truth often finds its way to the mind close muffled in robes of sleep," and then reveals matters which our "unconscious self-deception" keeps hidden from us otherwise. And this conception of the hidden truths of our own deeper minds, truths which we our-selves do not ordinarily know, is behind Hawthorne's state-ment, already quoted, of his purpose as a writer of romances: the kind of truth he was especially interested in could be reached only by "burrowing" far into the depths of our nature.

There were, Hawthorne was convinced, "strange and subtile matters" to be discovered by anyone with the courage to look into "those dark caverns" of the mind "into which all men must descend if they would know anything beneath the surface and illusive pleasures of existence." Self-knowledge so defined seemed to Hawthorne not only a profitable pursuit for the artist but in some degree a necessity for all men. It could be achieved, he felt, by the cultivation of what he called in "The Haunted Mind" a "passive sensibility." But there were dangers involved in this pursuit of the hidden, so that the position of the artist, conceived as fully conscious man, was highly ambiguous.

Hawthorne distrusted, and to some extent actively disliked, much of what we today think of as his best work. He professed not to know, in his later years, what he had meant by his tales, and it was as natural for him to prefer *The House of the Seven Gables* to *The Scarlet Letter* as it was to prefer Hilda to Miriam. Though he might define his purpose as a writer in terms that demand a psychological interpretation, he came increasingly to prefer the signature — the conscious elements, both personal or individual and social or cultural — to the archetype.* He had worked very hard both to create a self reasonably consistent with his ideal self-image and to adjust himself to the world he found as a prerequisite to opening an intercourse with the world; and once he felt he had had reasonable success in achieving these ends, he seldom felt any inclination to return to the dark cavern.

One approach, accordingly, to the problem of the decline of Hawthorne's power as a writer in the last dozen years of his life is in terms of the assumption that in the time of his success he tried to be a writer without paying the penalty. Some of the "strange and subtile matters" discovered by the passive sensibility were not pleasant or heartening, not designed to bolster a sagging optimism or minister to self-assurance. It is not accidental that the seers of myth have been pictured usually as in some way incapacitated: Tiresias blind paid for his insight with his sight. Hawthorne's lifelong desire to be perfectly adjusted — and only the adjusted can open wholly satisfactory intercourse with the world of their time — was partially in conflict with his desire to probe into the truth we do not want to admit.

As his provincialism decreased in the European years, as he became more aware of the currents of advanced thinking in the era of Darwin and Huxley and Arnold, the gap be-

---

* Leslie Fiedler, "Archetype and Signature: A Study of the Relationship Between Biography and Poetry," *Sewanee Review*, Spring 1952.

tween the truths discerned in the caverns of the mind and the truths which were acceptable, socially approved, widened. Visions of guilt and death made sense in terms of a framework of Christian doctrine that they could not possibly make in terms of mid-nineteenth-century secular optimism and the religion of the heart. The specters that haunted the mind not only "fitted in" with the general framework of assumption and belief in which Hawthorne had grown up, they could be conceived as wholesome reminders of man's essential condition. But if, as Browning, with whom the Hawthornes became friendly in Rome, wrote, "All's right with the world" because "God's in His heaven," and because, as Browning did not write but everybody seemed to believe, man is "naturally" good and need only trust his instincts, what was Hawthorne to do with or think of his visions of sin and death? Presumably they could only be symptoms of a quite abnormal morbidity, to be rooted out or explained away.

The more Hawthorne "caught up" with his age in the years after 1850 the more he learned to distrust his own gift, to feel ashamed of the products of the passive sensibility. If Melville's career has anything to teach us, it would seem to require a judgment as relevant for Hawthorne as for the creator of Ahab: that the typical liberal views of the period were useless for any artist who would not willfully blind himself to the existence of tragedy, and to the moral dimension required for the conception of tragedy. Melville's lifelong attempt to reinterpret Christianity so as to make its truths available once more may be seen as having various implications, but one implication we cannot easily avoid: the very integrity of an artist with a tragic sense and a concern for the moral dimension of experience was threatened by both the materialism and the "evolutionary optimism" of the popular currents of thought of the age. As Dostoevski also noted, nineteenth-century liberalism was puzzled and affronted by anyone who concerned himself with the "deeper psychology" and entertained in a state of passive sensibility the visions that have haunted the mind of men through the ages.

We can hardly avoid the conclusion that the price Hawthorne paid for opening an intercourse with the world was the blonde maidens and all that goes along with them in the later works; perhaps also the increasing disinclination, after 1850 and before conscience and financial need drove him to it at the end of the decade, to do any writing that did not actually have to be done. Melville, refusing to pay this price, wrote on in comparative obscurity. Hawthorne was glad to pay it, did not in fact consider that he had paid anything — he had simply got rid of a very troublesome alter ego. We do not know all that went through his mind in the last year of his life, but it is possible to surmise that he regretted his bargain at last. At any rate, in the last thing he wrote before his death he returned to the old manner and the old meanings, to picture, in *The Dolliver Romance*, a little child running toward an open grave.

5

A great deal of nonsense has been written about Hawthorne's relation to his age, mostly by writers of a "liberal" cast of mind who were alert for "social significance" and were disappointed that Hawthorne, despite his Jacksonian politics, was not a utopian materialist. What needs to be recognized now is that some of the very qualities that made Hawthorne seem, during most of his life, a little old-fashioned and even provincial make him seem today saner than those of his contemporaries who kept up more than he with the latest fashions in thought. He dealt, for instance, with the problem of the individual in relation to the group, as Emerson and Carlyle and Whitman and the others did. But he dealt with the relationship not in terms of glib generalizations about the infallibility of instinct and the need for the individual to be wholly self-reliant, or with Carlyle's dour insistence on the necessity of obedience and subordination, or with Whitman's substitution of feeling for thinking, but with subtlety, firmness, and depth. He saw, for instance, the moralistic and theocratic society of the early Puritans as "sinister to the intellect, and sinister to the heart," as he said in "Main Street," but he had a firm grasp on the fact that man is a social creature. He saw the dangers of alienation, and the necessity of it, for the artist or for anyone else who valued only that which is worth valuing. He saw the individual as inevitably alone, yet needing always to maintain contact with the magnetic chain of humanity. A case could be made for the idea that Hawthorne and Melville were the only American writers of their time who saw the problem of the individual and society in terms that still seem relevant today.

His treatment of the problem of fate and freedom is equally distinguished by his refusal to settle for easy half-truths. To his contemporaries in a period characterized by philosophies of freedom that tended toward voluntarism, he seemed a fatalist; to mechanists of the recent past he seemed old-fashioned in his belief in man's moral responsibility. He saw man as immersed in a mystery in which responsibility is at odds with fate. His own natural tendency was to emphasize causation at the expense of freedom, but he criticized and corrected his emotional bias and always returned to the unresolved paradox. "You emerge from mystery, pass through a vicissitude that you can but imperfectly control, and are borne onward to another mystery." We need only compare Hawthorne's insight into both the reality and the limitations of choice with the confused wavering between automatism and irresponsible freedom characteristic of Emerson's thought on this subject to see the degree of his sanity. He was not so philosophic as Emerson, he was in fact nearly as indolent about mental as about physical exertion. But he had the advantage of not supposing that nothing had been learned in the past.

And despite the essential conservatism resulting from his skeptical attitude toward reform, it would seem that the sanity of his handling of the problem of progress must be acknowledged by both liberals and conservatives today. In an age which, because it could see great progress in certain areas, assumed that progress was automatic and inevitable in all areas, he never shared either the shallow confidence or the blind fears between which his contemporaries tended to alternate. The implications of "Earth's Holocaust" and *The Blithedale Romance* and his other treatments of the theme are those of the Bible and Greek tragedy and Shakespeare: progress toward a better condition is not inevitable or automatic; it cannot be assured by any gadgetry, political or technological. Like Dostoevski, Hawthorne refused to choose either of the alternative attitudes presented by the spirit of the times: primitivism or progress. Groping toward a conception of history as cyclical, yet not necessarily futile or sterile, he moved toward our century's discovery that the death of civilizations is not a minor incident in a subplot but an essential part of the main story. Some aspects of his thought on this matter point toward Spengler, some toward Toynbee.*

The crucial dimension for man, Hawthorne thought, is always moral. Those who ignore this fact, no matter how lofty their aim, he saw as defeated by "an error at the very root of the matter." We have recently passed through a long

---

* There are also some interesting relationships between Hawthorne's thoughts on history and the neo-Christian interpretation offered by Herbert Butterfield in *Christianity and History* (New York: Scribner's, 1950). Douglas Jerrold has recently treated these matters with incisive brilliance, relating Toynbee to the historiography of Hawthorne's day and our own, in "Professor Toynbee, 'The West,' and the World," *Sewanee Review*, Winter 1954.

period when such doctrine as this seemed either meaningless or pernicious. If we are, as I suppose, coming into a time when it will not seem necessary to deny the possibility of moral knowledge and moral error in order to enhance the glory either of technology or of history conceived as a dialectic, Hawthorne is likely to seem more relevant to the next generation than he did to the fashionably advanced thinkers of the recent past.

"Man's capacities have never been measured; nor are we to judge of what he can do by any precedents, so little has been tried." Thus Thoreau. Emerson defined his position as that of an endless seeker with no past at his back. Hawthorne in contrast felt the presentness of the past. It is, he thought, in and all around us, it is what we have to work with and start from. From Hawthorne's point of view Emerson's metaphor of the past which was not at his back was wrong in the sense intended by Emerson and right in a sense not intended: the past is never at one's back but in one's blood and in the very shape of things; if it were simply behind us, we could walk away from it into a future completely of our own making. To escape completely from the past, Hawthorne thought, would be possible only if we could escape from the conditions of natural existence. The past can be transcended only to the extent that it is faced, accepted, and understood. This is the implication of "Roger Malvin's Burial," of "Major Molineux," of "Egotism," and of *The House of the Seven Gables.* Here too Hawthorne seems to me to have had more wisdom than Concord's futurists.

Finally, there is another Hawthorne theme that is perhaps even more relevant to our situation today than any of these. I mean his theme of the relations of head and heart, which takes so many forms in his work and is present almost everywhere in some form. It is the relation of knowledge to action, of knowledge to emotion, of knowledge to will, of science to wisdom, of fact to value. His treatment of the theme foreshadows all the essential aspects of the Prufrock situation. Abundance of knowledge, to Hawthorne's way of thinking, does not in itself guarantee right action, or indeed any action at all. Ethan Brand attains extraordinary knowledge and destroys himself. Chillingworth adds to his scientific lore a knowledge of the inmost secrets of another's heart, puts his knowledge to an evil use, and is destroyed. Coverdale is paralyzed by somewhat the same kind of knowledge that keeps Prufrock from acting purposefully.

Hawthorne was no obscurantist. He did not undervalue knowledge. Stanley Geist's epigram on Goethe and Hawthorne is valuable only if it is taken as pointing to a contrast between the two men: "The father of modern German literature died calling for more light; the father of modern American literature was born calling for more darkness."* Taken without qualification this could be misleading. The problem of Ethan Brand is not the only one in Hawthorne. Roderick Elliston's disease is cured only when the voices of both wisdom and love speak to him. There is no condemnation of knowledge in "The Birthmark," only of intellectual pride and lack of vision. Theologically Hawthorne stood squarely in the middle between medieval rationalist "natural law" theories and modern anti-rationalist "existential" theologies, between Aquinas and Barth. He was first and last a realist, unwilling to deny any part of his experience. His experience suggested to him the value of reasonableness but not of rationalism. The myth of Faust, who separated the good and the true and sold his soul for knowledge, is one of the fundamental myths of the modern world. Hawthorne's treatment of the *libido sciendi* theme has immense relevance for an age as profoundly Baconian as ours.

In short, there is a sense in which Hawthorne's very alienation saved him, during most of his life, from being swept along with the mere reactions of a troubled and confused

---

* "A Preface to 'Ethan Brand,'" *Hudson Review*, Summer 1952.

age. Less the "representative man" than Emerson and a host of other writers, he is more alive today. He pondered some of the permanent aspects of man's condition and created works of art that at their best are as alive now as when he wrote them.

6

If we are today moving out of a period very largely pre-occupied with quantitative knowledge and into a period when qualitative knowledge will once again occupy the center of our attention, as it seems to many that we are, Hawthorne's achievement as a writer is likely to seem greater to future generations than it has to those of the recent past. In the climate of opinion symbolized by the growing authority of Herbert Spencer in the decades following Hawthorne's death, Hawthorne's reputation could only decline. When, around the turn of the century, the naturalistic "aesthetic," which asserted chiefly that no aesthetic was possible or desirable, was widely accepted, it was difficult to know what to do with Hawthorne's works. When, later, materialism took the form of asserting the significance of large-scale social problems but denying the significance, or even the existence, of individual moral responsibility, liberals could only conclude that "progressive" writers were dealing with "reality," Hawthorne with chimeras. When "behavior" was thought to be more real than morality and "facts" more concrete than experience of facts, Hawthorne's work could only seem unimportant or exotic.

But in a time when Kierkegaard seems more profound than Spencer and Dostoevski more interesting than the novelists who tried to "reduce" moral problems to problems in biology or sociology, it is no longer necessary to try to "find a place" for Hawthorne. He can be recognized for what he is, a writer of the first importance, who often failed but sometimes succeeded, and when he succeeded produced great works. Standing at the beginning of the tradition later cultivated by Melville, James, and Faulkner, Hawthorne is not clearly overshadowed by any of these. His works initiate and define the great tradition in American fiction.

Index of Characters and Titles

INDEX OF CHARACTERS AND TITLES